AF528016

LHOPS (DOYA) OF BHUTAN

An Ethnographic Account

Lhops (Doya) of Bhutan

An Ethnographic Account

B. DEBEN SHARMA

AKANSHA PUBLISHING HOUSE
NEW DELHI

AKANSHA PUBLISHING HOUSE
R 37-B, Vani Vihar, Uttam Nagar
New Delhi-110059
Email: ektabooks@yahoo.com

Showroom
4649/21B, Ansari Road
Darya Ganj
New Delhi - 110 002
Ph.: 23269193 / 9811582579

Lhops (Doya) of Bhutan: An Ethnographic Account
© *Author*
First Edition 2005
ISBN 81-8370-006-3

All rights reserved. Including the right to translate or to reproduce this book or parts thereof except for brief quotations in critical reviews.

[he responsibility for the facts stated, conclusions reached etc. is entirely that of the Author. The publisher is not responsible for them, whatsoever.]

PRINTED IN INDIA

Published by M.P. Misra for Akansha Publishing House, New Delhi and Printed at Mehra Offset Press, Delhi.

To

My Wife

CHHAYA DEVI

Acknowledgments

It took four years of fieldwork and another six years of strenuous exercise of writing and rewriting the report amidst hopes and despairs having taken their own time to finally produce this report in this present form. My guide was always with me from a distant to inspire and encourage me whenever I drifted to despairs. I always missed a constant companionship of my guide although I had opportunities to have intense interactions with him in quite a few occasions during the work. The present report therefore, would be lacking in the minute nicety and technicalities of a standard ethnographic thesis of this nature. However, for the ethnographic value of the rarely available information about some people in Bhutan I am happy to present this report.

In making this report presentable to the academic society I have many debts to acknowledge. Firstly, I am greatly indebted to Prof. B.P Misra, Centre for Himalayan Studies in the North Bengal University without whose bold initiatives, guidance and encouragement this work would not have seen the light in the academic circle in the present form. The occasional personal interactions with him have been great learning and self-rediscovering experiences for me in not only the academic concerns but also in my own personal life and career. I revere him as a role model of academicians and a true guide and philosopher.

Secondly, I am also greatly benefited from the very candid and valuable observations and feedback received from Prof. R.S. Mukhopadhyay of the Department of Sociology and Social Anthropology of the University in enriching academic value of this work. I am very grateful to him for sparing his busy time and showing interests in my work. I am grateful to the University of North Bengal to have permitted me to register as a private research scholar for the work and also for having granted me enough time to gather myself to put things into final shape. I am thankful to Mr. J.M. Majumdar and Dr. D Boot of Documentation Centre for all the supports in accessing reference materials and computer services at the Centre for Himalayan Studies. I would also like to record my gratitudes to Dr. M.C., Arun, Assistant Professor, Anthropology Department of Manipur University who read the final draft and gave valuable advice.

Thirdly; I am also much indebted to the people about whom present the work is all. I was fortunate to have been allowed to live with them to see their ways of life from close quarters. Among whom there were many students, friends and elders who loved, cared and owned me as one of them. I thank all of them including all the deities of the Doyas for keeping me healthy and happy, and making my stay among them unforgettable experiences. And through them I beseech forgiveness for any unintentional trespasses into the sacred realms or privacy of the people and/or any blunders I might have done in my ignorance during the course of my inquiries to produce this document.

Fourthly, I am thankful to the Education Department of the Royal Government Bhutan for providing me the rare opportunity to work in a remote area among the people. I am also grateful to District Commissioners and District Education Officers who encouraged and provided necessary supports while working in the remote schools. I am also thankful to Mr. Jagar Dorji, the then Education Director, Royal Government of Bhutan who recognized my humble documentation on the Doyas. Through his good office I was able to get a rare opportunity of officially conducting a short survey work of different communities besides the Doyas in the area before leaving Bhutan. I am also grateful to Mr. George van Driem, Associate Professor of the Linguistics Department of the University of Amsterdam who came down to the Doyas on an official linguistics survey conducted by the Royal Government of Bhutan during my stay among the Doyas. From him I gained valuable knowledge on the Doya language. He also provided me some photographs of the Doyas taken during his survey.

The efforts of putting my work into prints right from the first draft have been from my cousin Ms. Subhra and her colleagues of Association for Food Scientist, Imphal, my nephew Biswajit, proprietor, Kaku Computers and his friends. I am grateful to all of them for bringing out this thesis in the present form. I am thankful to Mr. Phalguni and Gagan of Computer Pride for giving me the needful technical supports in printing and of scanning all the photographs, sketches and maps.

Lastly, I must also acknowledge the financial and moral support from WD-FGC, Imphal in completing the work. I must thank Capt. (Retd.) Ashok Y. Tipnis, Chairman WD, for doing the much needed language corrections and suggestions at the last stage. I was able to make considerable improvement on the grammar, structure and presentation style of this work. Mr. J.K. Shimrei of WD-FGC for their encouragement and support in completing this work. I am grateful to all other persons who helped me directly or indirectly in doing this work. Last but not the least, I thank my wife Chhaya Devi who merrily shouldered full responsibility of looking after my family and aged parents during the work.

B. DEBEN SHARMA

Contents

List of Tables

List of Sketches

List of Genealogical Charts

List of Maps

List of Plates

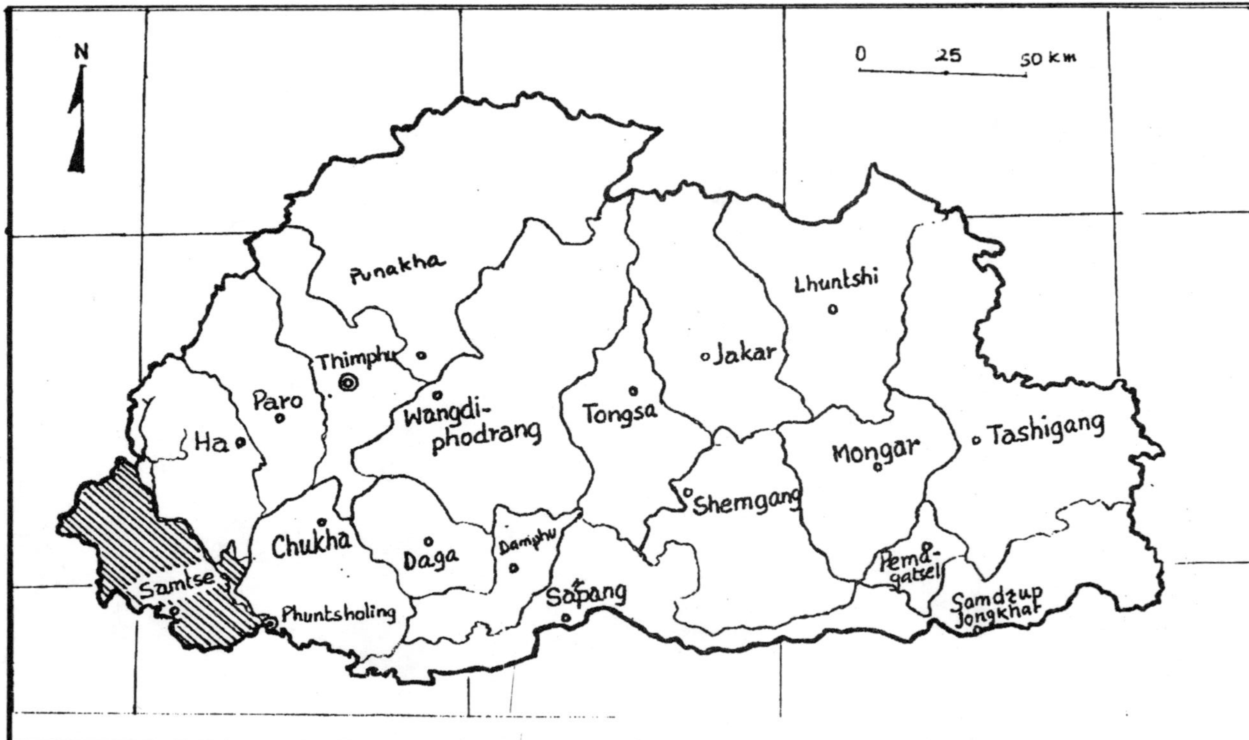

Fig. 0.1: Political Map of Bhutan

Introduction

The Land and People of Bhutan

Bhutan is a land-locked Kingdom in the eastern Himalayan hills. It has its own distinct cultural identity characterised by *Drukpa kagyu* sect of Mahayana fold of Buddhism. Numerous huge fortresses (Dzong) and monastries stand today to tell its past history of struggles to maintain its independent political status and identity. It is surrounded by Tibetan region of China in the north, Indian states of Sikkim in the west, Bengal and Assam in the south and Arunachal Pradesh in the east (Map 0.1). The country measure 46,570 sq. km. in extent and lies between 26°40' and 28°20' north latitudes and between 88°45' and 92°10' east longitudes. *Thimphu* is the capital of the country. There are 20 administrative districts called Dzongkhag (1995: 4).

Bhutan has several other names with which it has been known inside and outside the country. The several names seem to reflect different stages of cultural and historical development of the country. The name Bhutan itself has a Sanskrit root meaning high land or end of the land of Tibet (Bhot). This suggests a period of cultural influence from the south i.e Indian cultural influence over the north since earlier times, although, the brief political incursion of Cooch Rajas from the Bengal Duars into Bhutan could not withstand the Tibetan religious and cultural forces then, in Bhutan. The Tibetan influences into Bhutan gave it another name *Lho Mon*: the land of darkness in the south - at a certain period of time when the *Drukpa kagyu* sect of Mahayana Buddhism had not made much changes in the people's original way of life. In around the same period of time it was also known by another name *Lho Mon Tsenden jong* meaning southern mon country of cypress- a land of rich forest resources for the Tibetans at that period of time. Then, as Bhutan developed its own cultural traditions and political identity through a continuous process of cultural traditions and political

Map: 0.1 Bhutan and its Neighbours

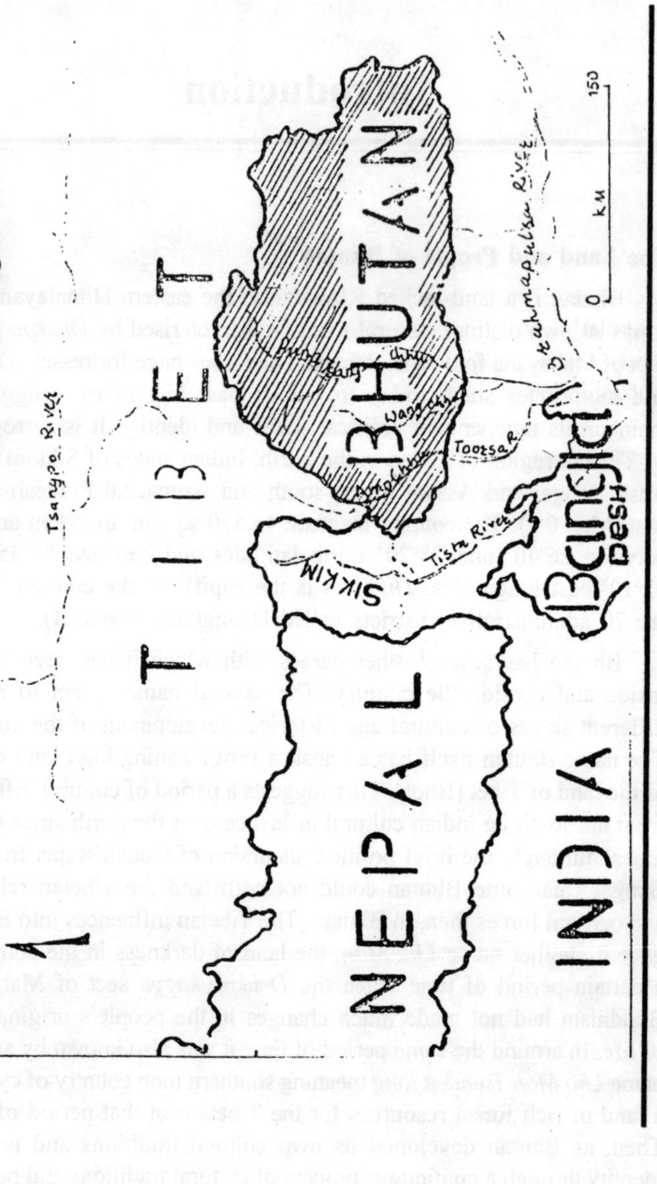

Map 0.1: Bhutan and its Neighbours

identity through a continuous process of cultural synthesis of its original *Bonism*[1] and that of Tibetan Buddhism it acquired a new name for its land and the people. Bhutan came to be known as *Druk Yul* - The Land of Thunder Dragon. The architect of Druk Yul was Shabdrung Ngawang Namgyal - religious leader from Tibet who migrated to Bhutan during the first half of Seventeenth century. This stage heralded the emergence of an independent and occassionally powerful country under the simultaneous leadership of two kings at two levels - spiritual and temporal, up to the end of nineteenth century. It fought many wars with the Tibetan and the British and grappled with many internal revolts. Druk Yul persisted and prevailed over all the odds and consolidate its sovereignty under the leadership of a single line of hereditary kingship, only since 1907 when Ugyen Wangchuk was popularly enthroned. Bhutan opened out itself to the outside world from a state of having been known as the *Land of the Sleeping Dragon* (according to some observers) towards stability, peace and prosperity. Until very recent times, Bhutan has also been described as the Land of the Peaceful Dragon by some authors. Yet, there are few other observers who sees the modern Bhutan developing into a *democratic monarchy with roots deeply entrenched in the affection of the people*, (1988: 222).

Physiography

Bhutan has 3 distinct physiographical units, viz: Sub-Himalayas, the Inner Himalayas and Great Himalayas. Foothills along the Indo-Bhutan border fall under Sub-Himalayan region. Most of the valleys including Thimphu and *Paro* fall under Inner Himalayas and the northern Bhutan with snow capped mountains along the Tibetan borders falls under great Himalayas.

The foothills bordering India from east to west rise higher and higher from south to north direction.

In between several valleys separate the southern foothills and Great Himalayas the mountain ranges. Most of these valleys run north to southerly directions. Some of the main valleys are the Paro, Thimphu, *Punakha, Wangdiphodrang, Tongsa, Bumthang, Shemgang*[2], *Lhuntse* and Tashigang. These valleys (Map 0.2) are in the Inner Himalayas. All the major rivers flow through these valleys.

AmMochhu or the Toorsa River rising from Tibet is a swift and narrow river. It drains Chumbi valley of Tibet and enters India at

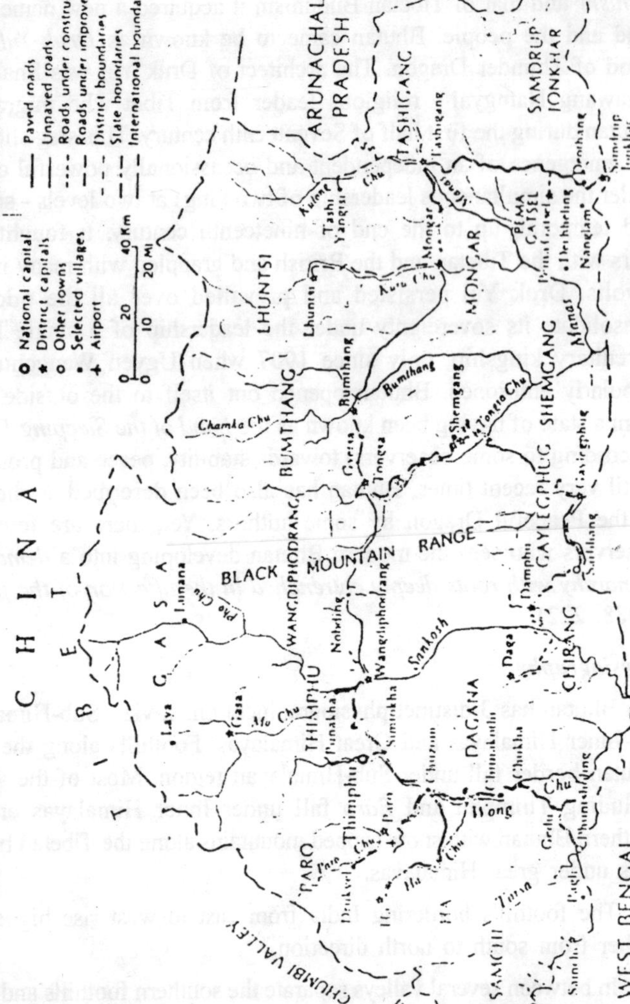

Map. 0.2 Bhutan Political Map: Valleys and Rivers

Phuntsholing after cutting across Samchi district southeasterly and further down joins the Brahmaputra River in the Duars.

Wangchhu or the Raidak River in India also rises from Tibet. Its main affluent are *Paro Chhu, Do Chhu, Ha Chhu*, etc. It drains the valleys of Ha, Paro and Thimphu before entering North Bengal and joins the Brahmaputra as Raidak. It is the longest river in Bhutan.

Mo Chhu or the Sankosh River rises in the Great Himalayan region. Their main affluents are *Pho Chhu* and *Mo Chhu* joining at Punakha valley. It passes through Wangdiphodrang and enters the Duar plains to join the Brahmaputra after assuming the name Sankosh. It is deep and a large river.

Dangme Chhu is the largest river in Bhutan. Almost the whole of eastern Bhutan is drained by it. Their principal affluents are the *Mangde Chhu*, the *Kuri Chhu* and *Dangme Chhu.* It enters Bhutan from eastern Indian frontiers and drains through Tongsa and Bumthang valleys. It further flows down south to India as the Manas and joins the Brahmaputra.

Important Valleys and Dzongs

All the valleys in Bhutan had been important power centres in the past at one time or other. There are huge Dzongs in these valleys at every strategic site. Important valleys in Bhutan starting from the west are Ha, Paro, Thimphu, Punakha, Tongsa, Bunthang Mangde and Tashigang.

Ha valley is the extreme west at an elevation of 8,700 ft. Ha Chhu flows through the valley. The valley is adorned with *Ha Dzong*. The present queen mother of Dorje families belongs to this valley. It has rich historical traditions and legends.

Paro valley is wide and lies at a height of 7,000 ft. towards the east of Ha. It has been an important cultural, political and commercial centre in Bhutan. Pa Chhu flows through it. *Rinchhen Pung* Dzong, *Ta* Dzong and *Drugyal* Dzong stand out in the valley at strategic locations. Paro had direct trade links with Bengal and Tibet. Paro valley has only airport of the country with regular flights to neighbouring countries and overseas.

Thimphu valley is situated at an average elevation of 8,500 ft. Wang Chhu flows through this valley. *Tashichhodzong* (often known as the fortress of the glorious religion) is the most modern Dzong of the kingdom and *Dechenchholing* (the king's palace) are situated in this valley.

Bumthang valley has *Byakar* Dzong. The valley is broad at an altitude of 9,700 ft. Bumthang River a tributary of Manas flows through the valley. Punakha valley lies towards the north-east of Thimphu at an elevation of 4,800 ft. Pho Chhu and Mo Chhu flow through this valley. It is at the confluence of these two rivers that the huge *Punakha* Dzong stands imposingly. This Dzong was the seat of power and politics in medieval Bhutan. Mangde valley is located in the east with the massive and imposing Tongsa Dzong at an altitude of 7,500 ft. on the banks of Mangde Chhu. The present king is the descendant of Tongsa Penlop who found monarchial and hereditary kingship in Bhutan in 1907. Tashigang valley lies at an altitude of 3,500 ft. Its Dzong is built on the bank of Dangme Chhu.

Climate, Forests and Agriculture

The foothill region adjoining the Bengal Duars and Assam plains has sub-tropical monsoon climate. This region has excessive rainfall with average temperature of 20°C and hot and humid throughout the year.

The region is abundant in deciduous natural vegetation. Wild animals like rhinos, elephant, guars, tigers, sambars, bears and many different species of monkeys are found. The forest produces different species of trees like sissoo, khair, sal, semal. Besides, the forest also provides space for large-scale cash crop cultivation like caradamom and orange forming a substantial wealth for the country. People in this region practice shifting and terrace field cultivation. Rice, maize, millet is a major food crop.

The central region, which lies within inner Himalayas, consists of high mountains, valleys and major rivers. The climate in relatively lower valleys of Punakha and Wangdiphodrang is moderate and it is extremely cold in Thimphu, Ha, Paro and Bumthang at higher elevation. This region is also rich in evergreen forest resources with different species of pine trees and wild animals.

Agriculture is mainly confined in fertile valleys like Thimphu, Paro, Punakha, Wangdiphodrang, and Tongsa. Rice is principal crop and apple is grown as cash crop. Major population is concentrated in these valleys.

The northern region lies in the Great Himalayas along Tibetan borders. High peaks- *Gangkar Puensam* (24817 ft), *Jomolhari* (23997 ft), *Masang Gang* (23756 ft) *Tsenden Gang* (23100 ft) *Melunghi Gang* (23100 ft) are located in this region. The lofty ranges above 16500ft remain snow covered and barren but alpine vegetation thrives to feed Yak, *Takkin*, cattle and sheep in summer. The climate is dry and cold. Birch, rhododendron, juniper, fir and spruce are found here. Population in this region is sparse.

People and Population

Bhutanese people may be said to be composed of different racial elements although people of Tibeto-Mongoloid origin with distinct features of cultural patterns. Drukpa Kagyu-form the predominant section of people in the national and political life in Bhutan. This section of the people of Tibetan extraction is known as the *Ngalom* in Bhutan. People of Indo-Mongoloid origin form another minority section of people with distinct cultural patterns. They are settled in southeastern part of the kingdom. They are popularly known as the *Sharcopa* in Bhutan. Yet another sizeable population is of the Indo-Aryan origin that flowed into Bhutan from Bengal and Assam. They are mostly Nepalese officially designated as *Lhotshampas*, who belong to many ethnic groups such as the *Rais*, the *Gurungs*, the *Limbus*, the *Bahuns*, the *Chhetris*, and the *Tharus*. There are also other minority groups like the *Brukpas*, the *Khengpas*, and the *Doyas* within the Indo-Mongoloid groups who speak different dialects and have distinct cultural patterns and ways of life (1980: 17).

According to an ad-hoc official census taken in 1969, the population of Bhutan was about 1,000,000 and urban population was about 30,000. The population of Bhutan was estimated at 1.26 million in 1988 (1992: 31) though in very recent times the figure is being quoted as 0.75 million[3].

Languages

The official language of Bhutan is the *Dzongkha,* although in the southern part of Bhutan Nepali language (*Lhotsham*) has also become an official means of communication and *lingua franca*. According to Bikrama Jit Hasrat, there are four major language groups and approximately 13 to 14 minor dialects in Bhutan. The four major languages are the *Chhoeki* in the northern part of Bhutan: the national language Dzongkha, derived from the former and spoken by the Ngaloms in the northern part of Bhutan. *Sharcopkha* spoken by the Sharcopas in the eastern part of Bhutan, and the Lhotsham of the Nepalese spoken as *lingua franca* in the southern part of Bhutan (1980: 19). No detailed information on the 13-14 minor dialects spoken in Bhutan were available till date.

Background to the Study

The Doyas have not been studied and documented anywhere so far in a systematic fashion. In this respect, they are less fortunate than many other ethnic communities who live in this part of Himalayan region. Not only they are one of the less known and minor ethnic community in Bhutan they also do not matter much in the sociol-political affairs of the country. They are also one of the most unexposed people in Bhutan. The present work is aimed at bringing to light the distinct socio-cultural identity of the people and report on their socio-economic situation.

From the late nineteenth century onwards the Doyas have been mentioned only a few times as a people of Bhutan by a very limited number of scholars and observers. However, no one attempted to write comprehensively of them. The only exception so far is the nine-page paper entitled: *The Doyas: A Small Community in Bhutan* by B. Majumdar, who set the target to present in his own words a *first hand account through his on-the-spot investigation...to Tapakhan, a Doyagaon situated 15 kms from Totapara in 1979*. He collected some general and some significant information about the livelihood practices, religious life, beliefs, festivals, rituals relating to birth, marriage and death, and social organisation, etc. in his report (1991: 141-149). Unfortunately, his report had its own limitations and suffered from the problems of over generalisation about the ways of life of the people. It also made some incorrect information on several counts about the people's ways of life needing critical review to rectify, clarify and elaborate wherever necessary. I consider that the problems in his report arose because of the limited opportunity of knowing the people and the methodology employed in his studies, which were inevitable given the limitations within which the study was made. Nevertheless, some clarifications need to be attended first. Places of Doya settlements in Bhutan like 'Tapakhan' and 'Lamteykhan' as mentioned in his report should have been *Taba* and *Ramteykha* (I have also come across the word 'Dramteykha') to the best of my knowledge. 'Dorkhasiddim' should have been read as Dorokha, which is the sub-divisional headquarters in Samchi district.

It also needs to be noted that no Doya settlement is there at *Dorokha* in present times[4] where the *Dogapa* and Nepali community reside at present. Further as has been noted by Majumdar himself that he could not contact the Doyas living in *Lotukuchu*. But, it must be mentioned that of the two settlements of the Doyas, Lotukuchu group of villages holds the central position, one reason of it being the larger concentration of population therein, the other being the proximity of the place to the historical relics of the Doyas, as has been mentioned by B.Chakravarti (1980). It appears from a close examination of his paper that the author, even while making a pioneering effort on the subject, was only casually familar with the people concerned, and did not have either the time or opportunity to pursue the subject as deeply as was needed.

The Doyas are a group of pre-literate people in Bhutan making barely 0.136% of the total population. However, it is very difficult to form a correct estimate of their relative importance because the total population of Bhutan, which was estimated at 1,260,000, is itself not beyond doubts (1995: 7). The Doyas have their own traditional ways of life and belief systems that persist despite the influence of Drukpa Kagyu Sect of Mahayana Buddhism that is officially being promoted in the state[5] and Nepali communities who live in their immediate neighbourhoods.

Very little is known about these people and practically nothing is known about their historical background because no mention is made in any of the older Chronicles and official records of Bhutan. The British and other Indian visitors to the kingdom, of course sometimes mentioned the Doyas, without any significant elaboration upon them. Under the circumstances there are many people in Bhutan and elsewhere who do not know anything about these people[6]. It was perhaps, for the first time that the Bhutanese National Weekly Newspaper, the *Kuensel* (1987: 25 July) brought out a report on these people attracting attention of administration and the general public towards their deplorable socio-economic conditions. The measures taken up for the development of these people by the Royal Government of Bhutan were also reported. The report recognised the Doyas as a distinctive ethnic community in Bhutan.

The Doyas live in two separate communities called Lotukuchu and Taba-Ramtey under Samchi Dzongkhag (District). They have been recorded under many different names such as *Doiya* or *Roiya* in D.Sunder's *Survey* and *Settlement of the Western Duars* (1895: i-viii), *Daya* in B. K. Roy Burman's *Dynamics of Persistence and Change of a Small Community Totos* (1958: 28) and *Dahyas* in Bikrama Jit Hasrat's *History of Bhutan* (1980: 17). However, in Bhutan while they are popularly known as the Doya and called as *Lhop* by the Ngalom (the Drukpa of northern Bhutan), the Doyas themselves prefer to be known as Lhopu.

Most of the historical accounts and reports relating to Bhutan and adjoining areas of 19th and 20th century available to me were disappointing by the absence of any descriptive account of the Doyas except for some general information and brief mention of ethnological propositions.

It is needless to say that description of any society is comprehensible only when it is portrayed in the context of a larger socio-cultural and historical context of the people and region that surround them. The point assumes importance particularly because the whole of northeast frontier of India along the southern Himalayan region has witnessed a continuous flux of population of different creeds and ethnic origins since ancient times (Hutton, J H: 1963). The cultural and political confrontations of different ethnic groups of diverse customs, creeds and colours must have also resulted in synthesizing number of mixed cultural and racial groups of people. This is precisely another problem area with regard to ethnic relation of Doyas with other tribes especially the *Meches*, Totos, *Koch* and *Monpas* in this region that requires further investigation.

However, for the purpose of the present work a review of certain historical and political antecedents of the country relating to the Doya region and the contemporary socio-economic and political situations of the country in which they find themselves would help us comprehend and elucidate the plight of the Doyas much better.

Historical Antecendents of the Country

About the earlier history of Bhutan Ashley Eden (1864: 108) records that Bhutan belonged to a tribe called *Tephoo* who believed to be people of Cooch Behar. They are defeated in fight with the

Tibetan Sepoys sent by the Lassa Government. Consequently, they left Bhutan leaving behind some of them[7].

Bose, K.K. (1815: 110) gives another account, which Eden claims to be a Booteah version. According to Bose, Bootan was at the time . . . ruled by a Raja of the Cooch Tribe. When the first Dhuram Raja came, he (Dharam Raja) performed many miracles . . . contrary to the observances of Cooch tribe, . . . at which the Cooch Raja was so terrified that he disappeared with his whole family and servants underground, and slaves of Cooch Raja . . . who remained were instructed in his (Dharam Raja) own religious faith and customs and ..their descendants still remain at Poonakha and form the caste or tribe called Thep (1864: 339). Subsequently, more and more Tibetans poured in and slowly and slowly they became a dominant religio-political power and started increasing their dominion in the neighbouring regions, Sikkim in the west and Duars in the south by domination over many ethnic inhabitants or driving them away.

Further, B. Chakravarti records, Some Koch were pushed south of Bhutan organised themselves again under the name Hajo...who ruled the western portion of Kamrupa. It is said . . . their policy was to coalesce with the Mech and the Kacharis so as to be able to defeat the comtemporary Koch and the Tephoo rulers of Bhutan (1980: 15).

At such juncture of historical formation in Bhutan, a process of creating an independent power centre around the tenets of a different sect of Buddhism was going on under the stewardship of the would be Dharam Raja. In the course of time, the migrant Tibetans of Drukpa persuassion into Bhutan amassed much of power and became a despotic and feudal society by subjugating ethnic tribes, practising wide spread slavery, indulging in forced labour and treacheries on dominated groups of people. Nirmala Das in her book Dragon country identifies this period as, . . . the period marked by the disappearance of original inhabitants and advent of Tibetan influence on the traditional culture (1974: 17).

At the backdrop of these historical premises there is a possibility of picturing out some ethnic minority groups of people who were culturally dominated, politically reduced to insignificance, demographically displaced, socially disturbed and economically exploited, taking shelter at many different locations in the deep forests of Bhutan. The process was accentuated by the consolidation of British rule in India. It is possible that Doyas may have been one among those communities that were affected first by the process of Drukpa consolidation in Bhutan, and subsequently by the advent of British rule in the neighbouring India.

Against this background, we can understand why some scholars feel inclined to trace an ethnic relation among many small ethnic communities in Bhutan. Michael tentatively traces some similarities between *Tok-top* who in turn are known to Bhutanese as *Mon-pa* of *Mang-sde-lung, Kheng and gZhong-sgar called Upper and Lower Toktokha* in the south of *Pagro* and the people living in *Taba-Dramten* and *Lotukuchu* in the area of southern Bhutan west of the border town of *Phuntshogslling* all as possible splinters of *gDung people who once ruled whole over Bhutan before the migration from the north* (1980: xvii-xviii). And B.K. Roy Burman relates Daya who lives 6 miles from Totapara in West Bengal bordering Bhutan. In his unpublished Thesis based on different oral versions of the past history of the Totos in the adjoining area of Bhutan he wrote, *Totos and Daya previously used to live together inside Bhutan. . . . Toto and Daya were once cousins . . . and Toto must have migrated from Bhutan. . . : Paro chief ordered Toto to settle at Totopara for porterage works, and . . . Toto migrated out due to out-break of war between Bhutia and the Mech, further, Totos . . .* have common origin with the Koch (1958: 55-56).

Extrapolating from the studies on the impacts of Bhutia political-cultural influence on Toto he further says, . . . *no traditional structure of the Toto existed at all. Toto was a new Tribe - a child of Bhutia state-craft* (1958: 86).

His observations scratched only the edge of the problem and it demanded a comprehensive explorative ethnography on all these seemingly related ethnic people for a meaningful remark on their traditional culture and relations.

The scholars are generally inclined to trace *Bonism* or some form of spirit and nature of worship as earlier religion of ethnic people of Bhutan before the arrival of Buddhism from Tibet. B. Chakravarti classified all the ethnic people of Bhutan into three major Linguistic groups i.e. the *Mon,* the *Khen* and the *Dzongkha* speaking people thereby subsuming rest of the ethnic minority groups of people under the three major groups denying a justice to socio-cultural particularities and identities of the latter. However, Doyas did not escape his observation, although it is difficult to find out to which group Doyas may be related. In his passing note, on the Doyas of Lotukuchu he made a very significant point about the historical background of the Doya not found in any other books. He writes, *they (Doyas) once ruled over this portion of Bhutan* (Western Bhutan foothills) *and the ruins of the capital of Doya kings are found at Demchukha* (Denchukha?), *northeast of Dorokha* (1980: 18). Incidentally, B.K. Roy Burman also traces the original settlement of the Totos in Deingche *garden* in Bhutan from where they were displaced after the boundary demarcation between the British and Bhutan Government, . . . *following an order from the chief of Paro* (1958: 54). Unfortunately for me it is difficult to say if the two names of places are at separate location or they are corruption in the pronunciation of the same place name by different people.

History of Bhutan has been marked by political instability, internal strife among rival political powers under the leadership of different Lamas from Tibet professing to spread different sects of Buddhism from as early as 18th century to as late as 19th century. The situation worsened when the responsibility of administration of the land went into the hands of Penlops, resulting in rivalries and continuous confrontations among them. Conditions of lower section of people were at the worst. Ashely Eden aptly described the situation:

> *The misery of the subjects of a Government thus constituted can hardly be aggravated and it is not to be wondered at that the country is rapidly becoming depopulated and relapsing into waste . . . (Penlops) exercise authority of life and death, but it must not be inferred from this that there is anything like judicial system in the country . . . (Revenue system) strictly speaking there is no system. The only limit on the Revenue demand is the natural limit of the power of the officials to extort more. Nothing that a Booteah possesses is his own,... The lower classes, whether of villages or public servants, are little better than the slaves of the higher officials. In regard to them no rights of property are observed, . . . No official receives a salary: he has certain districts made over to him, and he may get what he can out of them . . . a certain portion of his gains he is compelled to send to the Durbar, and the more he extorts and the more he sends to the Durbar the longer his tenure of office is likely to be* (1864: 115-118).

However, discounting certain extent of exaggeration by Eden in his book it is still apparent that the lingering of the past attitudes on the part of some of the administrators persists in remote areas like Samchi.

Contemporary situations of the country relating to the Doyas

From this, rather despotic socio-economic situation when Bhutan entered into 20th century, peace and a stable form of Government emerged under a single centre of authority. A hereditary Monarchy was institutionalised under a single centre of authority. A hereditary Monarchy was institutionalised under the leadership of the King Ugyen Wangchuk in 1907 by abolishing the system of government under the Dhuram Rajas, Deb Rajas and the Penlops. A sovereign kingdom was founded but much remained to be done in the hand of the first king to organise the whole administrative system and regenerate its economy by exploiting its resources for the development of the country. There was a dire need of manpower to exploit the rich forest resources, Bhutan started opening its doors to neighbouring countries, attracting manpower, co-operation and help to develop its economy.

Hordes of Nepalese from the neighbouring regions immigrated and fulfilled the labour requirements. They were given land freely to settle and participate in the development works (1993: 3), in a relatively secular environment. Decades passed when Nepali population swelled up to a considerable proportion and posed a percieved cultural threat to Drukpa-kagyu way of Bhutanese national culture and demography. A political crisis surfaced in the whole of south Bhutan in 1990 when the Nepalese took to streets demanding greater democratic rights of representation in the present governance of the country. The age-old cultural and political identity of the country was questioned. It was a movement for re-defining the national cultural and political identity of the country. Under the circumstances, the slogan of One Nation One People was not only raised by the Royal Government of Bhutan, but it was seriously sought to be implemented by them causing opposition among a large section of the Lhotshampas.

Loyalty of the people particularly in the southern Bhutan (where maximum migrants lived) to the sovereignty of the country and the king was in question. A clear line emerged between Bhutanese denizens and other sections of people who acted against the interest of the nation. The latter group of people was popularly known as the *Ngolop* or the anti-nationals. In the ensuing political crisis in the southern Bhutan ethnically affined people, who otherwise, largely remained neglected and unheard got ever-greater attention of the administrators. Doyas as one among them came into the spotlight. Concerted efforts were on to uplift and integrate the least known ethnic people of Bhutan with deliberate attention from the government. There were attempts to rename the *Sengten* Primary School as Doya *Sengdhyen* Primary School and many other attempts were made to rename places and people in the southern Bhutan that had some kind of Nepali cultural shed. These changes affected the Doyas as well.

Boarding facilities in the only primary school at Sengten, which used to be opened to all the communities without discrimination became to be reserved for the Doya children exclusively for their upliftment. Nepalese children who were in the boarding were asked to attend the school as day-scholars. Around 50-60 Doya youths were picked up for militia training for maintaining the security of the area against anti-national militants and miscreants. Many a high ranking security personnel, officials and religious heads often visited the school and inquired into the security and development concerns of the Doyas, in particular. Strict land regulation ceilings were enforced. Active efforts were on to open a motor-able road to the Doyas in 1992 and 1993. Special national language classes were organised at several places in the Doya villages during 1992-93 for national integration causing immense heartburns to the neighbouring Nepali communities. This was done to promote the use of the national language as against the popularity of Lhotsham language among the Doyas. Adult people were also trained on the national code of conduct (*Driglam Namzha)* in the school premises and emphasis was laid on the national cultural forms of dance and songs in the school as part of the curriculum.

The Royal Government of Bhutan also encourages them to assert their identity as Lhop to highlight their cultural affinity to the Bhutanese mainstream and to differentiate them from the Nepali community in the context of the present socio-political situation of the country. Encouraged by these efforts the Doyas began to deliberately register their wards names with the title Lhop in the school registers instead of the common use of the title Doya or their preferred title Lhopu. The reason is, people who matter in the school were the Drukpas. It is possible that the title Doya may go into disuse from the common parlance soon in Bhutan. However, the social reality is that they are still popularly known as the Doya and fewer people call them Lhop in Bhutan. In this study, I would be using the same name Doya more often to prevent further confusion and Lhop and/or Lhopu in certain contexts only although, it is still difficult to say which is the endo-ethnonym of the people themselves.

It is in this context an ethnographic account of the Doyas gains its importance to understand the changing processes that the society is undergoing. A reference point has to be there to see the changes in time to come. There has also to be a meaningful dialogue to guide the developmental needs of the people lest they should suffer from an identity crisis later.

Today, Doyas are poised for a change under pressure from the government and Doyas also seem to respond positively to the changing factors even at the cost of losing peace and harmonious relation with their neighbouring Nepali community. They now strongly feel that the Nepalese had forced their way in their locality and that they are being dominated by them. It is feared that an ethnic conflict between the communities may ensue in the region in near future.

Objectives of the Study

Doyas have not been properly understood largely because they have lived in the shadow of dominant cultural groups inside Bhutan. Their cultural and political identity has been systematically undermined as a minority group in the course of nation-building processes of the country. They have remained inaccessible to the outside world for wide ranging social intercourse due to cultural, geographical and political barrier between India and Bhutan. The little information available about the people are mosty based upon secondary sources and rarely, if ever, a visit to Taba which is easier to access. The Lotukuchu group of Doya represents 70% of Doya population but they have not been studied so far. Hence, the picture of the people that emerge out of the little information is hazy and incorrect. Moreover, prolonged socio-cultural intercourse of the people with the dominant national culture and the influence of the Nepali culture in their immediate environment seem to have affected certain changes in the traditional ways of the pre-literate Doya people. Most of them speak fluent Nepali outside their communities. The people have been exposed to modern education: occupations and the fast growing market economy only during the recent past. The political upheavel in southern Bhutan has also affected the Doya people, and there are conscious attempts to assimilate the Doyas to the dominant national culture of the Drukpas. Doyas as an ethnic minority are disposed to further change and we may have nothing on record about their traditional culture. Therefore, the objectives of the present work were mainly four.

Firstly, it was to present a first hand ethnographic account of the Doya ways of life. Secondly, it was to make an attempt to understand the past and present socio-political situations of the country and the region that affected the Doyas. Thirdly, it was to study the basic structure and nature of Doya social organisation through their kin terms and relations. Fourthly, it was to study the traditional economy and the livelihood pattern of the people and the impacts of the changing socio-economic situation of the region on the traditional economy of the people.

Although the present work was intended to give a fuller picture of the Doyas touching upon almost all aspects of the people's ways of life it has its own limitations also. The religious and political aspects have been inadequately explored and in-depth studies on several areas of social and cultural life were overlooked.

Geographical Location of the Study Area

The area of study is confined within the Dorokha subdivision of southeastern Samchi district of Bhutan. The study was mainly carried out among the Lotukuchu group of Doyas comprising of five contiguous settlement areas namely: *Satakha, Sanglung, Upper and Lower Lotukuchu,* and *Lotok.* In addition, three neighbouring Rai villages namely: *Bisgaon, Lapcheygaon* and *Lumbey* were also studied for comparative purposes. These villages are located along the slopes of Sengten hills. At a later stage, a general survey of the whole region including Dorokha and *Denchukha* located on either sides of AmMochhu river was also done touching upon the socio-cultural aspects of the *Hapas, Dogapas, Nepalese, Lepchas*[8] and Doyas of Taba-Ramteykha communities.

This study area, in particular the Doya region is kept under restricted category by the Royal Government of Bhutan. Outsiders without proper permit are not allowed access to this region.

Approach, Method and Techniques

Doyas for me was just a fortunate encounter when I voluntarily took up a teaching job on contract under the Royal Government of

Bhutan in the beginning of 1990. I just wanted to earn for myself while seeing something new and exciting in a strange land after doing Master's Degree in Social Anthropology from the Delhi University in the early part of the same year.

As a student I always stood in favour of the oppressed and neglected for justice and humanity. It was this concern of mine that interested me to voluntarily undertake the study of the Doyas in particular and their neighbouring communities in general in the kingdom of Bhutan while serving as a fulltime teacher in the Sengten Primary School in the remote Doya region, for use in posterity.

The present work therefore, is the result of a very personal and conscious effort of knowing the Doyas, their ways of life in particular and their neighbouring communities in general in an attempt to give an inside story of those who have been undermined and neglected for so long.

This report presents a factual account of the people in the way they see their ways of life and I as a student of anthropology and a concerned outsider understand of them from a very close personal interactions, observations and occasional participations in their personal and social life activities during my four years of stay among them. 'Therefore, certain extent of Doya biasness cannot be ruled out in whole narration as against others in their surrounding. Further, with due respect to all other communities mentioned in the text, I have deliberately used the general geographical titles to refer to group of people like; *Ngalom*, *Lhotsham*, *Sharcop*, etc. to avoid unnecessary misrepresentation of specific communities in this report.'

It is a humble attempt to present the Doyas ways of life in as much as it was an explorative nature to give an enthnographic account of the society and economy of the Doya people. Since, it was a maiden and a private venture for me in a virgin area, the work was carried out in very peculiar and difficult circumstances. There were lots of limitations and constrains during the field and thereafter in writing up this report in the present form.

In the first place, there was no body that could understand and appreciate the anthropological concern for the people while in Bhutan. There was no guidance, support and encouragement from any quarters during the fieldwork for the first two and half years. I was often taken as a crazy fellow at the best or a suspicious character sometimes, inquiring about people's social affairs beyond what was subject of banal discussion about people in general. I also discovered, later that the Royal Government of Bhutan does not necessarily encourage any outsider to research in Bhutan.

Secondly, I did not have a chance to update my knowledge of Anthropology during the research and after, first because of my employment as a primary school teacher in a remote corner of Bhutan, and then because I did not qualify for academic profession in India. Even when I managed to register myself as an external Ph. D. candidate at the centre for Himalayan Studies of the North Bengal University it was not possible for me to seek regular guidance from my supervisor, as I had to take up a job in a voluntary organisation immediately after leaving Bhutan.

Thirdly, because of the full engagement in the school on all the working days there was limited option to adopt the Participant-observation method of field research even while I tried to maintained the basic approach by taking residence among the Doyas, sharing food and shelter, participating in their activities and observing the spontaneous events of life unfolding whenever and where ever chance happened. I always tried to be in the village - reaching out to every nook and corner on all holidays and off the school hours.

Therefore, the method followed for the study falls in the borderline of participant observation in the fashion no longer that much in vogue, of the classical anthropological inquiry into a virgin territory. Information were collected through observations of and informal interactions with the people as intensively and extensively as was possible and without any conscious efforts to select only few respondents from among the people and yet to be so close with the people to be seen as one of theirs. However, the Royal Government of Bhutan also thrust an opportunity upon me to conduct a formal survey of the people in March 1995. I utilised the opportunity to supplement my study by collecting some data on some aspects of economy and kin terms of the Lepchas, Dogapas and the Rais for comparative purposes.

Rapport with the people

I landed up in Sengten without in any preconceived notion in mind. All that I knew was that I was there to see something new.

Once at Sengten, it took sometimes to adapt to the local environment and the exotic life-style. My colleagues in the school helped me to know the place and also the people. I had to go slow as I was not conversant in Nepali, which was the commonly spoken language, there. It took some five months to pick up a workable knowledge of the local language with the help of my colleagues, school children and Doya staff (non-teaching) in the school. By the end of the year I could manage to speak some Doya language with the help of Doya children in the school. During the same year, my colleagues also took me around the Nepali and Doya villages nearby the school. We were always welcomed with drinks and presentations. While being at Sengten I became quite acquainted with almost all the local people as many of them used to come to the school premises for some work[9] or the other.

Children in the school and villages were dirty and unkempt. Some of them were afflicted with common diseases, which could be easily attended. I took up the responsibility of looking after the health of the children in the school and provided personal care to all of them. This responsibilty brought me very close to the children that in turn helped me a good deal in developing close relation with their parents at home. I always kept in the company of the children who taught me their language and educated me about their place and ways of life. They often took me to their homes for seeing sick person in the village and also for showing me their homes and villages.

They became good friends, teachers and guides for me in learning about the Doyas. My command over the *Lhokpu* language delighted the people and they developed a special liking for me. Doya children used to call me *Pang,* which meant paternal uncle even while in the school. However, it was not enough for an ethnographer who was also a schoolteacher working from morning till evening although the interest and ability to talk in the local language and also the first-aid services I was providing had created a special place for me in the village. I was deliberately looking for an opportunity to take shelter in one of their homes. But there were two problems. One, the traditional houses did not have space for an outsider. Two, my colleagues were discouraging me as they could not make any sense of my adventurism. They also considered Nepali villages were a better place if taking shelter in village was so desired. Nevertheless, their was a will and so there was a way.

Education as a state subject was free in Bhutan. Doya children in the school were given stipend to encourage them pursue high school level education. Dropout problem of Doya children and their parents' reluctant attitude to education was acknowledged as a big problem by the district administration. I volunteered to take this opportunity to stay in the village among people for special admission drive of Doya children in the school. And thereon, I continued to stay but in the village at different places and different times in Lotukuchu between 1991 and 1994. The Headmaster of the school was convinced and I succeeded in obtaining a record enrolment of Doya children in 1992 session. *Dasho Dzongdag* (District Collector) and other heads of department in the district visited the school and the Doyas during the period. I had opportunity to express my interest in the development of the Doyas and I was acknowledged as one of the Doya sympathisers. In 1992 I was able to send a preliminary report on the Doyas entitled *Doyas: Past and Present* to then Director, Education Department of the Royal Government of Bhutan (Appendix I). By the end of 1993 the Director wrote back appreciating my report and at the same time seeking my help in developing a document of the people under a standing order from the Home Ministry of the Royal Government. After a brief follow up communication and personal meeting with him, I was given an order to formally and officially conduct a short but very productive survey for twenty days intensively among the Lotukuchu group of Doyas and a general socio-cultural survey of all the neighbouring communities including the Dogapas, Lepchas and other Nepali communities across the AmMochhu. A thirty five-page document to support and elaborate upon the previous report was submitted to the Director as result of the survey work.

Things were not so easy for me. My personal attachment with the Doyas and taking shelter among them was seen as a sort of detachment from the rest of the Nepali communities. They expressed their feelings by often calling me "Doya *juwain*" or "Doya *Bura*", meaning a resident-husband among the Doyas or a Doya old man. On the contrary, Doyas themselves found in me a *Chan* (son) for the elders, a *Pang* (*Patenal* uncle) or a *Pu* (elder brother) for the children and younger ones while I would always wonder why I was not addressed as *ku* (maternal uncle). It was a struggle to maintain a balance between the two communities.

I tried to maintain good relations with each and every *Karbari* (village Heads) of neighbouring Nepali villages and also with some of the Nepali *Bijuwa* (Sorcerer) who frequented the Doyas for their healing services. I had occasions to accompany them in their night performances. I learnt a great deal from them about the Doyas, as they knew them also. They liked me, trusted me and even wanted me to take a Nepali girl for my wife.

While in the village I tried to reach out to everyone in every nook and corner of Lotukuchu group of villages with children as my guides and friends. I was affectionately welcomed at their homes. I used to get current information on every small and big incidents ranging from childbirth, funeral services, religious activities, family quarrels and seasonal activities in the villages. Sometimes the villagers would approach me seeking my help and intervention into their small or big personal problems. There were occasions when I received marriage proposals from among the Doyas also. There was an occasion when I announced my desire of adopting a young widow with a minor kid in Lotok village which however, remained unfulfilled.

Tools and Techniques of the Study

The major part of the study was carried out in very informal manner without using any of the conventional tools and techniques of interview. Much of the information collected in day-to-day interactions and personal observations and experiences were religiously recorded every day in personal dairies. Some of the genealogical charts and maps were worked out with my Doya friends and students. Wherever possible on the spot investigations, observations and participations in most of the social events were made to record facts about peoples' way of life. Home visits, round-the-fire discussions on matters of mutual interests over a drink and being of some help at times of crisis and needs also helped gain much insights and knowledge about peoples' perception and way of life. At a later stage, camera and tape recorder were used to record some social and cultural activities, folklores and songs of the people. Number of biographies were taken from a number of companion friends in informal interviews (Appendix II).

The draft report of all my findings about the Doya ways of life was presented to some of the learned elders and very few educated Doyas for necessary final crosschecking and verifications. The basic findings about them were appreciated and approved by Doyas at the last stage before leaving Bhutan in 1995.

Plan of Presentation

I have made a major focus on the social organisation, Kin terms and relations and livelihood pattern of Doyas in comparatively greater detail because of certain urgency that beset the present work.

Firstly, the traditional ways of life of the people are currently exposed to a fast changing socio-political scenario in the country. The little tradition of the Doyas is greatly influenced by the great tradition of the Drukpa cultural mainstream patronised by the Royal Government of Bhutan for their development. They are being weaned away from the influences of the Nepali culture into their ways of life in their immediate neighbourhood as part of national integration. The modern education through the schools and Health Service Centres in their vicinity and market economy is also affecting their ways of life bringing a change in their tradition and culture.

Secondly as this monograph is going to be first of its kind to give a first hand account of the people, I have also tried to give an overview of their ways of life touching upon all relevant aspects in relation to their immediate environment in an attempt to clarify many of the misleading information current among ethnographers and curious audiences outside.

The main report is distributed in five separate chapters besides the general introduction and the concluding sections. A general introduction to the land and people of Bhutan collected from differernt sources books and also my own knowledge and experiences relating to the historical antencendents and contemporary situation affecting the Doyas have been given in the Introduction chapter.

Chapter 1 presents the geographical location of the Doyas, their village settlements and social relations with other people in their surroundings, their demographic situation and oral account of demographic trends in the past, their family organisation, household articles, dresses, occupation, daily activities, food habits, health situation, recreational activities and recent educational development and modern occupation of the people.

Chapter 2 gives an account of their social organisation, origins of different lineages and associated deities, the nature of Doya matriliny and matrilocality, marriage rules and development cycle of a consanguinal family.

Chapter 3 describes Kin terms and relation of Doya society to a certain depth to show how an individual born is identified with certain roles and status with respect to sex of a person as s/he passes through the whole schema of social matrix of the society. An attempt is made to classify the Doya system along the Murdock, Lowie and Krichhoff typologies. At the end of this chapter an attempt is also made to compare and contrast the Doya system of kin term and relation with other systems existing in the neighbourhood of the Doyas in Bhutan to further elucidate the Doya system of social relation that makes them different from others.

Chapter 4 describes the rites and rituals that give meaning and essence to Doya ways of life during the transition of an individual from Birth to Death. It also tries to articulate the Doya philosophy of life and death from the way they respond to questions relating to different life situation.

Chapter 5 describes the economy and livelihood patterns of the people in relation to their natural environment and people around them. In this chapter, I have also tried to give a comparative study of means of livelihood and food production level among the Doya villages with that of a neighbouring Rai village with the help of exhaustive statistical data. Impacts of the market economy on the traditional economy and livelihood pattern of the Doyas are also discussed here in brief. An exhaustive data on household economy of each residential unit is provided at the end in several annexures.

Each chapter ends with a summary note and a brief summary and reflections of my experiences and learning from the Doya society and economy is given in the Summary and Conclusion at the end of the chapters. Correspondence with the Royal Government of Bhutan relating to my official involvement in the study of the Doyas and the persons and personalities who were closely associated with me during the whole length of my stay among the Doyas are also given in separate Appendices I and II, respectively at the end. Relevant documents and supporting information and data are provided as Annexure at the end of each chapter wherever, necessary. Other information and data that are not directly related to the present studies but provide important clue and insights to the racial background of the Doyas and their linguistic classification are provided in Appendix III. I am sure this information might provide some important clue to future researches in the region. A detail genealogical chart of one of the major matrilineage among the Doyas that helps in elucidating the descriptions on the Doya social organisation and relations in chapters 2 and 3 is also given in a separate Appendix IV.

A detail list of local terms, words and local names of places often occurring in the text is reproduced in the Glossary.

References cited in this text follow simple style of putting only the author and page number of the source book in parenthesis. A detail list of select bibliography is given at the end of the chapters. Maps, sketches and charts are inserted at appropriate places while photographs/plates are given at the end of the book. Lists of all the illustrations are provided separately indicating the page numbers between which they are located in the text. Table are inserted inside the text at appropriate places. The local names of places, terms, words and phrases will be in *italics* only when they are appearing first time in the text. To distinguish the Doya names, terms and words from other languages spoken in the country the particular language is often indicated in parentheses in the text.

NOTES AND REFERENCES

1. Chakravarti (1980: 30) claims that before the advent of Buddhism in Bhutan people had an indigenous religion, which was based on naturalistic belief in the sky gods (lha), water gods (klu) and the earth gods (sabdag) and mountain gods (gnyans)
2. Spellings of names of several places in Bhutan have been recently rewritten according to Dzongkha phonetics. Some of these alternative names have been listed in the Glossary.
3. See also Himal (July/August 1992: 17) and Dorji, C.T.(1995: 7).
4. However, there used to be some Doya settlements around two to three hundred years ago says Guman Singh Gurung, a local respondent of Maney Gaon at Dorokha on my visit. The only remnant of the Doya at present times at Dorokha is the ruins of *Maney Chhorten* standing in the mid of paddy field. It is believed that the Doyas erected it. Local Nepalis residents including the Hapas (who migrate seasonally in the Doya region) believe that a powerful deity reside in the ruin of mud and stone structure which is still standing today. They worship the deity by offering meat, food and drinks every year.
5. At least three children were being imparted with religious education in the Lamaic tradition in different Monastries of the country although role of the Lama in the ritualistic life of the people was not in vogue.

6. It is surprising to note that a very recent publication on the *Political and Religious History of Bhutan* by a Bhutanese author recognises the *Monpas as a mongloid stock as the original inhabitants of Bhutan living in the dense forests of southern Himalayas.* It also says that *a tribal people known as Tabab - Damteb (Doya) lives on the bank of AmMochhu under Samtse Dzongkhag* indicating resemblance with *the Todas race of north Bengal having different clothes and customs from all other people in Bhutan.* Further, the author claims that there are *eleven languages in Bhutan* among which *Lhobi-kha* (which would literarily mean language spoken by people in south) *in Taba and Damtey villages under Samtse Dzongkhag* (1995: 8-10). It must be borne in mind that there is no indigenous people called *Tabab-Damteb* and also that the people in the north Bengal bordering Bhutan are known as the Totos and not as *Todas* (Todas are infact a south Indian tribe) as far I know. The author also does not seem to have any knowledge about the race relations of many indigenous people in Bhutan as described by Michael Aris (1980).
7. *Tephoo, generally believed to have been people of Cooch Behar . . . a fight ensued with Tibetan sepoys sent by Lassa Government, Tephoos gave away and went down to the plains with an exception of few who remained in a mental capacity . . . whose descendants are to be found still holding the lowest offices about the Forts . . . their appearance clearly indicates their plains origin* (Eden, Ashley: 1864).
8. A minority group of Lepchas live in Denchukha hills just opposing the Sengten hills across the AmMochhu. Hapas are a migratory pastoral group who migrate into the Doya region seasonally from northern highlands of Bhutan. Dogpas were also migratory people from the northern highlands but they are settled permanently in large community at Dorokha sub-divisional H.Q.
9. A School Management and Development Committee comprising of the Headmaster, teachers, Block representative leader and heads of villages belonging to both Nepali and Rai communities used to meet at the school regularly to look into the labour and material requirements of the boarding school.

CHAPTER 1
Physical and Social Setting

Location and Geographical Features of Doya Habitat

The Doyas live in two physically separate hills in the southwestern district of Bhutan, Samchi, bordering Sikkim in the west and *Jalpaiguri* district of West Bengal in India to the south. Road communication to Samchi district is only from the Indian side. The National Highway No. 31 and the North-Eastern Frontiers Railway lines run parallel to the borderline between India and Bhutan providing basic communication to all the southern districts of Bhutan. The nearest approach to Samchi on this national highway is at Banarhat, which is at 12 km from the District headquarters. There are local taxis and bus services to go to Samchi via a market called the *Chamurchi* on the Indian side. There is regular road communication between Samchi and Phuntsholing - a commercial town and the main Gateway to Bhutan from India. There are also regular bus services between Phuntsholing and *Siliguri* - a commercial centre also known as the Gateway to the India's northeast. Phuntsholing is under another southern district of Bhutan called *Chukha* neighbuoring Samchi district on the eastern side.

Samchi is also a hill district gradually rising to a height of 3000 to 3500 ft. approximately, from the Tea gardens in the Duar plains bordering India. The district has basically no road communication except for a stretch of 42 km of black top road running parallel to Indian borderline. This road connects the district H.Q Samchi with another sub-division called Sipsoo located along the Bhutan foothills in the extreme southwestern corner of the district. All communication inside the district is done on foot and ponies.

The biggest river that passes through the interior hills of Samchi district is AmMochhu originating from the Tibetan region in the north.

It cuts across Samchi southeasterly and flows down to India as Toorsa from Phuntsholing town (Map 0.2). The river flows very swiftly and is shallow in Bhutan. There are several other small rivers and streams like *Jalđhaka*—originating from Sikkim hills, *Jiti* and *Damti* (Chamurchi Khola in India) originating from a large watershed in Samchi hills that drains out into the Indian side in the south (Map - 1.1). The two Doya settlements under Dorokha *Dungkhag* (subdivision) in Samchi district are located on either side of AmMochhu (also called *Moti* by the Doyas) on the hill slopes. One settlement on the southern side of the river is called Lotukuchu located in the interior hills and the other is Taba–Ramteykha[1] located near Phuntsholing town. Lotukuchu is approximately at a distance of 30-35 km from Samchi headquarters and 15 km from the Dorokha Dungkhag. To go to Lotukuchu one has to start on foot right from the district headquarters, track along the Damti river cutting across it several times for about a distance of 15 km and finally climb on the hills to a height of 3000 m walking along a further stretch of 15-20 km. One path breaks away from this route at a place called *Sangguri,* that leads to Lotukuchu at 6 km. Another path leads to the Dorokha sub-divisional headquarters towards the north direction. The first path continues along shoulder and ridges of hill ranges in the southern direction to finally reach Lotukuchu. It usually takes 7-8 hours of walk to reach Lotukuchu and 8-9 hours of walk to reach Dorokha headquarters from Samchi.

Taba-Ramteykha is easily approached from Phuntsholing town on foot. Taba and Ramteykha are two separate settlements. Taba is located at the AmMochhu riverbank on the foothills at a distance of 10-12 km from Phuntsholing. Ramteykha is located on the hills along the river at an altitude of about 1500 ft approximately. It is at a distance of about 20 km from Phuntsholing. One can also go to Taba-Ramteykha from Lotukuchu on foot but the path is rather difficult and dangerous. The distance between the two settlements is 35-40 km approximately, taking minimum nine hours of trekking along the river AmMochhu, crossing over number of ridges of *Panbari* hills before finally entering Taba after crossing the turbulent river on a raft. Ramteykha is another 6 km walk on the hills. *Totopara,* the village where the Totos reside in West Bengal, India, is located along the Indian border at a distance of 12-15 km from Taba.

The Dorokha subdivision can be physically divided into four main hills Dorokha proper, Denchukha, Sengten and Panbari hills. River

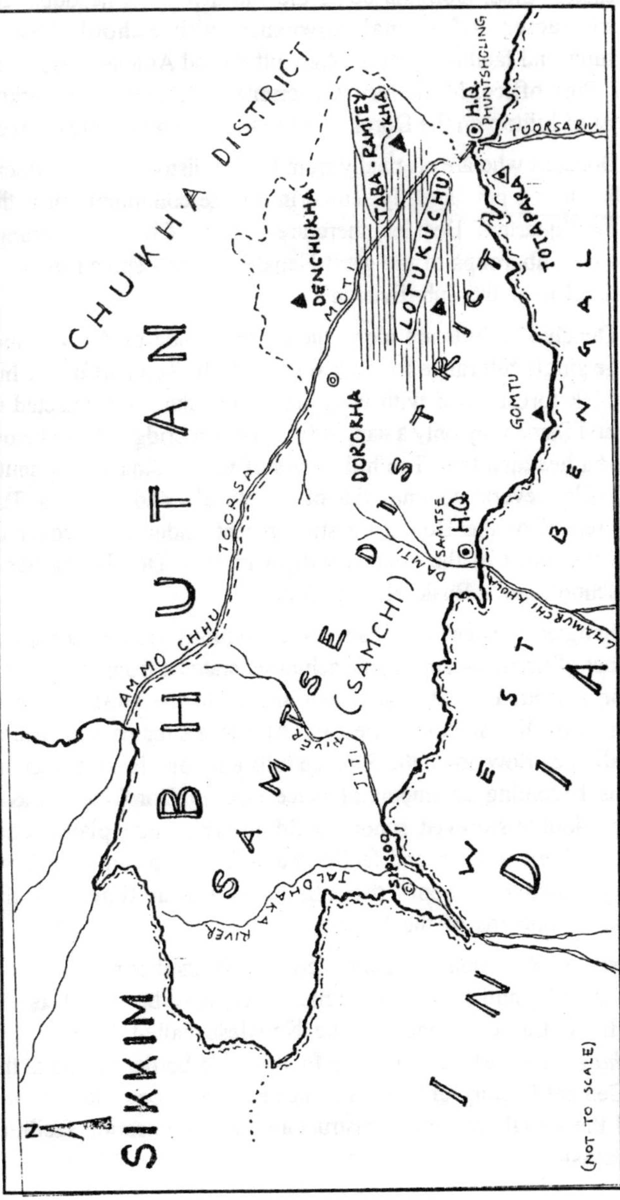

Map. 1.1: Samchi District showing Doya Settlement Areas

and streams separate them. Dorokha , Sengten and Panbari hills are on the south-western side of AmMochhu river and Denchukha is on the northeastern side. Dorokha being the sub-divisional headquarters has the characters of a small township with School, Health infrastructures and facilities, Forest, Agriculture and Animal Husbandry out posts, Post office, Monastery, Government Quarters and market. Large areas of hilltop on the Dorokha hills still have good forest cover.

The Dogapas who are originally from the Ha district in the northern part of Bhutan are permanently settled in a large community near the Dorokha headquarters. Besides, there are Bahuns, Chhetris, Gurungs and Rais—all subgroups of the great Nepali society—spread over the hill slopes all over the sub-division.

The Denchukha hills are along the northern side of AmMochhu. It is a large single hill range running southeasterly. Top part of the hill still has thick forest cover with wild life. Denchukha is connected to Dorokha and Samchi by only a hanging suspension bridge[2] down below the Dorokha headquarters. The hill slopes of Denchukha facing south is inhabited by several communities of the Nepalis and Lepchas. The historical relics[3] of the Doyas are still present under thick cover of bushes in the midst of the Lepcha settlement area. Denchukha has a Primary school and a Basic Health Unit.

The Sengten hills consist of several contiguous hillocks separated by a number of small streams. AmMochhu separates it from Denchukha in the north, from Dorokha by *Kamti* stream in the west and from Panbari hills by *Yeti* stream in the east. All these streams and several other small ones flow down the Sengten hills and join the AmMochhu. Sengten is becoming an important place next to Dorokha. It has a permanent double-storeyed school building with large playground, Basic Health Unit services and facilities and few shops on the hilltop. The school also represents the administration at times for the development concerns of the Doyas.

Across the Yeti stream in the eastern side is another range of hills south of AmMochhu bordering India, which may be called as the Panbari hills. Large villages of the Nepalese called Panbari and *Lapchakha* are located there. On the foothill side bordering India, the *Penden* Cement Factory of Bhutan is located at a place called *Gomtu.* It has all the social services infrastructures, communication facilities and a market.

Settlement Pattern

The whole of existing Doya settlement area is confined within the inner side of Sengten hills facing the AmMochhu (Moti) river in the north, *Kamti* and *Yeti* streams in the west and east respectively. Lotukuchu is a group of 5 distinct residential territories spread over the hill slopes below Sengten hills downwards to the Moti riverbank. There are also three Rai villages called Bisgaon, Lapcheygaon and Lumbey situated in a column from top down to the bank to AmMochhu intervening the two Doya residential territories (Map 1.2). The present locations of Doya community would comprise a very little space of what their folklore has to say about the expanse of their territorial area in the past.[4] The geographical region where these two communities can be located is approximately around the intersection point of 27°. 2' north and 87°. 1' east. The region lies at the junction of Sub-Himalayan foothills and Inner Himalayan zone at an elevation of about 3500 feet. Many streams and rivulets draining through the habitation slopes join AmMochhu at the foothills. The climate is moderately cool throughout the year. Average temperature does not exceed 20°C. Cold and dry season is very short. Wet season is longer with high humidity. Maximum average rainfall of 1600 mm has been recorded during my stay in June-July, 1992-93 at the school premises.

The region is covered with evergreen tropical forests. Varieties of broad-leafed trees, sal, bushes, shrubs and Savannah grasses grow. Many species of animals like rhesus monkeys, variety of rodents, squirrels, snakes and pythons, barking deer, wolf, wild cats, boar and jaguar live here. The region is abounding with ubiquitous variety of leeches. Tiger, leopard and bear do not live here anymore. Folktales reveal that once upon a time giant creatures otherwise of the form of human beings called *'Mihgoe'* lived there.

Most part of the habitat is uneven, stony and sloping hill surfaces. There are very few areas where terrace fields can be developed. Soil is loamy and black and acidic but once the vegetation is removed the soil fertility loses very fast. The relative difference in the temperature between the upper hill and lower hill slopes, along the AmMochhu River allows cultivation of different crops continuously within a seasonal cycle at different places. Most of shifting fields are also located in the upper and lower slopes. Land in the Upper regions where most of the residential sites are located is not as fertile as the lower foothills. Most of the permanent terrace cultivation fields are developed in the middle and lower parts of the slopes. Orange orchards abound in the lower hill slopes where relatively hot and humid climatic conditions prevail. Most of the cardamom fields are located along sides of streams in the upper part of the hills.

Lotukuchu is a group of three physically separate residential territories namely (starting from the west end side of the hill slope) Satakha, Sanglung and Lotukuchu proper with its extension village Lotok (Map-1.2). Lotukuchu is the biggest village of all. It has upper and lower divisions. There are therefore, 5 administrative units of residential territories each under a Karbari (Head of a village in Nepali). All these villages are taken here as Lotukuchu group of villages for our social analysis in juxtaposition to Taba-Ramteykha group of villages consisting of two separate villages for the purpose of the present study.

Lotukuchu group of villages is organised in five administrative units, which seems to be matching with their social and territorial sub-grouping within their social and territorial boundary. The five administrative units are (starting from the western side) Satakha, Sanglung, Upper and Lower Lotukuchu (A and B) and Lotok the last residential area bordered by the Yeti stream in the eastern side. Satakha people are known as *Satank* or sometimes *Danchat*[5] and they live in the western extreme end of the residential area. People of Sanglung, the second largest residential territory are known as *Guchat*. A hill ridge sloping down the hill and corresponding a stream called *Kamchal* separates Sanglung from Satakha. On the western side of Sanglung residential territory there is a flattish ridge on the eastern side on which the three Rai villages are located separating Lotukuchu and Lotok from Sanglung and Satakha on the western side. There have been cases of inter-marriages between the Rais and Doyas.

Lotukuchu proper is the largest residential territory among the five. The residential area is spread over 1 km in width in the upper part of the hill slope and the whole area runs roughly 2 km from top to bottom on the hill slopes. Lower part of the settlement area towards the AmMochhu River has gentle slopes.

People of Lotukuchu are known as *Binchat* and further among themselves, people residing in the lower part of the village are known as *Leysant*[6] and those in the upper part of the village are known as

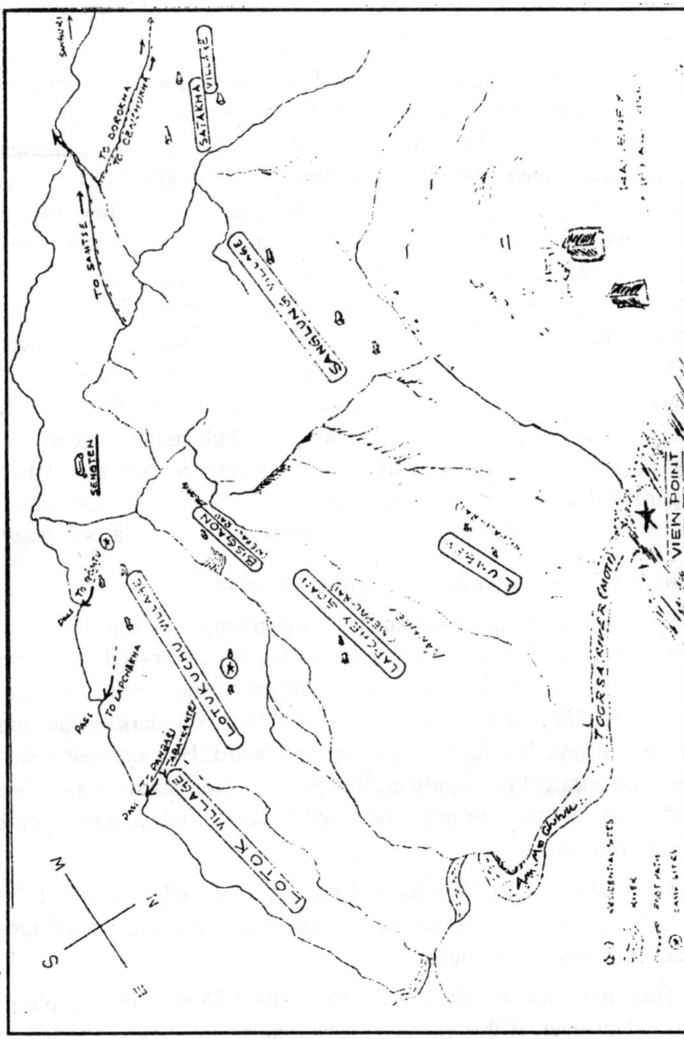

Map. 1.2: Sengten Hills showing Doya Residential Territories

Rosant.[7] Further, people of Lotukuchu group of villages as a whole is known as *Gonkey* to Taba-Ramteykha group of Doyas, who in turn are known to the former as *Sarmi* (eastern dwellers). There is an antagonistic feeling apparent between the Gonkey and Sarmi.[8]

All these named groups seem to connote certain social categories also in relation to one another although they were basically territorial groupings. These groups have established intra and inter-territorial social relations among themselves and with others in their surroundings. Rai who live in their immediate neighbourhood are known as *Dan* or Danchat, Drukpas who are looked upon as superior as they are the ruling class of people known to the Doyas as *Lhakey.* The same term is used for *Hapa*[9] (people of Ha district in the north of Doyas) and Tibetans alike who across the snow capped mountains in the north. They do not distinguish between the Tibetans, Drukpas and eastern dwellers *Sharcop* by name *although they have different experiences with each of these communities.* Hawkers in the regular *Haat* (weekly markets across the national border in the foothill plains) who are mostly Bengalis and *Biharis* are known to them as *Jaadan,* and they know tea garden labourers in the foothill plains as Madesi and others inhabiting the foothill plains of north western Duars of India as *Lehdan.*

Physical Features and Demographic Situation

The Doyas are predominantly of the mongoloid stock by race although among them some Austric features are also noted. They are short and strong people. The average height of the people does not exceed 5 ft. Their skin colour varies from relatively dark to fair and their bodies have less hair, moustache and beard. Hair on their heads varies from straight to slightly curly type. However, many of my close friends told me that their ancestors used to be tall, fair and handsome like the Tibetans.[10]

Total population of Doyas in 1992 approximately stood at 1720 that included 1100[11] heads for the Lotukuchu group of Doya villages residing in about 150 houses.

This figure hardly makes 0.137% of the 1.26 million[12] people in Bhutan. However, if this figure is seen against what was reported in 1987 in the country's National Weekly,[13] . . . *total population of Doyas is little under* 1000, . . . *with almost equal number of male and female* . . . *in about* 100 *households.*

The population has shown a growth of about 100 heads per year over a period of 6 years, at an average. Until the year 1987 no population record of the people was publicly available. However, local folktales have this to say that Doya population had a fluctuating trend in the past. It had its climax when their ancestors lived in vast areas of hills of the present Bhutan and adjacent plains of India.

That was perhaps, a time about 400 to 500 years ago. They say that Totos were also their people with whom they lost social contact ever since.[14] What marginalised such a large population to a few hundred souls now that confined them into small pockets in Bhutan? Investigation in this regard in the absence of any historical documents about these people is difficult proposition. Nevertheless, folktales reveal that a great decline in their population was due to war, flood and evil spells of supernatural powers such as Sun and Water[15], and that the present population of Doya is regeneration from the last survivors of the population, downfall 5 *Mitchis*[16] ago.

Table 1.1: Population of Lotukuchu Group of Doyas

Sl. No.	Name of the villages	No. of Households	Total Males	Total Females	Total	Birth	Death
1	Lotukuchu-A	33	117	126	243	11	0
2	Lotukuchu-B	33	123	147	270	15	2
3	Lotok	18	72	67	139	8	1
4	Sanglung	30	126	156	282	15	1
5	Satakha	13	57	78	135	5	0
	Total	127	495	574	1069	54	4
	Average	25.4	99	114.8	213.8	10.8	.8
	Percentage	-	46.3%	53.7%	-	-	-

**Sources*: Sengten Basic Health Unit, Sengten, 1990.

The elders of the present generation ranging between 70 and 100 remember that in their young days there were just 9 houses of Doyas; 4 in Lotukuchu, 3 in Sanglung, only 2 in Satakha villages and no one settled at Lotok. The population of the whole Lotukuchu group of villages would have been much below 200 heads then, in early 1900s. If the base population is taken at 200 in early 1900s, the population has grown 5 times in its initial strength over the years. However, the growth may not have been so smooth as we suppose. Elders often talk about untold miseries of death and diseases and their general helplessness to counter the misfortunes. Birth rate may have been quite regular but high mortality rate must have resulted in slow and irregular growth rate in complete absence of medical facilities and faulty remedial practices pertaining to beliefs in supernatural forces. Until the year 1986 there was no medical facility available nearby to these people. A classified population record taken in 1990 for the Lotukuchu group of Doyas gives a total of 1069 head counts in a total of 127 household units which gives an average of 8 to 9 heads per household unit in the Lotukuchu group. Data available (Table 1.1) show that now, there are on an average 25 households in each residential territories. These territories have a minimum of 13 households in Satakha and a maximum of 33 households in A and B parts of Lotukuchu. It shows little higher average of female population in all the territorial groups except for Lotok. On the overall average 8 females for every 7 males and 10 to 11 children born in each village against a total of 4 deaths recorded in the year 1990.

The excess of females seemed to have caused multiple marriages in the society ensuring a steady growth of population in the present generation[17]. Although, there is no strict prohibition against multiple marriages it is definitely not encouraged in Doya society. There were about 10 cases of multiple marriages involving 2 to 3 females to single male(s) contributing a large number of offspring in the present generation, which also included inter-marriages with Nepali community.

Further, sex-break up analysis of the present population (Table 1.2) reveals that out of the total 574 females in the population, 284 (49.47%) were in reproductive age group (15-49 years), 218 were girls between age group of 0-14 years comprising of 37.97% and the rest 72 females (12-54%) included those who were above the reproductive age group, spinsters and imbeciles.

On the other hand, out of the total 495 males 353 (71.31%) were adults (15-above years) and 142 (28.68%) were boys (0-14 years) including a minor group of imbeciles. It means that for every 4 females in the reproductive age group there were approximately 5 adult males that is contrary to the overall high ratio of 8 females to 7 males. This ratio in reproductive age group is again counter balanced in the first generation of 0-14 age group. There were 3 girls for every 2 boys for the following generation.

Table 1.2: Population Sex Breakup

	Females			Males		
Villages	Total	15 & above	Girls	Total	15 and above	Boys
Lotukuchu-A	126	76	50	117	80	37
Lotukuchu-B	147	97	50	123	94	29
Lotok	67	36	31	72	36	36
Sanglung	156	102	54	126	96	30
Satakha	78	42	36	57	47	10
Total	574	353*	221**	495	353	142
Average	114.8	70.6	44.2	99	70.6	28.4
Percentage	100%	61.5%	38.5%	100%	71.3%	28.7%

* Females in reproductive age (15-49 yrs) is 284 (353-284 = 69 are above 49 years and imbeciles).

** Total girls (0-14 yrs) include 9 imbeciles. Therefore, the total number of normal girls is 218 and total number of females over reproductive age and imbeciles are (69 + 9) 72 females

What possibility we can infer from this statistical analysis is males competing for females in the adult age group and, on the contrary, females competing for males in the subsequent younger generation of boys and girls.

But what actually occurred in the adult group did not quite follow the statistical prophecy. My own genealogical studies in 1992 among the Lotukuchu population recorded 280 women married against 260 men. It indicated that for every 14 married couples there was a man with two wives. This was quite in contrary to the male-female ratio in the adult generation. The pattern of marriage alliances and the subsequent demographic situation out of the male-female ratio in the younger generation will also be subject to the marriage rules. However, it is still difficult to predict the pattern of marriage alliances in the next generation. It will suffice here to say that the demographic situation did not actually decide the reproductive pattern of a society but on the contrary, it was the social rules of marriage ability that mattered.

Further, the village-wise demographic records (Table 1.2) show different situation in different villages. It must be borne in mind before analysing that Lotukuchu-A (Lower) and B (Upper) are physically contiguous villages along the slope of a single hill although, there was an apparent social segregation between the two. Lotok is a horizontal extension of Upper Lotukuchu-(B).

The demographic situation in Lotukuchu-A (Lower) a total of 243 heads in 33 households. There was an excess of 9 females on the whole, but males outnumbered the females by 4 in the reproductive age group, while females outnumbered the males by 13 in the children group. The major difference was in the younger generation. Lotukuchu-B (Upper) shows a total of 270 heads in 33 households. It has an excess of 24 females to the total males with a marginal difference of just 3 females in the adult section of the population. The major difference was an excess of 21 girls against the total boys.

Lotok had a total of 139 heads in 18 households with minor difference of 5 females from the total males in the population. It had equal number of adults but had 4 excess boys to the girls in the younger generation.

Sanglung with a total of 282 heads in 30 households had an excess of 30 females on the whole. It had a minor difference of 6 excess females to the total males in the adult section and a major difference of 24 girls in excess among the younger section.

Lastly, Satakha village had a total population of 135 heads in 13 households. It had an excess of 21 females on the whole. There was an excess of 5 males in the adult section but an excess of 26 girls over the boys in the younger generation.

It may be mentioned here that the total excess of 4 males in lower Lotukuchu of the adult section may account for spinsters and old aged people, etc. The total excess of 9 males in Lotukuchu-A and Satakha and the total excess of 9 females in Lotukuchu-B and Sanglung in adult section of population may account for the minor portion of spinsters, bachelors and imbeciles. The present adult section of the population reproduced a very disproportionate sex ratio among the younger generation.

The excess of 79 girls to the total number of boys who were gradually entering into the active reproductive phase would decide the

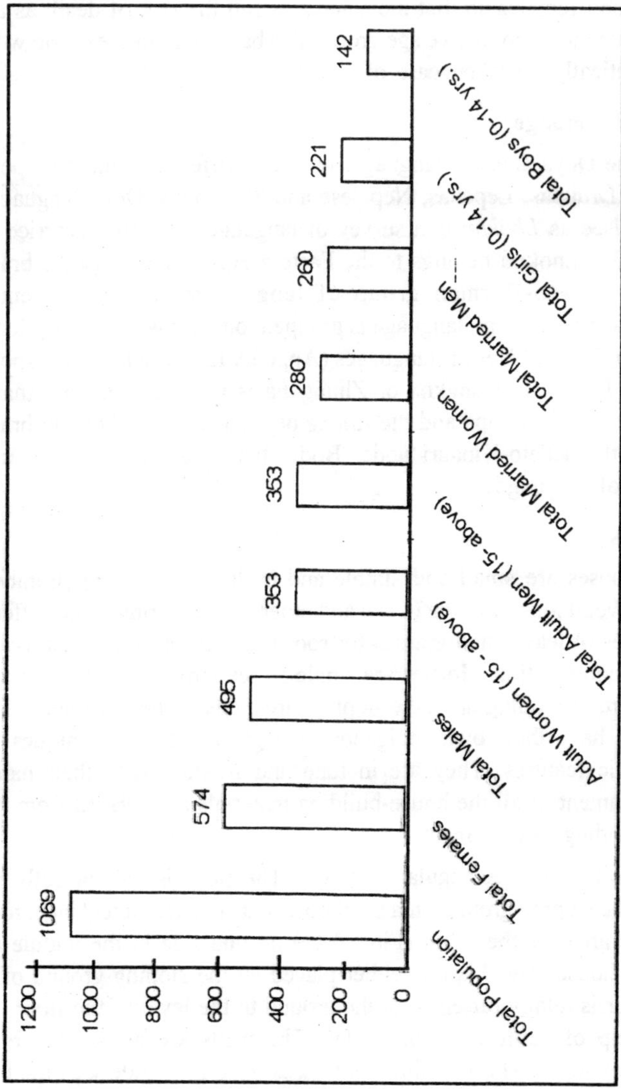

DEMOGRAPHIC SITUATION OF THE DOYA

future demographic and social situation of the Doyas. Of course, if there was a significant difference in the age-specific death rates for males and females so that more females run the risk of death as they approach the reproductive age group. The balance in the sex ratio would automatically be taken care of.

Doya Language

The Doya speak a language, which is different from that spoken by the Drukpas, Lepchas, Nepalese and Sharcopas. Doya language is recognised as *Lhokpu* in a survey of languages in Bhutan carried out in 1993.[18] Lhokpu belongs to the Eastern Himalayas of Bodic branch in the Tibeto-Burman group of languages. In this system of classification Lhokpu language is grouped together with that of Monpa, Lepcha, Rai and Newari languages (Appedix III). The language spoken by the Drukpas Dzongkha or Zhungkha is put together with that of Tibetan, the Sharcopa and the *Kheng* belonging to another sub-branch called the Tibeto-Kinauri under Bodic family in the Tibeto-Burman group of languages.

Houses

Houses are small and simple and built with *Ba-sing* (Bamboo), *Sing* (Wood logs), *Li-sing* (Cane and other creeper strings) and different varieties of leaves and grasses for roofing. Mud or clay is not used in house construction. Houses are single storey structures, mostly facing eastward depending upon the sloping directions of the hill slopes. Their houses have their own indigenous design, building techniques and aesthetic features. They are in tune and friendly with their natural environment as all the house-building materials are derived from their surrounding environment.

Houses are rectangular in shape. The floor is half or fully rose from the sloping ground on a bamboo/wooden platform leaving a rough square area for the *Jikpu* (Fire place) on one side in the middle part of the house. The Jikpu is either placed on the sloping ground of the earth or is totally raised from the ground to the level of the floor with the help of earth and stone piles. The walls are made with broad bamboo strips. These traditional houses have no window as the rows of bamboo strips leave slit open spaces in between to facilitate adequate ventilation in the house in all seasons. The walls without plaster also allow a good watch outside from inside the house in daytime and moonlit nights. Anybody sitting inside the bamboo strip-walled houses can see what is happening outside the house but an outsider approaching the house would not see anything inside the house unless, one peeps through the slits on the walls or looks through the entrance door. To a question once I asked why they don't plaster their walls like the Nepalese in the neighbouring villages, they simply told me that people would die if all the walls of their house were plastered!

Front entrance is opened along the side the hill slope. The entrance normally has no door wings. A piece of cloth or a thin bamboo mating is put up to close the house. The Jikpu has three stones standing in a triangular formation for mounting cooking pots. Above the Jikpu a squarish bamboo frame with bamboo matting *(Tab)* is hung from the ceiling as a rack for smoking meat and other food items. Besides, the hanging rack, there are also many bamboo baskets of different sizes and cloth pouches storing seeds and food grains, etc. Left over food, pots and pans also go into these baskets.

Inside the house there is a semi-partition of bamboo strips in the middle part, which divides one half of the room into two equal quarter rooms. The inner quarter room is a sort of private or sacred room where they say resides the household deity. If there are more people in the house this room is also used for sleeping. Visitors are received and entertained in the front quarter of the room at the entrance. Any ritual performance is also done in this front quarter of the room. Outside the house is a hut raised on four tall bamboos covered with thatch grass or leaves. This hut, though small, is normally raised taller than the main dwelling house. This is called *To-kim.* Food grains and seeds such as millet, maize, and sorghum are preserved here protected from wet ground, rainwater and rodents. The size of such grain stores may be 1 m × 1 m × 2 m by volume and 4 to 5 m tall. These granaries were not often seen full with food grains. The sizes of the present-day granaries attached to a house seem to be indicating the decreasing production level of foodgrains. In olden days, the To-kim used to be as large as main living houses.

Type of Houses

In larger families this To-kim is often used for sleeping when it is empty. In Lotukuchu area there are largely four to five types of houses.

Kim: A relatively small house in which only one half of the room is raised on a platform with a semi-partition inside. The Jikpu is on

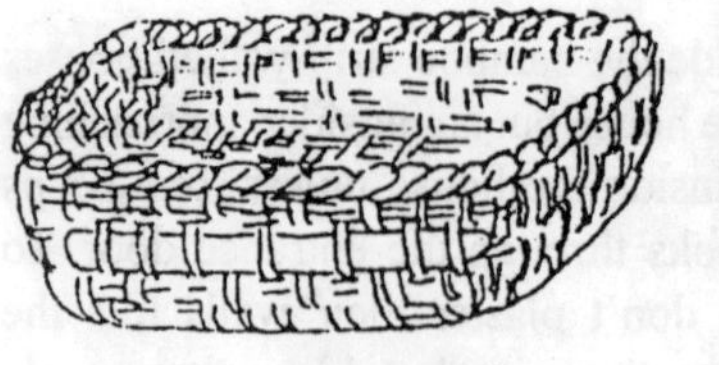

Fig. 1: ***Tol***
Length: **51 cm**
Breadth: **23 cm**
Depth: **15 cm**
Material: **Cane and Bamboo**
Uses: **A baby carrier**

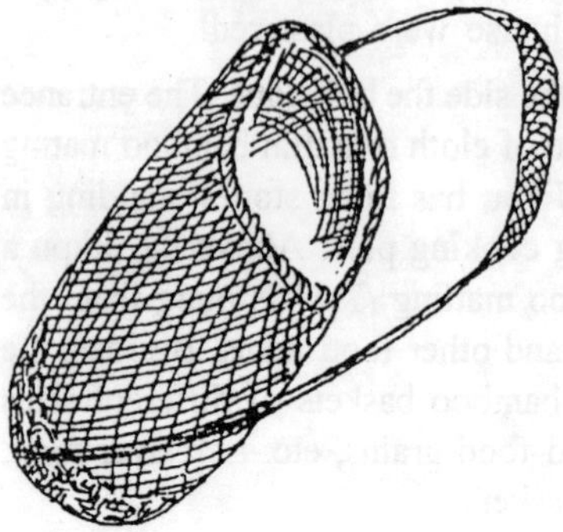

Fig. 2: ***Wang***
Material: **Bamboo**
Uses: **A Basket carrier**

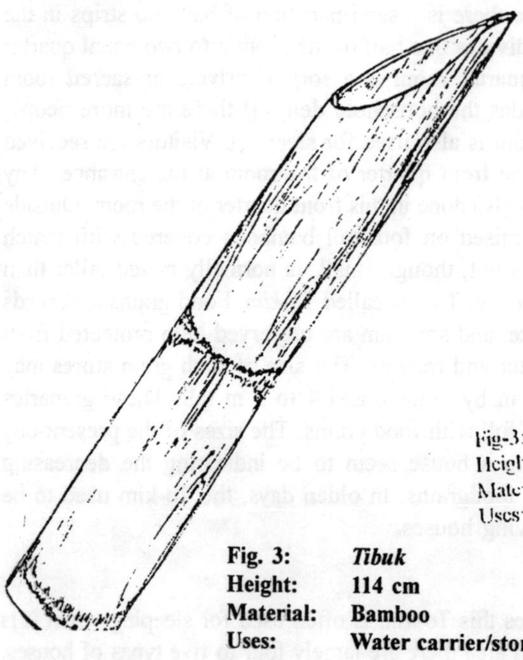

Fig. 3: ***Tibuk***
Height: **114 cm**
Material: **Bamboo**
Uses: **Water carrier/storing**

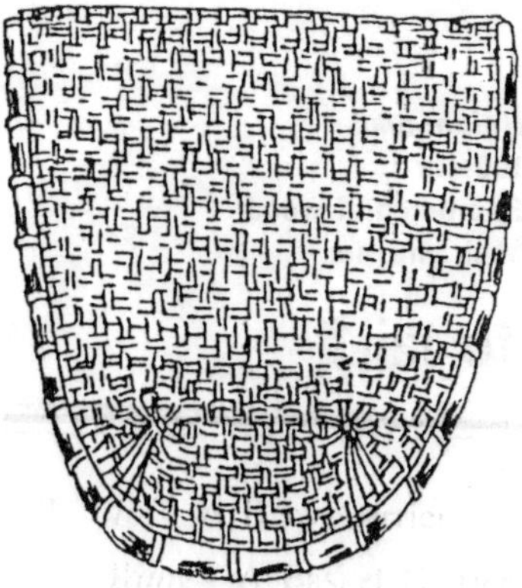

Fig. 4: *Tra*
Length: 76 cm
Breadth: 58 cm
Material: Cane and Bamboo
Uses: Winnowing Basket

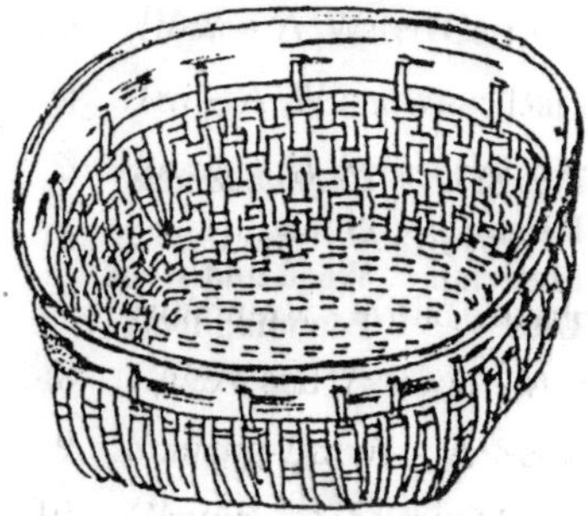

Fig. 5: *Roung*
Diameter: 36 cm
Depth: 15 cm
Uses: Measuring grain

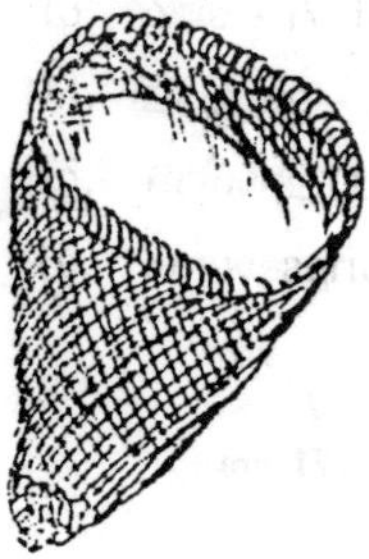

Fig. 6: *Chachang*
Length: 45 cm
Diameter: 28 cm
Material: Cane
Uses: Sieving

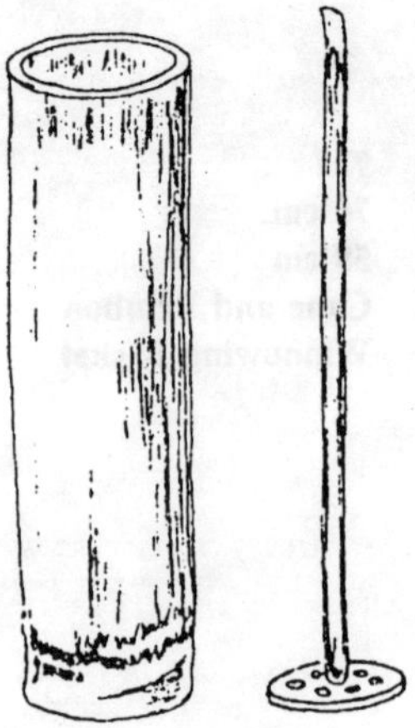

Fig. 7: *Halum-tok*
Height: 120 cm
Material: Bamboo and wood
Uses: Milk churner

Fig. 8: *Chiptok-tombu*
Height: 20 cm
Material: Wood and stone
Uses: Pounding tools

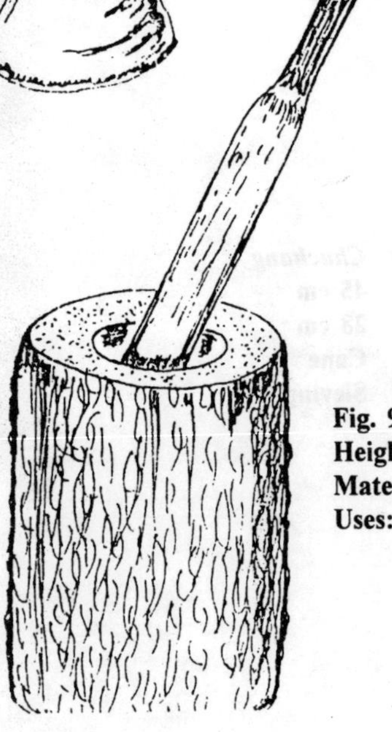

Fig. 9: *Simteng-dahol*
Height: 57 cm and 171 cm
Material: Wood
Uses: Pounding grains

the ground. This type of house is called Kim where an extended family of a married couple resides with their kids. A Kim measures 10 × 15 ft approximately.

La: A temporary (make-shift) hut made in the same fashion as a Kim with certain simplifications. This type of hut is called *La.* It has no walls, the half platform on the sloping side of the hill is raised higher to shelter young calves underneath and sleeping bunker above. A La measures 5 × 10 ft. approximately on ground and maximum 6 ft. tall. La is built far away from homesteads in grazing grounds and pasturelands. A small family often stays in this hut looking after cattle and crops. They would abandon the hut when they have to move to another pastureland or to attend to some other works.

Makim: This is the third type of house. It is little larger than a Kim to accommodate joint families of young daughters. In this type of house the whole room is raised on a bamboo/wooden platform except for the fireplace. This type of houses is old type. The floor and walls are of wooden planks in some of the very old houses. The entrance has replaceable door wings of wooden planks. Most of the ancestral main houses are of this type. They are called Makim (Main house) in which all the descendant members of the matrilineal household worship the ancestral and lineal deities at times together. This house normally measures 15 × 30 ft approximately on the ground and as tall as 7 to 8 ft from the ground.

Tokim: There is another type of house, which is basically a large granary rather than a dwelling house. It is also known as Tokim. These types of houses are seen only in Lotok village at present. Since early times Lotok village has been known for its productivity. They say the name itself is derived from the nature of land and its productivity. In this type the whole main room of the house is used for storing food grains in big bamboo baskets on a raised wooden platform. A small family with or without kids who guard this granary live in little extensions in front and back of the house. On the front side a little portion of the extension is raised on a low bamboo platform leaving some space in the middle for the fireplace. The sleeping platform is called *Tonk.* This granary measures 30 × 12 ft. approximately.

Modern Houses: The fifth type of house, which has become a status symbol among the richer people, is a permanent structure of stone, mud, wood and tin sheets. They are most often double-storey structures. This type of house is at present coming up in the whole region. Building of these houses require time, specialised skills and considerable amount of money as compared with the traditional types which are wholly built from local materials. During my stay in Lotukuchu, Doyas had built six such houses which belonged to those among them who could make best earnings out of the orange and cardamom sale off in recent times. These modern houses have also become a status symbol among the Doyas.

The houses in Taba-Ramteykha are different from the ones in Lotukuchu. The Taba-Ramteykha houses are larger in size and they are fully raised on bamboo platform higher than those in Lotukuchu. The Jikpu is also arranged on the platform by laying layers of earth and stone. The front side of the house has a large open area on the platform. Pigs and cows take shelter below the platform. A fairly big size stump of a tree with steps dug out on one side of it is leant on a side of the platform. One can step on this dug out stairs to board on the platform and approach the house. This platform provides a safe and comfortable space for all the household chores and social activities.

Household Articles

They possess very little household articles. Most of them are indigenously manufactured from materials derived from their natural environment. Bamboo and wood are chiefly used in making most of the household articles. Some of the commonly used household articles can be classified under different categories according to their usages such as carriage articles, implements, storage and vessels.

Some of the carriage articles are: *Tol, Wang* and *Tibuk, etc. Tol* (Fig. 1) is basically a cradle made of cane and bamboo strips. It measures 60 × 22 × 20 cm, approximately. It is used for carrying baby while going to a work place and markets. The cradle with the baby is carried on the back harnessed by a cane string around the chest and forehead. *Wang* is also cane and bamboo woven basket carrier (Fig. 2). *Tibuk* is a long hollow cylinder closed at one end. It is cut out of big bamboo by knocking out one of the nodes. It measures approximately, 120 cm in length and is used as water carrier (Fig.3).

Some of the implements are *Tra, Roung, Chachang, Halum-tok, Chiptok-tombu, Simtengdahol, Goish* (Fig. 16: Sickle), *Chatub, Chabu*

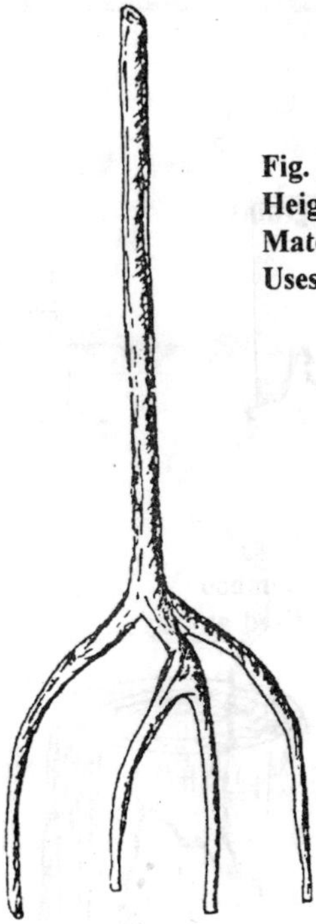

Fig. 10: *Chatub*
Height: 20-30 cm
Material: A forked branch
Uses: Mixer tool

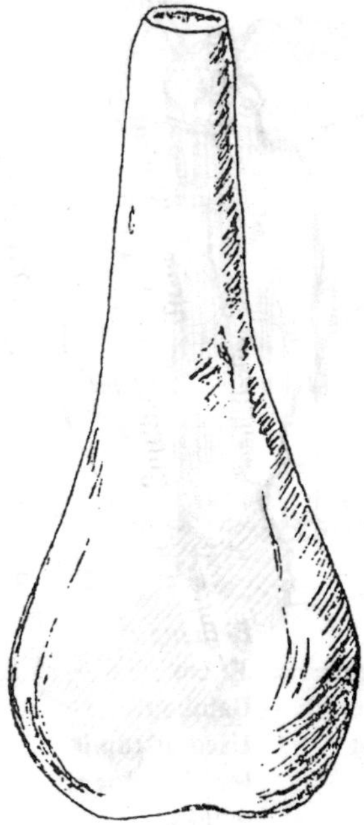

Fig. 11: *Jopsey*
Height: 83 cm
Material: Bitter guard shell
Uses: Storing seed

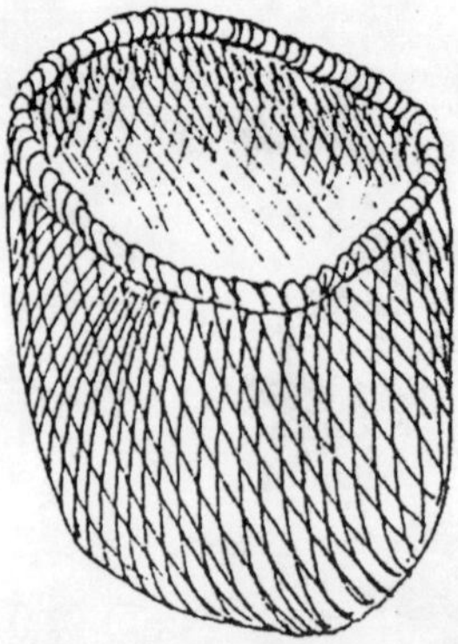

Fig. 12: *Jiten*
Material: Bamboo
Uses: Storing grains

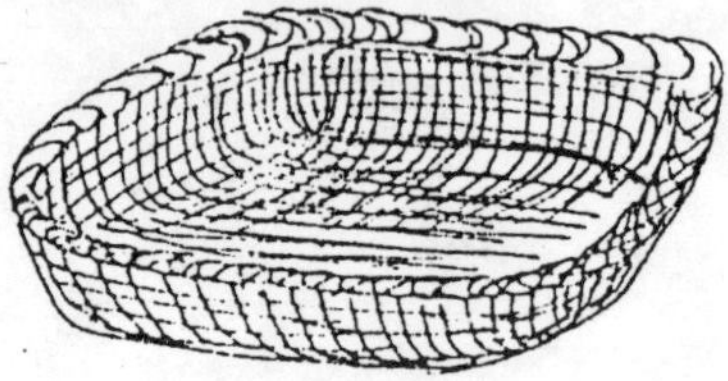

Fig. 13: *Sele*
Material: Bamboo
Uses: Used as tray

Fig. 14: *Belheng*
Height: 30 cm
Material: Bamboo
Uses: Used as tumbler for local drinks

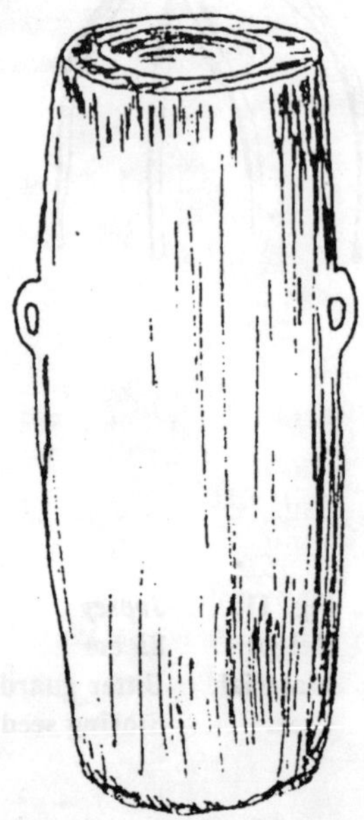

Fig. 15: *Belheng (Large)*
Height: 80-100 cm
Material: Wood
Uses: Storing/fermentation

(Fig. 16), *Jaru* and *Kulik* (Ladles), etc. *Tra* is U-shape winnowing basket made of cane and bamboo. It measures 68 cm in length and 58 cm in breadth, approximately. The people for domestic uses are still locally making these only (Fig. 4). *Roung* (Fig. 5) is a standard measuring basket (38 cm in diameter and 14 cm in depth, approximately). Highly skilled craftsmen make these. Very fine and complicated weaving is done on it. Almost all the *Roung* I have seen in village are pretty old but they are in good conditions. Nobody in the village makes this article but they say their ancestors used to make it. *Chachang* (Fig. 6) is a sieve made of very fine bamboo strips. It is conical in shape and measures 25cm in diameter and 40 cm in length approximately. It is used for filtering tea and local brew. *Halum-tok* is a pair of long hollow cylindrical bamboo made of a large size bamboo and a pestle with valve like structure at the end. The cylinder is 70 to 80 cm long, approximately. This is used for churning and processing sour milk to produce local cheese and butter (Fig. 7). *Chiptok-tombu* (Fig. 8) is also a pair of mortar and pestle. The mortar is made out of hard wooden stem and the pestle is often a longish piece of stone measuring around 20 cm, approximately. It is used for grinding chilli and salt at every meal. *Simteng-dahol* (Fig. 9) is a pair of pounding implement made of cylindrical log measuring around 60 cm in height. It is used for pounding food grains. It is a pestle made of a hardwood log measuring around 170 cm length and weighs around 3 kg. *Goish* is a sickle. It is procured from outside. Sickle is also all-purpose weapon for them. Outside the house it is a handy tool for cutting and protection. Inside the house, it is used as kitchen knife. Once outside the house women are always seen with a sickle. *Chatup* (Fig. 10) is a mixing instrument made of a hard branch of a tree or shrub with 5 to 6 forking branches. It is used for dispersing butter in tea by rolling between palms. *Chabu* is a chopping knife. It is one and half to two feet long and it is bought from markets. It is used for cutting trees and slaughter of animals. Men folk would always be seen with a knife at their back. *Jaru* is a service spoon made out of bamboo. *Kulik* is a ladle made out of bamboo. This is used as stirring implement in cooking food.

Some of the storage articles are *Jopsey, Jiten, Sele,* and *Belheng,* etc. *Jopsey* (Fig. 11) is a bitter guard shell of different sizes. Big ones are used for storing seeds and for fermentation of millet for local drink *(Yu)*. *Jiten* (Fig. 12) is a carrying basket made of thin bamboo stripes.

Sele (Fig. 13) is a flat open tray made of thin bamboo strips. It has a conical shape and measures 25 cm in diameter and 40 cm long. It is used for keeping meat, chilli and vegetable over the fireplace. *Belheng* (Fig. 14) is a very important tumbler made of a big bamboo with fairly wide curvature. It measures 25 cm in height. It is used for drinking local beer with a bamboo straw. There is another Belheng, which is larger in size. It is carved out of wood trunk and it is used for fermentation of local brew.

Some of the commonly used vessels are *Belheng*, *Gemba* and *Rog*, etc. *Gemba* is a pot made of clay. These are procured from distant places. They look very old and considered a very precious possession of household. It is also used for millet fermentation and as ritual gifts. *Rog* is a cooking pot. These are of different sizes. It is made of different metals. These are all imported items but they have become essential commodities. *Rog* is used for cooking. *Porr* is a dish made of aluminium. It is procured from markets. *Loha* is round bottom frying pan of cast iron and it is also procured from outside. This has become an essential item in a household. *Tal* is an aluminium plate procured from outside. It is used for eating food.

Clothing

Doyas have their own traditional dress called *Ga-da*. It is a white piece of coarse cloth of about 3 × 2 metres in size. Putting on the cloth is very simple although it looks complicated.

The cloth is folded in the middle length. The two corners of the free ends are held in left hand and the middle fold end in the right hand around the back of body. The three edges are brought together over the right shoulder by running the cloth from below the left armpit and across the chest and back. From this position one free end of outer side of the cloth is released to fall under the left armpit behind the body. While the other three edges are held together by the left hand over the shoulder, the right hand reaches out for the fallen cloth edge and it is picked up from below the right armpit, taken across the chest and over the left shoulder. From this position all the three edges i.e. the two edges of the free ends and middle fold part are held together and adjusted at the centre behind the neck. The two edges are fastened at the middle fold point together with the help of a bamboo spindle called *Rim*. In this position the upper cloth border makes an X-cross around the neck in the front side and the body is well covered all around. The cloth runs in two layers from side to side around the body leaving the arms large and free from the armpit region. Next, the cloth is adjusted properly on both sides. Then the cloth is pulled up above the knee length and fastened tightly with the help of string around the waist. Once it is fastened properly the lose cloth makes a sizeable pouch in the front part of the body to carry many things inside.

Women also put on their clothes in the same manner but it covers their body from shoulder to the middle part of the calf, leaving a smaller pouch on the front side along the upper part of their body. They do not need any carrying bags in their traditional dress. Now a day, the traditional dress of the Doyas is being fast replaced by the national dress *Gho* and *Kiyra*[19], under an active campaign for promotion and preservation of national cultural identity by the Royal Government of Bhutan. Doyas use very few clothing at home. Gho and Kiyra are all-purpose clothing worn all the time for them. Most of the men and women do not have another set of clothes for a change. A piece of clothing is worn as long as it can cover their body for warmth and carry some weight. They do not at present weave or knit their own clothes. Any wear and tear in their cloths is repaired/stitched very roughly with the help of indigenously made bamboo needle.

Rim and thread *Jin made* out of plant fibre. Steel needle and mill threads from the markets *are* fast replacing *the* Rim and Jin.

Occupation and Daily Activities

Doyas are semi-sedentary agriculturist people. They start their day by preparing the *Rihto* (morning meal). The preparation works include collecting water from nearby *stream,* pounding *cereals* or preparing boiled roots, making strong tea and processing *fermented* millet for a morning drink. They take the Rihto by around 7 O'clock in the morning right after which they start to their respective work places. Ask anyone walking by in *the* morning with knife or sickle in the hand and something in their front pouch.

Hey, Nang katt-a no? (Hey = where, *Nang* = you, *katt-a-no* = *are* going). The answer invariably is: *Ka-nga La hut-la Katt-an: (Ka-nga = I, La = work, hut-la = to look after, Katt-an = going)*

The type of works they normally attend to are looking after their *Yonk* (shifting fields), collecting firewood, and other things for food from Jungle, etc. There is hardly any body at home during the daytime except for some children, nursing mothers and sick ones. Most of *the time,* the whole family can be seen together in a field along with newborn babies.

Towards the evening before sunset they are all back to their houses. Once at home they begin to make fire, collect water in the bamboo cylinders and pots, a*nd* prepare *Hin-to* (evening meal) which generally consists of roasted and flattened maize, sometimes or *Lohbol* (Tapioca) or *Burr* (Kochu or *Colocasia)* or some food left over from the morning meal. And some tea or *Yu* after which it is leisure time and the time for drinking and talking. Most of the inter-personal talks, meetings and visiting each other, conveying messages, sharing news and events occurring around them take place. It is often said that most of the quarrels also take place at this time.

While elders drink leisurely with their friends and neighbours around the fire other family members prepare *Lip-to* (night meal) starting right from pounding, grinding, winnowing and collecting water and so on. Nothing at home is ever kept ready for next meal.

While this type of pattern activities generally remains as day-to-day routine works during the short winter season they are relatively free from agricultural works. It is the time after they harvest most of the crops and they are relatively free from agricultural works. This free time of theirs has always been exploited for free labour services in various development works of the Royal Government involving construction of roads and buildings and trading activities of the state.

Now, in the contemporary times they actively engage themselves in earning hard cash through porterage of oranges from interior orchards to foothill markets. Almost everybody from very young boys and girls to very old and aged people carry baskets of orange down the hills. The money thus earned by direct selling and carrying oranges is immediately utilised in procuring basic commodities such as food grains which include essentially millets for making local drinks, some new clothes, oil, salt and luxury items, etc. Rest of the money is used in loan redemption from others and a what-so-ever remains is immediately consumed in drinks at the market. Most of them including women have a habit of making their first expenditure in terms of buying liquor and millet for home brew.

At the end of the orange season there is hardly any savings left with them except for some new clothes, few bags of food grains, and cheap varieties of watches, radio tapes and some ornaments. For further requirements of food grains, other commodities and essential expenditure for the remaining months of the year they begin to borrow money from better-off among themselves and neighbouring Nepali brethren or sell their next season's crops in advance. This is also a time for marriages among young boys and girls. Neighbouring Nepali brethren often say orange season is also Doya marriage season. They say so because young boys and girls often are seen going together and mixing freely while on travel during the orange season. This may however, be a contemporary change among people. People are being increasingly influenced by market showing indications that their traditional subsistence economy has been greatly influenced by cash economy.

Food and Drinking Habits

Food consists of varieties of cereals, roots and different kinds of meats. Cereals such as *Kersey* (Buckwheat), *Ra-am* (Maize), *Jar-to* (Millet) and *Chak-to* (Sorghum) are popular food grains. Chak-to and Jar-to are two essential and indispensable food items in their life and rituals. Chak-to is boiled the way rice is cooked and taken as main food. *Jar-to* is used mainly for making *Yu*, and women mainly do the preparation. Buckwheat is ground in a *Ra-tag* (a stone mill) for *Bee* (flour) and taken as *Roti* (flat bread). They eat all sorts of meat and fish except snakes. Pork, beef and meat of wild animals are their favourites. They talk of *Madesis* (Tea garden labourer in the Indian plains) with disgust because they say that Madesis take snakes.

Once, I talked to an old woman aged around 50 years about different types of meat. Talking about snake meat she said, *how can one take snake meat? It kills People. If you eat snake, will you not die? We eat monkey meat, fox and wolf meat only, etc.*

Even though they are not particularly fond of vegetables, they sometimes consume *Pa-em* (Bamboo shoot), *Sa-em* (edible variety of fern), *Chuisey* (squash), *Jungka* (Pumpkin), *Sengsey* (Beans) and *Sa(n)-ag* (spinach, leafy vegetable), etc. They do not like pulses. Taking pulse with their food was very rare occasion during my stay with the people in the village but their liking for meat is striking. They do not mind taking stale meat infested with worms. Once, I expressed my anguish over their liberal appetite for stale meat. They told me coolly:

Sir, these worms come out of the meat itself so what is the harm in taking meat infested with worms[20].

Cooking is very simple process of boiling. They do not use much oil. Most often any food item is boiled simply in water and consumed with salt and chilli. Sometimes, if they have some oil or butter they put it while it is boiling in water. Frying vegetable or meat is not their habit. Food is not mixed with curry while eating. Both are taken separately in turns. They can consume substantial amount of food with only some *Dii* (salt) and *Muris* (chilli).

Health and Sanitation

Doyas have very poor sense of sanitation. They live in a very poor condition of health and hygiene. They live at the pleasure and mercy of their spirits who have control over their health and general well-being. Talking to Jamio (80+years) of Satakha and Sakab (70 years) of Lotukuchu about their past and present health and hygiene conditions, they say:

There was no medicine, many people used to die due to diseases and sicknesses and also due to food poisoning, sometimes. Once, one of my sons ate some roots he found in the Jungle. He collapsed unconsciously. We ran to Panbari Nepali village and got a local medicine from a Nepali Bijuwa (Sorcerer in Nepali language) *and with that he was saved.*

But don't the people know some locally available herbal remedial practices?

No, none of us know very well about that. But, I know there is one root called Konio. Its milk cures loose motion. There was no one in our village that practised local medicines.

They believe that evil spirits who have been neglected or disregarded by the victims in their ignorance causes sicknesses and diseases. To cure the diseases or the sicknesses a *Pama* or Bijuwa (Sorcerer) has to be *consulted* to reveal the particular spirit or deity, responsible for the same. They have to be appeased through ritual performances, offerings and sacrifices of animals. A Pama is born and gifted in the art of sorcery. They believe that not anyone can become a Pama unless he is born differently with the requisite talents. The belief in supernatural power is so deep that people give much importance to sorcerers for magical cure of all their health problems.

As said earlier, people have very little knowledge about local herbal medicines and practices.

Pama is Lhokpu term for witch doctor or a sorcerer. It is *'Geypa'* in the national language. There were few Pamas among the Doyas, who were adept in sorcery and witchcraft. They used their knowledge to secure personal gains, because of which they were exiled out of the village with the help of Drukpa Lama[21].

There are many elder persons who have goitre, a iodine deficiency disease. Many young children are afflicted with angulostomatitis dysentery, diarrhoea, and upper aspiratory tract infection. Skin diseases, fungal infection and internal and external viral infection are very common health problems among the people. Often they suffer from epidemics like Chicken pox and Measles. There are several folktales where reference is made to such epidemics.

Neatness and cleanliness are generally neglected in every walk of life. Women often suffer from venereal diseases[22]. They do not wash their hands and feet before and after food unless things get very dirty according to their standards. Very little water is used at home for general cleansing as they fetch water in small containers enough for cooking and drinking only. They do not wash their pots and pans properly after meals as the neighbouring Nepalese do at their homes. They freely share in of each other's food and utensils while eating without any inhibitions. Since, basic hygienic care is not taken in day-to-day life there were often high chances of contacting communicable diseases among the people.

Now, the situation is improving with regular exposure to modern education in the school and health education from the Basic Health Units from time to time[23]. Old habits die hard. They seldom clean the surroundings of their houses. They do not possess a broom at home. Cock, hens, dogs and pigs have easy access inside their houses to lick and pick on their plates and pots. Sometimes, hens and cocks snatch food from their food plates and pots but they don't mind. They had no safe latrines until the Basic Health Unit was opened in the area in 1987. Under a strict supervision of the Health Unit and School staff they were made to make safe latrines.

When someone falls sick she is left alone at home unattended while others go out for work. If young ones fall sick elders would just think of what is to be taken and what is not to be taken according to the type of sickness. They would not bother to come to the Health centre unless the person becomes very serious, and sometimes, they rather prefer to invite the health workers at home.

They would look for health workers' help only when all other local methods and practices of appeasing responsible spirits and worship of local deities failed to cure the sickness. Every disease is associated with certain beliefs and practices relating to their food restrictions, a few of which are given below.

Chuteck (Measles)—One must not eat fried things from market places, salt, meat, milk and its by-products. One must not drink Vu. One must take only loosely prepared simple food.

Semah (Chicken pox)—One must take boiled roots of *Lahara* (local medicinal plant). One must not move in the open air. One must sit in the sun. One must not take roasted things, meat, drinks, milk and its by-products.

Recreational Activities

Doyas do not play any game, as there is no free time for games and sports as such in an organised manner. Of course, when some people gather for night stay on someone's death, few persons play a game with maize seeds called *Kauri,* which is also not their traditional game. Leisure time is the time when they retire to their homes after a days' work in the fields and jungles when they like to sit, drink and talk about something amusing and about day-to-day affairs, events, incidents, and general gossips about other people and things. Posters of popular film stars, photographs, radio and tape recorders have become popular means of entertainment for the present generation. They like to listen to popular Dzongkha and Nepali songs. More and more young people are being attracted to film shows at Samchi market.

***Loh* Festival**

Doyas celebrate only one festival in a seasonal cycle. The time coincides with harvesting of Chak-to and Jar-to, which are their favourite cereals for food and drinks, respectively. The festival is called *Loh* and often falls between 7th and 8th month according to Bhutanese calendar. The word Loh literally means a year and the festival starts from *Gutok* that is 29th of the month and ends on the 3rd of the following month[24]. Mainly drinking, eating meat and worshipping their household, local deities and ancestors to celebrate the festival. Killing of cows and pigs is a must for this festival. They offer cock's head and blood to household deities *Eechan* and *Tenglha.* The cock's head can be noticed erected on a stick on the ridge of the Makim. During this festival sons visit their parents house with gifts of food and meat. People in the village visit each other eat, drink and sing songs. One very popular song often sung on this occasion clearly mentions the time but they still have very clear local specific reasons for difference among themselves. It goes like this:

Oi loko lawa daw chuni wa-i

Sake tida chobjet le rangni loko lawa daw chuni Dawdi gube chibe ya che le-o

Dawdi geba jube jokople rangni loko lawa daw chuni

Dawdi guba chibe ye ya chile-o

rangni tengi wo gowa luse-en

Rangni nangi lada laying se-eh

Dawdi gube chibe ye ya chi lu-o rangni mase eh guna me em-bey Rangni loko daw chuni ein.

(Meaning in 12 months Loh comes once only in 18 twenties[25] days Loh comes once only, in the last 8th month and beginning of 9th month is our Loh. We must worship and give offerings to all Gods and deities of our land during Loh. We must offer and worship cock's head to our household deity and ancestors during Loh from the 9th month onwards we must worship all our deities. 'o' - we are innocent beings. This is our 12th month Loh.)

Children's Games

Children are often seen conscientiously playing certain games when they are left to themselves in free times. My friendly relation with the children gave me a rare opportunity of closely observing their games and behaviour undisturbed. Children below 12 play lively games of enacting the roles of their parents. They gather and collect small sticks, stumps, twigs, leaves, branches, strings, stones and chips, and pieces of bamboo. Out of these collected materials they make small houses (Kim) and makeshift hut (La) big enough to crawl in and sit inside. They use different materials to simulate all those things in a household family and emulate all the elders' way of life and works. It make belief they maintain a house as mother and father with some children, they cook food, collect water, look after cows and calves, milk the cows, so on and so forth.

One afternoon, Lhasang (6 years girl), Rimpen (5 years girl), Nunu (4 years boy), Passalham (9 years girl), Desing (3 years boy) and I went down to the paddy field just below Dillang (last residential site in Lower Lotukuchu) for a stroll. The moment we were on the field Lhasang jumped around after crickets *(Zigma)* and so they all spread all over the length and breadth of the field to catch Zigma. Vimb (9 years girl) another girl of the locality spotted us on the paddy field from a distance where she was looking after their cows. We hooted at each other and she soon joined us at the field leaving behind her cows. Lhasang and Rimpen were most active; they swung all around and caught many Zigma without missing a single. The moment the insects were in their hands the hind legs were removed to prevent them escaping from their hands. These captive powerless creatures were then passed on to me to carry, except for Rimpen who carried the insects for herself. Lhasang did not like it she told Rim to pass the insects to me but was not readily heeded to. After some persuasions from Lhasang, Rim submitted a cream colour legless one but very unwillingly. Rim caught some more zigmas but declined to pass on to me. This disturbed Lhasang and she said loudly, *Rim is not giving it because she likes to roast and eat them alone at home.* All this while I was watching their expertise and skills in catching and detaching the hind legs without missing a single one. I was also wondering why after all these poor creatures were being caught amputed so mercilessly. As we were climbing up from the fields Lhasang told me that they were going to play cow *(pik so-ane)* rearing game with the zigma. She further told me that with the strong hind legs it is difficult to get the restless zigmas under control like cows. The zigmas were released on the veranda of Lhasang's house and she began to look after them like cows by steering them here and there. Suddenly all our attention towards the game was distracted by Passalha, who attracted our attention towards rabbits[26] copulating nearby in a cage. They quickly rushed near the rabbits leaving Nunu to look after all the cows. Nunu was happy with all the cows around until suddenly something clicked in his mind. He picked up two crickets and held them closely along the ventral sides. He was fully absorbed in this experiment for some time closely watching the strange behaviour of the two poor insects held between his hands.

When Lhasang, Passalham, Kinjong (6 years boy), Diku (6 years girl) and Vimb came back they began to play a different game. Lhasang, Kinjong, Diku and Nunu became cows and bulls according to their wishes. Nunu and Diku were happy to be ferocious bulls. They began to play bullfight while Lhasang and Rim became mild cows with ropes tethered around their necks. Kinjong became the most ferocious bull. He began to bellow and challenge all other bulls around. Soon the bulls were head on against one another and fight ensued. Vimb who became the one to look after the cows came in between two bulls whenever the fights were getting uncontrollable to prevent hurting one another. When it seemed that the fighting bulls were getting tougher she tethered them all with ropes and separated them physically. With the ropes around the neck the bulls were showing their anger against one another by staring furiously at one another, scratching the ground with forelegs and picking on the ground with their horns. After tethering the bulls it was time for Vimb for milking the cows. When the cows stood ready one behind the other, Vimb fetched a calf by the ear and let it suck the udder for a little while and then tethered them away to proceed milking the cows. By this time temper of all the bulls had calmed down and they sat down licking and scratching their wounds and muscles. It became almost dark and we retired to our homes for the night.

More grown up boys do not like to indulge in such childish games. They prefer adventures in the jungles, fields and pastures with a catapult and/or a chopper in their hands. They like climbing trees, hunting birds and monkeys, fishing in the streams and explore the jungles for whatsoever interests them. In fact play, amusement and games go side by side, hand in hand with their daily routine works in the fields and at home. They are good audience; they do not mind spending a whole day watching something new and strange or anything that looks extraordinary to them.

Modern Education and Occupational Change

The Doyas were basically pre-literate ethnic community in Bhutan till the early decade of twentieth century. Very few elders among them began to learn the Devnagari scripts as a formal means of written communication when the migrant Nepalese began to influence over the socio-economic and local administrative affairs of the region[27]. In the past Lamaic traditions of education in the monasteries remained restricted among the elites in Drukpa society. During the middle of twentieth century the kings of Bhutan began to lay special emphasis on modern form of education. Royal Government of Bhutan is making considerable efforts to reach out the light of modern education using tri-lingual formula of English, Dzongkha and Lhotsham. The government established Primary Schools in far and remote corner of Bhutan even before constructing any road communications and infrastructure in most of the regions. Hundreds of Indian teachers were being employed to teach in these schools.

The first school for the district that came into being was one at Samchi HQ in early 1950 and another at Dorokha sub-division in 1956 with boarding facilities. It was only then the first batch of Doya children was put into the schools in 1962. The first batch of children who went to school at Dorokha consisted of nine boys all from Satakha village. The Sengten (Sengdhyen) Primary School came into being from the year 1987 for the children of Lotukuchu area with lots of local initiatives and supports from all people in the Lotukuchu area.

With the advent of modern education among the Doyas and the changes in Government's attitude towards them some Doya men (mostly those who studied up to middle class) and few women were encouraged to take up different jobs outside their villages. As a consequence certain extent of social mobility set in otherwise conservative and isolated society. This occupational mobility was confined to few individuals who had to face resistances from the closely knitted traditional society (see Jochung's case in Appendix-II: Persons and Personalities).

Since the inception of the School in 1987 as many as 152 Doyas have attended Sengten Primary School. 130 children were on the current school register in the year 1994. Based on the enrollment figures up to the year 1993, an approximate percentage of fourteen of the total population of Lotukuchu group of Doyas have attended primary schools. Female and male literacy uptil the year stood approximately at 7% and 22.4%, respectively. The dropout rate recorded uptil the year 1993 was 10-15% per year. The actual literacy rate particularly among the male population would be higher. There were many elders among the present generation who know how to read and write in Nepali language which is Devnagari script and few other who knew the national language Zhungkha. These literate people did not attend any formal schools but they learnt by experience and practice as they had to communicate some how in the past. To find out the actual literacy rate may require a separate survey work.

Table 1.3: Doyas in Different Occupations

Sl. No.	Occupations	No. of Persons		
		Males	Females	Total
01.	Teaching	1	-	1
02.	*Gelong (Monk)*	5	-	5
03.	Forest Guards	2	-	2
04.	Agri. Field man	1	-	1
05.	Royal Body Guards	2	-	2
06.	Royal Bhutan Army	6	-	6
07.	Police Wireless Operator	1	-	1
08.	Businessmen	3	-	3
09.	Contractors	2	-	2
10.	Drivers	1	-	1
11.	Peons	3	-	3
12.	Watchman	3	-	3
13.	Cooks	2	-	2
14.	Servants (House)	4	1	5
15.	Wage Labourers	-	2	2
	Total	36	3	39

Source: Field Data, 1993-94

Out of a total 152 literate persons thirteen persons were engaged in Police and Security Services, Forest and Agriculture departments of the country at different places. There were another twenty six (Table 1.3) persons who did not attend Primary schools, but they were literate working in private and Government services at lower grades. These people who were working outside were mostly unmarried singles. Those who are married left their families at home.

They do not easily get married outside their community. Of course, there were exceptional cases like Sakab who worked in Phuntsholing district as a Forest Guard and got married with a local Tamang Nepali woman. Soon after he quit his job, brought home his wife and succeeded in settling at his ancestral land despite lots of social resistances.

The range of services Doyas were taking up were teaching as the most coveted and latest development, spiritual services as monks, state security services, forest and agricultural field workers and few in business. Some of them have already quit their jobs premature to settle with their families at home.

Summary

Doyas live in remote corner in the hills under Dorokha subdivision of Samchi district without any modern communication facilities. They are located in two physically separated habitations without any social interactions between the two.

Doyas have indigenous names for all the geographical features in the surrounding which amply proves that they are the indigenous people of the region with their historical past embeded in their oral tradition.

Of the two habitations, Lotukuchu group of Doyas live in the interior region of Dorokha subdivision, hence they remained even more inaccessible to outside world. Today the Doyas live along with many other communities of the Rais of Nepali communities, Dogapas and the Hapas, who migrated into the region. The settlement areas of the Doyas have been reduced to few square kilometres from the vast area of territories their forefather once lived.

Lotukuchu is a group of five territorially and socially distinct groups. Similarly, Taba and Ramteykha are also two physically separate locations and social groups.

The territorial groups in the Lotukuchu side are identified with distinct titles. Certain number of lineages resides in a residential territory although few lineages are commonly found distributed in at least two adjacent territories. The territorial titles are mostly related with geographical features of residential sites and / or directions. They consider themselves as a distinct ethnic group in comparison with other people in their surrounding who they identify with distinct titles known to them.

Shifting cultivation coupled with hunting and gathering have been the mainstay of their livelihood like any other hill tribes in the Himalayan region, although in the recent past they have also adopted more settled way of life by erecting terrace fields for cultivation and raising cash crops under population pressures and ecological constrains in their surrounding. Their staple foods are sorghum, maize, roots and millet consumed with varieties of meat, salt and chilli. They are also inveterate drinkers. They brew their own drinks at home.

Doyas have mixed physical features although they are predominantly mongoloid. Their population is showing signs of improvement from near extinction. Lotukuchu group of Doyas comprises 64% of the total population of Doyas at present. The present sex ratio of the Lotukuchu population is showing an excess of female proportion to the total male population.

Doyas live in environmental friendly houses built with locally available wood, bamboo and leaves. Of late some the richer families have begun to build permanent houses with stonewalls and tin sheets.

Doyas speak a distinct language identified as the Lhokpu by linguists, recently. Lhokpu is clubbed together with Monpa, Lepcha, Rai and Newari languages in linguistic classification.

The modern education and occupations are exposing the Doya people to new and alien status, role and position in the larger society outside their own community. This is a land-marked change from their general status of having been porters' community en block placed in the lowest rank of the larger society until recent past. Despite, resistances from the rest of traditional community modern education and government jobs are gaining importance among the younger generation. Few government employees among them are becoming role models and change agents in the community. These educated and salaried and/or richer people put up better houses, maintain better living conditions and understand the value of modern education national culture and as such are treated as respectable persons. They are fast catching up with the new ways of life. Some of them have very negative attitude to their own traditional way of life.

A conflict has emerged in the Doya society between the old and new generation in which the new tradition of market oriented modern society is gaining its ground. The Doya society is passing through a transition phase. We shall try to understand the old social values and tradition in the following chapters.

NOTES AND REFERENCES

1. Taba-Ramteykha was previously under the Chukha district administration but later in the year 1990 it was put together with Lotukuchu group under the jurisdiction of Samchi district administration.
2. This bridge provides a very important communication link for the migratory people of the district and it used to be an important trade route also for Paro Penlop in earlier times.
3. Doyas generally refrain from going to Denchukha to visit their historical relics as though it is a forbidden place for them. One reason they said whenever I asked for their company to visit the place was that in 1980s one Doya man from Satakha died mysteriously right back home after he ventured to visit the place.
4. Elders narrates about their territory in the past like this -*Tangpu tangpu la rang k a pon Mih ya- an. Tangpu tangpu la jang Salela nang Lhop Jalpaiguri tuk-tuk, sar Seti chio nang Nup Jiti chio tuk-tuk Lhopu ka ewui ka Mih ya-an* (Long long ago we had our own king. Lhopu villages were located in the vast territory extending between the first snowline in the north and Jalpaiguri in the south, between Jaldhaka river in the west and Seti river in the east.
5. *Danchat* is a social category among the Doyas meaning descendants of inter-marriages between Nepali and Doya. They are socially segregated from the rest of the society.
6. *Leysant* literally means residents of lower part of hills (*Ley* = lower/ down, *sant*= residents/dwellers). This is also taken as social category.
7. *Rosant* also means residents of upper part of hills *(Ro* = upper/up, *sant* = residents/dwellers). This is also taken as a social category.
8. The local elders told me that the Gonkeys and Sarmis had been serving different Penlops in earlier times as royal porters and labourers. And that whenever, Gonkey women happened to travel through the Sarmis villages they received maltreatments and in another couple of instances Sarmi women had forcibly taken Gonkey men for their husbands. An apparent distrust and mutual fear between the two groups of people were observed during my study also. The Doya children of Taba-Ramteykha who were brought to Sengten School never had friendly relation with the Lotukuchu children even when staying together in a common dormitory.

9. *Hapa* are migratory pastoral people of Tibetan stock. They speak a corrupt form of the national language *Dzongkha.* They keep herds of cattle and fleets of horses and make seasonal migration towards the south foothills of Bhutan passing through Doya region during the winter season staring from Sept.-Oct. to April-May every year, from their cold habitats in the north of Bhutan.
10. My Doya friends often showed me Pa Tshering an old man aged 80+ years, who stands at 5.6 ft. and has fair skin, broad shoulders as an example of Doya physical features in earlier times.
11. These figures were obtained through an interview with a Doya clerk working at the District Census Department, after 1990 National Census operation. These figures were cross checked and endorsed through my personal door-to-door survey in February and March 1992. However, detail analysis on demographic situation was done on a figure of 1069 heads from the Sengten Basic Health Unit.
12. 1988 population estimates. Source: *A Geography of Bhutan,* CTDD Department of Education, Royal Govt. of Bhutan.
13. *Kuensel,* July 25, 1987 vol. 2, No.29, p5.
14. Nepali people along the 'Jiti' khola (a stream in the western boundary) at Pinjuli and Sipsoo also corroborated the same story about the past of Doyas. They said that the Doyas were separated from the Totos after Indo-Bhutan boundary demarcation. This was recorded during my short posting at Pinjuli Primary School in 1995.
15. People generally believe that evil spirits causes death and diseases. They say, "*at times their people were destroyed by Sun, at other times by evil spirits of water at another time by a great epidemic.* "Basic Health Unit outpost sources at Sengten say that this region is endemic in dysentery and diarrhea.
16. One *Mitchi (Pusta in Nepali)* is equivalent to time period of a persons lifetime which is roughly taken as a 100 years according to local standards of life expectancy. The time roughly coincides with second half of 19th century when British were enroute towards the northeastern frontiers of Bengal and Bhutan and in the course of which Bhutan was engaged in continuous war with the former over the occupation of the Duars. The population down fall of the Doyas is conspicuous by the absence of any mention about them in the historical records and travelogues of the British although, mentions are made of the Lepchas, Bhutias, Nepalese and Tibetans, etc.
17. Almost all the forefathers of the present generation had two to three wives when the population was just below 200 towards the end of 19th century. One such example is of a man called Pincho who lived in one of the two houses in Satakha. He married 3 wives including one Rai

(Nepali migrant) woman. Descendants of these parents now make 66.6% of the total population (135) of Satakha (Table 1.1) they often say people of *Satakha* or Satank are sons and daughters of Pincho-ganpa causing far reaching social consequences in the small society.

18. George Van Driem, an Assistant Professor in the Linguistics Department of the University of Amsterdam who was appointed for linguistic studies by Royal Government of Bhutan. He visited Lotukuchu in April 1993 to do linguistic study of the place and identified the Doyas language as Lhokpu in a personal interview with him at the Sengten School.
19. National dress *Gho* and *Kiyra* is part of the National customs and code of conduct *(Driglam Namsha)* being promoted among the people through schools and colleges currently to preserve national identity of Bhutan against the influence of western culture. Laws are being enforced to use national dress in all public places and Government offices.
20. The Totos are also known for their habit of liking stale meat infested with worms.
21. Not long ago, a complaint was lodged against one Jiwa Doya a professing as local doctor (Pama), for indulging in malpractices of sorcery and witchcraft, to the head Lama in Thimphu. The matter was referred to the local *Gumba* (monastery) authority at Dorokha Dogap (Sub-divisional religious body). All the professing local doctors, both Nepalese and Doyas of the region were summoned at the Monastery and they were made to take oath of allegiance to the Supreme Lamaic Body of the country's religious institution and to use their knowledge benevolently for the people. Jiwa Doya was asked to wash off his hands from the profession by keeping away from the village. In compliance with the order of the religious body Jiwa Doya now stays out at Thimphu and never comes back home in the village.
22. Official visitor as a part of local hospitality often sexually exploits most of the young women both Doya and Nepali. Some of the women often attended the Basic Health Unit near the school for venereal diseases.
23. During my stay in upper Lotukuchu in one of the house, I saw a conscious attempt of my host to keep the surrounding clean in my presence. I decided to join their kitchen but most often I cooked separately as their food habits did not suit my stomach for every day. They gave me all the possible help and tried to keep clean. I often shared their food. My pots and pans were always washed well than I could manage myself and kept dried in safe place. When I asked for the pot and pan they would wash it again and then only give me. If I ask them to cut vegetable or clean rice they would consciously make it a point to wash their hands before they touched any of my things when I never told them to do that way. I knew that they never take all these care of cleanliness for themselves during the long consociation with them.

24. However, there is a division among the people in timing this festival since 1980s before which time they used to celebrate together. After 1980 more and more people are celebrating *Loh* a month later i.e. between 8th and 9th month of a year according to local calendar. Some elders say that the difference had come due to their engagement in the free labour service of the state during the New Year time leaving no responsible persons in the village. Meanwhile the dispute remains and people are divided into two groups i.e. one who celebrate early Loh and other who celebrate late Loh. The matter was taken to sub-divisional headquarters in 1980. The officer wisely advised them to sort it out among themselves. Meanwhile, the celebration continue at two different occasions amidst controversy as is reflected in the folk song sung on this occasion.
25. 18 twenties is a period of a year as they follow the Lunar calendar (18x20s = 360 days). Twenty is a unit of counting bigger number.
26. Rabbits are not found in the region. Rabbit keeping was also not known. Once my landlord express a strong desire of keeping some rabbits at home. Not much later, I was able to get him a pair of Rabbits and that became a piece of exhibit among the people. Many turns up to see them at Lower Lotukuchu.
27. There is local history surrounding the present Samchi district. Reliable sources among the Nepalese in the district say that there was a very influential Gurung family at Samchi. He was a prosperous contractor on behalf of the Paro Penlop who gave him responsibilities for labour organisation to exploit the forest resources in the region and facilitate trading and economic development of the country. Over a period of time, it is said that the Gurung family became very influential and powerful in the region. He assumed monopoly in the socio-political affairs of the area so much so that he wanted to create a political domain of his own much to the displeasures and uneasiness of the Penlop. He even started constructing a large palace with 52 doors for him on the Samchi foothill. His increasing power was not appreciated by the Penlop: Once, he was summoned to the Paro Dzong for a discussion and it is said that a serious quarrel took place with the Penlop. Ever since he did not live to return to Samchi. It is assumed that he is dead.

CHAPTER 2
Social Organisation

The Doyas have lived with their own ethnic identity over time immemorial. They have retained a distinctive culture and social organisation of their own amidst the politically dominant Ngalom and culturally influential Lhotsam communities in their immediate neighbourhood. Doyas form a distinct social unit in the socio-cultural environment within which they find themselves. Their relation with the Ngalom due to geographical barrier has been partial and master-servant like in nature through private and personalised contacts or as groups of porters/labourers for the rulers. The Doya occupies a receptive position at lower level of social strata in Bhutanese society. They don't protest if Ngalom take away their women as the latter do not necessarily treat them as equals and accord legitimacy to any offspring out of a sexual intercourse with Doya women. There have been instances when Ngalom have taken young males and females for their domestic services through their administrative and trading contacts with the people. When the males, who are picked at their young age, come back home they retire without spouse and children, as they would not readily find mates in Ngalom society.

On the other hand, Doya's relation with the Rai among the Lhotsam communities can at best be described as harmoniously symbiotic but socially exclusive. Rai as a part of great Nepali cultural extract present themselves as culturally superior and potentially impressive social group capable of considerable influences on the Doya ways of life. Rai in general feel that their Doya brethren needs to learn a lot from them to improve their living standards and change some of their social customs. Incidentally, the Doyas also seem to have adopted certain cultural traits and techniques through years of close social interactions with the Rai and subsequent changes in their ecological environment. In turn, the Rai found amicable the people and place to settle down and prosper. Yet, both the societies maintain a social boundary between them by virtue of their intrinsic socio-cultural tenets and different perceptions. In this connection it may be remembered here that the offspring of inter-marriages between the Nepalese and Doyas form a distinct category in the Doya society called Danchat *who* are socially segregated from others.

Doya social organisation is based on Matriliny and Matrilocality and that of Durkpas and Rai are based on the principles of Patriliny and Patrilocality[1].

Thus, a social boundary line can be delineated for the Doya with respect to the Rai and the *Drukpa* societies. The Drukpas, on the one hand as the ruling and dominant cultural group, trace their origin from Tibet. On the other hand, Rais as the lower caste in Nepali society trace their origins from Nepal and form a distinct cultural group with local variations and consider the Doyas as an indigenous minority group of people having inferior lifestyle and language. The Doyas therefore, present a distinct ethnic group in the socio-cultural environment of the region for an ethnographic investigation.

Riihs, their Origins and Deities

The Doya society is organised through number of matrilineages. Individuals born in the society is identified with a matrilineal title that is transmited through female lives. A consanguinal group of people with such a lineage title with a distinct origin transmitted through only female line of descendants is called a *Riih.* There were at least 13 Riihs known to the people with different titles in the Doya society. They are *Namba, Kordang, Himajang, Laskey, Ruischat, Humchat, Dupsot, Metchat, Binchat, Ding chat, Dohtag, Asonk* and *Konsiring.*

Members of the most of these *Riihs* trace their origins from different sources while some of them did not have clear idea of their origins. The *Riih Konsiring* had no descendant family left among the Lotukuchu Doyas.

Among the existing Himajang, Laskey, Ruischat, Humchat, Dupsot, Metchat, Binchat seem to have origins of earthly nature amongst which the former five Riihs trace their origins from some form of land dwelling animals and the latter two trace their origins to specific geographical regions. We can have at least six Riih groupings on the basis of some similarities of their origins among those whose origins were known (Table 2.1).

Table 2.1: Riih(s) and Their Origins

Riih Groupings	Name of the Riih(s)	Origins
1.	*Namba* *Kordang*	Sky. A branch of Namba riih.
2.	*Himajang* *Laskey*	*Pey-chop:* An insect that infests the stems of Acorn tree.
3.	*Ruischat** *Humchat* *Dupsot*	*Bup-sop:* A land dwelling snail with whitish shell.
4.	*Metchat*	The origin is not known. They are also believed to have come from a place called *Todey-tankha* in the south.
5.	*Binchat*	From *Bindin:* an ancestress deity, revealed and worshipped by a famous Pama. The descendants of who became associated with this deity and came to be known as Bin-chat.
6.	*Dingchat*	Their origin is not known. Members of this clan are known as high hill dwellers.
7.	*Doh-tag*	Origin not known.
8.	*Asonk*	Origin not known.
9.	*Konsiring*	No descendants left.

*People of this clan are believed to have come from Sikkim.

Himajang and Laskey share a common origin from a stem borer insect called *Peychop.* Ruischat, Humchat and Dupsot also share a common origin from a land dwelling snail called *Bupsop. Namba*[2] *is said to have originated from sky along with another Riih called the Kordang* being a sub branch of the former. It is also said the Doya kings of the past belonged to Namba Riih. Origins of Ding chat, Dohtag and Asonk Riihs could not be known during the studies. Ruischat (although sharing common origin with Humchat and Dupsot) and

Metchat are said to have migrated originally from Sikkim and *Todey-tamkha* (a place said to be in south of the present Doya habitat). However, different may be the origins of each Riih the Doyas as an ethnic community all together seem to have at least three mythological stories that accounts for a common origin[3].

There are several high gods called *Lha* among the Doyas. These Lhas are believed to have control over their lives, properties, fertility and natural environment. There are three different important Lhas namely, *Tengtha*[4], *Zibdag* and *Nehdag*. All the Doyas generally worship these once in 3 or 5 years period in different residential territories with the cooperation of all the matrilineage descent members. However, Namba and Kordang Riihs were more closely associated with Tenglha, and Laskey Riih to Zibdag deity in ritual observances at the time of worships. These Lhas are believed to be residing in the rocks and top of hills. There were however, no signs of idols but they could point out the abodes of these deities in their territories.

There are also several deities associated with the natural resources In the residential territories. Some of the popularly known are *Orhung, Lhungma* and *Uripemo* deities residing in different parts of Lotukuchu territory *Uripuda, Yuhma* and *Chohminh* are other territorial deities in Sanglung. *Kenduma*[5] is another deity in satakha territory and Bindin[6] in Lotok. There are certain sacred spots preserved where these deities are believed to be residing. They are worshiped every season before and after seed sowing for productivity and well-being of the people[7]. It is believed that these deities exercise their control over the land fertility, productivity, rain and wind and also over the health and well-being of the people. These deities are to be appeased and worshipped occasionally also by the local people when something seem to be going wrong in their normal live.

The Doyas have yet two other deities closely associated with their residential households (Makim) and matrilineage. One is called *Echan* and the other *Gyenea.* They are associated with residential households and one's matrilineage. Both are to do with the welfare and solidarity of the ancestry and descendant lineage members under a Makim.

All the Doya households in general worship these deities every year between September and October marking the beginning of a new year *(Loh).* All the descendant members of a lineage segment who may be found under different territorial units have to be present on this occasion. They are bound together under a deity specifically associated with each Riih. The unity and solidarity among the segments of a lineage find expressions in the annual worship Riih deities. This worship of Riih deities is performed once in 3 or 5 years with sacrifice of cocks *(Kek),* or a Pig *(Pank)* or local ox *(Pik)* or an ox procured from tea garden labourers from the Indian border[8]. This requires co-operation in cash and kind contributions from all the Riih members of lineage[9]. Some such names of Riih deities are; *Gomchen* deity for Namba Riih and *Jimpey* deity for Kordang Riih.[10]

I once had an occasion to witness the local deity worship in Sanglung territory along with Hirrang Maila, a popular Rai Bijuwa of Bisgoan neighbouring to Sanglung. It was 2nd May in 1992 when the maize crop had grown 3 to 4 feet tall on the Jhum fields along the ridges and slopes of the hills. Representatives of eighteen households who had their fields *(Yonk)* around the stretch of hill slopes there. Hirang Maila was also invited as he had a patch of maize field on *Adhiya*[11] (50:50 share) basis with a Doya family in Sanglung.

They had contributed to arrange two pigs, some hens and cocks and eggs for offering to the deities. The place of worship was on a ridge running west to east direction on which maize was already sown. Nine small platforms raised on four sticks, one to two feet from the ground were erected around the ridge facing different detections. Elders including women were gathered to do the worship. The deities that were worshiped on the day were as follows; *Zibdag:* supposed to be male deity was offered with pig. He has control over life and death, and general health of the people. He can cause all sorts of body aches if neglected by the people. *Yuhma:* supposed to be a female deity was also offered with pig. She has controls over wind and rain and also on the health of the people particularly health problems related with digestion and breathing. *Chirrgan* and *Sing:* supposed to be a female deity. She was offered Hens and Cocks. She controls over the crops grown in the shifting fields. *Lung char* and *Gangchen:* Spirits of death people supposed to be residing in the hilltops. They are offered hens and cocks facing the western direction. *Chopdut:* another female deity of the local area. She was offered hens and cocks. My informant friend did not reveal her influence in the local environment. *Chohminh:* another female deity. Her abode is at a pond in the upper part of Sanglung territory. The pond like a spring is a perennial source of water drained by streams down hill though the length of Sanglung territory. The deity has control over this source of water and also responsible for fever and skin diseases, if neglected. She was offered eggs. The last two deities that are also worshipped are *Pandigang* and *Yuhma.* They were offered hens and cocks. Their influences were not revealed very clearly to me. The ritual performances of the day were as follows:

The nine platforms at different places were covered with freshly cut banana leaves. Seven trident figures made of dough called *Sebu* were kept on the platform for *Zibdag* along with a small bowl made of the same stuff filled with fermented millet was also placed. On a bark of tree incense smoke with dried pine spruce leaves was kept. Some boiled eggs were placed on the platform for *chohminh* along with chanting of appeasement and sprinklings of local brew. The chanting translated goes like this: "You are our benevolent guardian. You have been worshipped and respected by our ancestors since long. We beseech you to guard us against misfortunes and diseases. We are offering you things that we could manage." This way all other deities were also appeased with their particular offerings separately one after the another for better productivity, good health, good weather and continuous water supply, etc.

Offering of the pig: A person caught the pig by the two hind legs, while the others/preacher chanted with a cylinder of jar in one hand. At the end of the chanting an elder signalled to spear the pig through its heart and lungs. The blood smeared pointed knife was shown on the offering platform while the pig died soon out of bleeding. The pig was then roasted a little on fire to clear its fur after which the hind finger-nails of all the four legs were cut off, a part of tail, lower lip, the eyes, ear, nose, tongue were also cut off and kept separately on a piece of leaf. Two long parallel cuts were made running from the armpits and meeting around the genital. This piece was cut off along with the sternum leaving the stomach and abdomen exposed. The whole of alimentary canal, heart, stomach and liver were cut off and kept separately. From this lump again a piece of liver and lung were cut off and kept on the leaf. The pelvic bone was broken to cut into four major portions; 1. Head. 2. Forearm region with the two legs. 3. the middle part including the chest and vertebra. 4. The hind region with two hind legs. These major portions except the head was further cut into four small pieces each. The middle part was cut along the vertebral column and a piece of spinal cord was taken out and kept on the leaf. These two pieces were again cut into three pieces each. The hind part was also cut in the same manner in three pieces each. The head was cut vertically into two symmetric parts and the brain was taken off, then another cross sectional cut was made between the jaws and the tongue was taken out. In all, twenty-two pieces were made of the pig. These pieces were boiled and offered along chanting and sprinkling of Yu in chorus.

The hens and cocks are also offered in the same manner. After all the offerings were made they partook the meat and drinks. They said that the alimentary canal and lungs couldn't be given to any outsider to eat: they have to eat it themselves.

Ewui[12] (Organisation of Residential Territories)

A look at the composition of Riih(s) in a particular residential unit *(Ewui)* would reveal that there are at least two groups of people belonging to different Riih (Table 2.2). However, the fact that some Riih(s) share a common source of origin may also throw some light in understanding the composition of a particular Ewui formation (Table 2.1).

Table 2.2: Riih Distribution and Territorial Titles

Residential Territories *(Ewui)*	*Riih(s)* found	Titles
Satakha	Ruischat, Humchat, Dohtag	*Satank*
Sanglung	Laskey, Dupsont, Asonk Ruischat.	*Guchat*
Lotukuchu (A and B)[13]	Namba, Laskey, Kordang	
Lotok	Metchat, Binchat, Himajang.	*Binchat*

And the fact that people residing in a particular residential unit are known under different names, viz., Satank, Guchat and Binchat[14], worshipping respective common deities also shows some kind of territorial solidarity in the social organisation.

Moreover, there is an apparent aggregation, segregation and regroupings of the people based on common territorial residence, lineage, Riih and cultural difference. An interesting aspect of grouping phenomenon can be observed, reflected in the grouping behaviour and attitudes of school going children of the place[15].

Residential groups of people within a common territory are known with distinct territorial titles such as Satank for the people of Satakha, Guchat for the residents of Sanglung and Binchat for the people of Lotukuchu and Lotok. The territorial solidarity by virtue of sharing a common residential area is expressed by worshipping the local deities from time to time for the general well being of the residents and productivity of land and food grains.

Matrimonial relations within and amongst the residential groups present a particular pattern (Table 2.3) despite possible deviations due to demographic situation. An analysis of the pattern of matrimonial relations of 160 cases revealed that there is a tendency of intense intra-territorial matrimonial bonds rather than that of inter-territorial bonds.

Table 2.3: Inter- and Intra-Territorial Conjugal Patterns

Residential Territories	Satakha	Sanglung	Lotukuchu	Lotok
Satakha	54 (71%)	16 (21%)	-	-
Sanglung	-	110(66%)	-	-
Lotukuchu	11	4	276 (88%)	-
Lotok	-	-	8	8

The table above shows at least 54 (≅71%) cases of intra-territorial matrimonial alliances out of 76 adults males and females and another 16 (21%) had relations with adjacent neighbouring village Sanglung and no relations with Lotukuchu and Lotok which are physically apart. Sanglung being the oldest and second largest village with vast territorial expanse has 110 (66%) matrimonial alliances within the village out of 176 adults. Lotukuchu as a whole has 88% of intra-matrimonial alliances and a few relations with sanglung and Satakha. Lotok as an extension to Lotukuchu has equal intra and inter-matrimonial relations within the village and with Lotukuchu.

These figures were calculated in terms of males taking residence to wife's households.

The inter-territorial alliance seems to be the result of the imbalance in the sex ratio. The little excess of females in reproductive age seems to have received the excess of males in Satakha as the two residential territories were contiguous to each other. Similarly, the excess of adult males in Lotukuchu seems to have gone to find their partners to Satakha and Sanglung. However, there are also other social reasons to explain this phenomenon. It has also been observed that there is an intense intra-Riih matrimonial bond rather than that inter-Riih ones (Table 2.4). The patterns of inter and intra-Riih conjugal relations that emerged out of the field data show interesting results. The samples included married couples of eleven different Riihs and out of which at least five Riihs were found to be practicing intra-Riih conjugal relations.

These Riihs were Laskey, Namba, Metchat, Humchat and Dohtag. In the sample of 113 married couples collected during the study 62.2 % belonged to intra-Riih couples of Laskey Riih (as compared to 37.8% of *inter-Riih* marriages with Namba, Metchat, Humchat, Dohtag and Kordang Riihs), 7.9% couples belong to intra-Riih marriages of Namba Riih, 5.3 % belong to intra-Riin couples of Humchat Riih and single cases (0.8 %) of intra-Riih marriages with Metchat and Dohtag Riihs. Out of a sample of 22 cases for Namba Riih 40.9% were of intra- Riih marriages and the rest inter-Riih with Laskey, Metchat, Humchat, Dohtag and Dingchat. Metchat and Humchat Riihs had inter-Riih marriage relations with Laskey, Namba, Humchat, Metchat and Dohtag.

Makim: An Abode of Matrilineage and Matrilocality

To disentangle and understand the inter-twined complexity of Doya social organisation within and without let us look at domestic level consanguinal family unit which reproduces its members and perpetuate the relations. This consanguinal unit is called Makim. In a Makim (main household) mother, her husband, married daughter her husband, unmarried daughters and small boys and girls live together. But seen in any household, these consanguinal units can be found with varying compositions such as:

A. Mother, her husband, with one or more married daughters and their husbands along with unmarried daughter(s) and son(s) may be found in a Makim.

B. Newly married daughter with her husband may still be a part of a Makim taking shelter in a budded structure on one of the side of the main house.

C. Married daughter with her husband and children may be found in a small house called *Kim* built nearby the Makim or in a *La* at the shifting field.

B and C groups would always be found linked to an ancestral house through matrilineal descent thus these two family units do not necessarily occupy a Makim. Unit A can often be found occupying a Makim forming a matrilineal corporate group (a *la Maine)* in continuity of its Riih. All individuals born in this group, identify themselves with the particular Riih title. Descendant females transmit the Riih title through her children. Males retain their Riih identity in their lifetime and end with it when they eventually die. From a consanguinal family of the unit A matured son takes residence in his wife's ancestral house with parents- in-law and other resident husbands.

This situation may be quite alike Robin Fox's Model-1 derived from ethnographic materials of *Nayyar, Navaho* and *Yao* tribes, in solution of his 4 Principles[16] but we cannot afford to overlook the cultural specificity of other society.

The Doya situation presents a specific case in particular the question why must only females stay put on the ancestral land? And why must only females transmit the Riih title and not males? Who exercises control over the ancestral land? These questions require us to look into the history and traditional law of inheritance in the Doya society. Here, we will look into the land owning system first.

What the local folktales account for the way land came to be owned by them in the past corroborates the land revenue system in the 19th century in Ashley Eden's book (1864). Doya folktales reveal that they did not enjoy an ownership right to the land on which their ascendants lived. Until 1956 Land Reformation Act of the Royal Government of Bhutan the land belonged to the Penlops and Rajas. Doyas were allowed to use forest and land resource freely in lieu of free labour services in transportation of goods, tending ponies, cattle and construction work through *'Gon-do wula'*[17].

Illegally in the eyes of the rulers but internally, they had well defined legitimate land ownership and inheritance pattern. In the vast area of richly forested land on the hill slopes they practised mainly slash and burn/shifting cultivation, wherever it was suitable. They moved from place to place within their territory and slashed and burned

Table 2.4: Inter and Intra-Riih Conjugal Patterns

Riihs	Laskey	Namba	Metchat	Humchat	Dohtag	Dingchat	Kardong	Binchat	Ruischat	Himajan
Laskey	33	3	2	6	–	–	2	3	–	1
Namba	11	9	3	–	1	–	1	1	–	–
Metchat	1	6	1	1	–	–	–	2	–	–
Humcha	2	1	1	6	–	1	–	–	–	–
Dohtag	2	1	2	2	1	–	–	–	1	–
Dingchat	–	2	–	–	–	–	–	–	–	–
Kordang	4	–	–	–	–	–	–	–	–	–
Total	53	22	9	15	2	1	3	6	1	1

(Random sample size: 113)

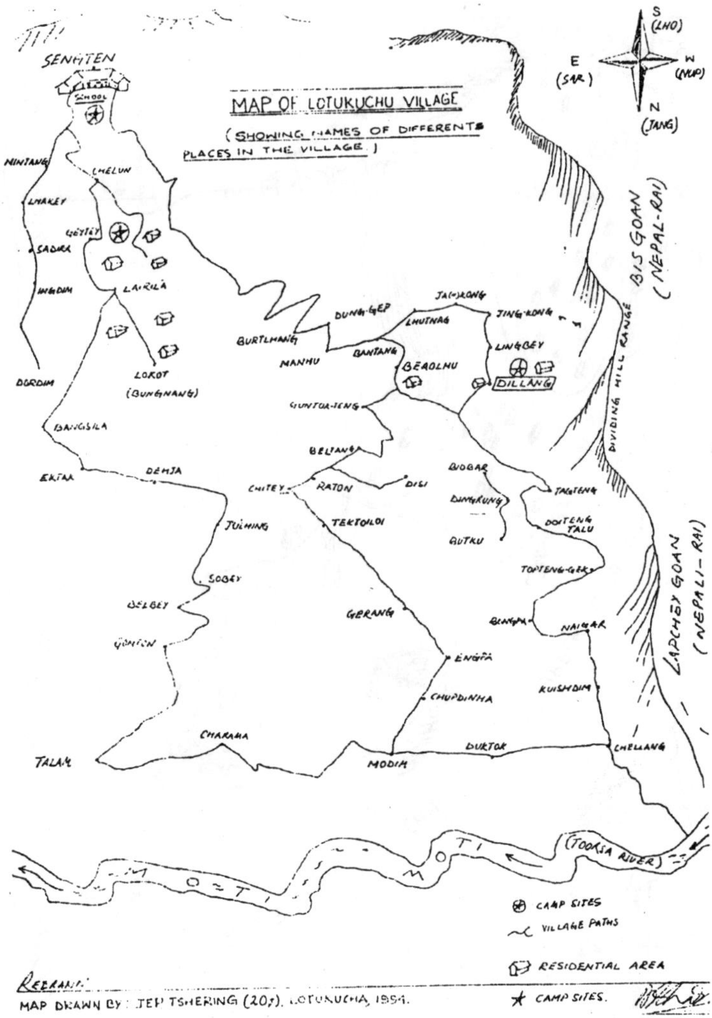

Map. 2.1: Lotukuchu Proper: A Native's Version

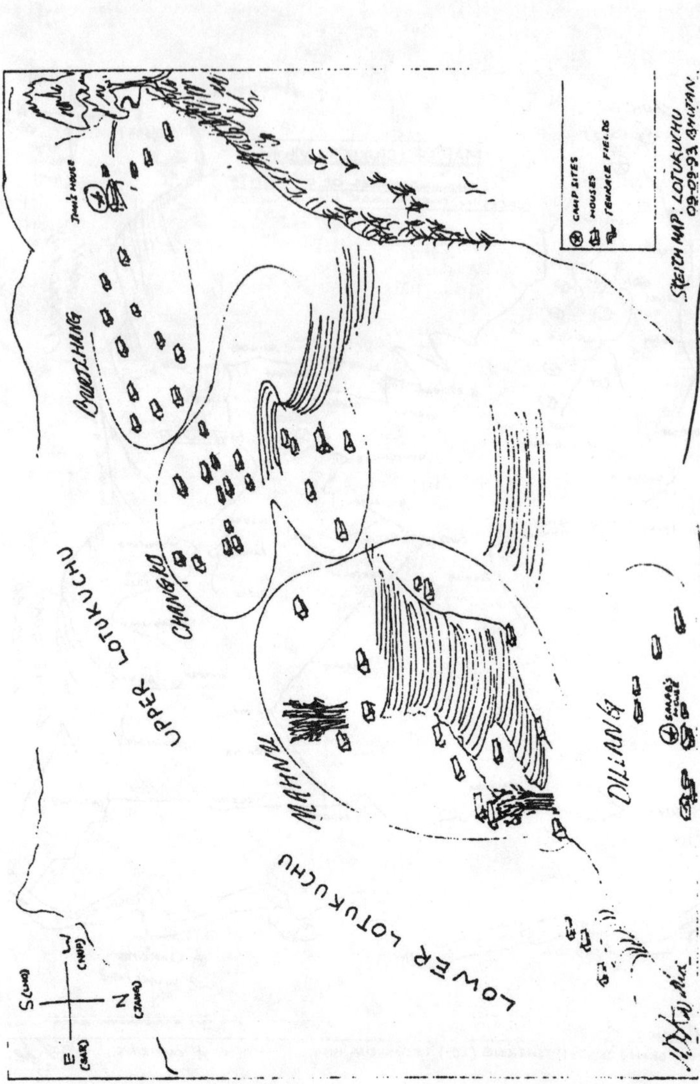

Map. 2.2: Lotukuchu

parts of hill slopes, at many different places. And whosoever, did the work first, the land belonged to him or her lineage and got inherited through generations. Thus, each and every ascendant primary lineal family began to possess land they cultivated and possessed. The more each primary lineal family procreated, the larger and the more of Jhumming fields as they had the freedom to exploit their environment. Although both male and female worked at par, a popular folksong called *Nangsey*[18] is sung by females for its magical effects on the work progress in clearing the fields. These lands owned at many different places were named after important landmarks of the area (Map 2.1: Native's Version).

Given the historical antecedents and given the type of Doya family organisation (*la Malinowski* and *Firth, R.*) with respect to land it does not make sense to talk out land ownership as such, it would rather be meaningful to talk in terms of and *authorship* and subsequent maintenance and inheritance pattern of the land through the descendant consanguinal lineage group, who seem to corporate to use and maintain and extend it wherever possible/needed for their future descendants.

In the above situation it goes without saying that who ever group authors a piece of land develops a sense of attachment towards it and consequently a sense of collectively owning it along the matrilineal residential group. For a descendant consanguinal family among many other different such lineal groups, to maintain such a piece of authored land it becomes necessary that the land remains within matrimonial group and not to others. Therefore, to this effect the consanguinal family as a corporate body has to see that the lineal reproduction is ensured within close kin groups through generations. This is the main problem of matrilineal corporate body for which there are customary rules relating to conjugal alliances that ensure continuity of the land and female line through generations.

Given the understanding of this kind of situation and to set out to analyse the Doya social organisation would be indigestible if Robin Fox's Principle-3, which says, men usually exercise control, is not heeded to, at all. But for any analytical purpose I would like to see the male(s) for men because the word is more often value laden in a particular cultural context. Let the image of men emerge out through the analysis of their situation.

Rules relating to Conjugal Relations

Rule-I

A. **Son must go for brother's daughter and daughter must bring brother's son** (females' perspectives) or in other words, **Daughter must bring sister's son and son must go for sister's daughter.**

B. **Consanguinal daughter must stay put together in mother's natal house and son must take residence in wife's natal house.**

These are the ideal rules of residence and conjugal relations for eligible males and females to reproduce the lineages, which they try to adhere to the problems of finding conjugal partners due to imbalance sex ratio in the community it is often difficult to adhere to the ideal rules in practice. Therefore, here are also some alternative rules in the spirit of the former. First, we will look into the operations of the first set of rules and resultant problems by taking up two consanguinal families of Unit-C[19] (comprising wife, resident husband and their children) in which the wife and her husband are grandchildren of a mother in the preceding third generation. In ideal situations, the children in the two-consanguinal families will grow up into matured males and females. They will then begin to look for their conjugal partners according to the first set of rules and they establish conjugal bond with their own mother's brother's son or daughter, and/or father's sister's son or daughter.

In this situation, son of a sister will take residence at brother's wife's natal house or brother's daughter's natal house and sister's daughter will stay put in mother's natal house that is also brother's natal house. This relation affects some sort of sons exchange between the two families of brother and sister. The case studies of Challamo and Chedojis will illustrate the point at the end of this chapter. Son goes to none other than his own mother's brother's daughter and daughter gets back her own mother's brother's son (the bone and seed theory in Chapter 4) to the matrilineage, to further perpetuate the line of descent. The son provides his labour in both his wife's maternal land and his own maternal land and contributes his share of grains to his conjugal family. He is also entitled to a part of whatsoever property such as livestock or land that his mother's brother *(Ku)* raises for his children during his lifetime. Whereas, mother's brother's children also have an access to a part of the matrilineal land for use that may be allotted through a joint decision taken by parents and married sons and daughters of a matrilineal group. The males of the family help to make and extend the matrilineage through generations by his sex right mobility. His role and status is embedded in this social matrix. He plays an important and responsible role in facilitating decisions relating to the matrilineage in different social occasions. However, he does not necessarily dominate over the decisions. He is equally responsible to his sister(s) and her children who enjoy a special relation with him different from their own father's brothers and father. He plays an important role in organising and performing rituals relating to the matrilineal household deities and deities associated with their Riih and territory and at the time of familial crisis. In the time of misfortunes and at the time of rituals of life, he is always the one to look upon[20].

From the following observations and analysis a deviation from the principle-3: *men usually control* is irresistible. And equally irresistible is an idea of commonality of interests amongst the consanguineous lineal members in its perpetuation and maintenance of the authored land within a Riih *vis-a-vis* other Riih(s), which may be seen, reproduced through generations in the Doya social organisation on the whole.

For the time being we will continue to concern with our consanguinal family. Daughters of sisters establishing connubial relations with brother's sons serve the same purpose. In that the husband who is mother's brother's son comes to no alien household other than his own close aunt. Working and procreating in that household also serves the common interest for the future generations. If he is able to author some more land, he does not become a rich man but he becomes resourceful male to have had more of which some part can be shared to his own children and some part to his sister's sons. One of them gets more who gets chance to carry his *(Ku's)* dead body in his funeral rites.

However, in reality it isn't possible to get one to one relation for every FZC and MBC to reproduce and maintain the matrilineage and the land according to the Rule-l. More often than not many of the prospective matured males and females fail to have their prescribed opposite sex partners due to various practical reasons which are out of their control such as:

1. Unequal sex distribution, 2. age differences between the prescribed partners, 3. individual adventures, etc. To counter such practical problems pertaining to the basic tenets of the society alternatives are provided in Rule-II.

Rule-II: One can seek connubial partners with mother's sister's children (MZC) also in the third generation by direct descent.

This rule provides an alternative to the Rule-1 within the same scope and parameter. But in this case both the conjugal partners will belong to the same Riih. Moreover, they may also be residing in the same territory but living in separate households belonging to a lineage segment. Nevertheless, this relationship brings the groups even more closely and consolidates on their corporate land and property ownership. But for the small size and limited pool of members belonging to a particular Riih or for that matter a lineage and also for the general morbidity of children and presence of some imbeciles many a conjugal relations were found affected even among the first and second generation of parallel cousins in the direct descent. Such relations are considered as deviance from the norms of the society however; the party concerned and their children are legitimised and accepted only after paying *Nama*[21] to a congregation of elders in the residential community.

Nevertheless, neither the Rule-I nor Rule-II is able to contain and satisfy the problem-3 as listed above and the strict adherence conjugal prohibition among the parallel cousins on the father's side up to *7th* generation. This is apparently adhered to by the absence of such matrimonial cases notwithstanding very rare exceptional cases that resulted to social ostracism.

Non-adherence to the prohibited rules and non-payment of *Nama* in case of pardonable social offences, they say are ostracised from the society and lineage land. Such cases have not occurred among the Doya but application of such a sanction on prohibited relations involving individuals from among the people is apparently considerate[22] although they are labelled with different identity.

However, the problem of finding one's conjugal partner given the sort of rules and the demographic difficulties seem to have allowed situation where individuals to personal adventures courted marital relations with the Nepali women in their neighbourhoods from earlier times. Almost the whole of people in the Satakha territory is often said to be descendants of such deviant inter-marriages. It was found that these people suffered from social ostracism for long time. They were differentiated from the rest of the society by labelling a derogatory title.

Observing and talking to all these people who face social sanctions relating to conjugal relations it was confirmed that they lead a secluded and left out life. They authored new land on their own or bought land from others and started a life anew on their own. Descendants of these parents are not all together forgotten and pardoned. They are collectively separated from the rest of society and labelled as Danchat (children of Nepalese)

Now, let us look into the consequences of the execution of the Rule-II (Females must stay put at matrilineal house). Obviously, the execution of this Rule will best serve the purpose of the corporate body wherein the lineal individuals and land will be intact. For this matter why should not the children of sisters be allowed to form matrimonial bonds in the second or for that matter in the first generation itself without having to pay *Nama*? Why should there be prohibitory rules against it? I put this question to many of the people. The answer I get is a frank affirmation, *"Pahela-pahela to hundeiy thiyo, cheli-maiti ko bich-ma puni. Abota hundeina."* (Speaking in Nepali they say," Long ago, there used to be, even between sons and daughters of sisters also. Now, it is not done.") There was an apparent uneasiness on the part of respondents in further talking about the matter. We look into the prohibitive rules on the father's brother's side. Under the prescriptions of Rule-II, and I brothers of a consanguinal family will seek matrimonial ties with:

1. MBDs, or
2. MZDs in the third generation, or
3. Other females within the society.

The first two (1 and 2) will best serve the purpose of their common interest but in case such options are ruled out, he will go for the third option (3). Even this will serve the common interest provided his wife's house or the land is in the same territory (Table 2.4). Now, let us assume another situation where two brothers get into matrimonial bonds to see how the common interest in the corporate body is maintained. This can happen in two different ways: One - brother getting married with same lineage females and Two - the two brothers getting married with females belonging to different lineages (*Riihs*). The fact that males do not transmit lineage title through their progeny and that they take residence in other's corporate consanguinal families only help us to say that males are to help in procreation and perpetuation wife's matrilineages. Therefore, the prohibition on matrimonial ties between parallel cousins on paternal side until 7th generation is justified. What is implicitly conspicuous in this analysis of consanguinal family is that the absence of any negative or positive (must or must not) rules against inter-*Riih* (lineage) and for that matter inter-territorial matrimonial ties. The implication of this fact seems to cause the very development, existence, sustenance and perpetuation of each and every lineage (*Riihs*) and also Doya society as a whole.

The worst situation is when a lineage is reduced to a mother (over her reproductive age) is left with one son only or the situation where execution of Rule-II and I of matrimonial alliances is out of question. The implication can best be illustrated through another rare social practice involving a woman to change her matrilineage for good among the Doyas. This rare phenomenon can be termed as *Matrilineage transmutation* of a woman to others matrilineage, which is facing extinction in the absence of female descendant.

***Matrilineage Transmutation*[23]**

Having no *Metchan* (a daughter) born/left in a matrilineage is a great crisis and extremely crucial situation that may lead to extinction of a lineage, which is also linked to certain deities. This cannot be allowed to happen in all consciousness of the collective conscience when there are possible ways of finding a woman in the situation to work out a solution within the society. All the possibilities are to be explored collectively and it is often not so easy for the woman is central to every lineage. Each woman is sacred in her own lineage with transcending relations the supernatural realms. As such they are firmly rooted and immovable like a piece of land in their matrilineage being responsible for the continuity of the lineage in normal circumstances. Corollary, how can anybody in a close society like the Doyas lay claim over a piece of land that has already been authored and owned by a lineal group? Even if it happens a serious conflict will ensue and the consequences will have far-reaching and irreparable impacts (see Setah and Chapey's case *inf.*). Although, the situation here does provide a room for such conflict the social collectivity sees to it that the problem is resolved amicably involving negotiation at societal and supernatural levels. It is time taking and painful emotional processes for the woman but the society shares it together. The details are as follow.

First, a lineage group will have to be found out who can spare a daughter to help procreate others lineage and a process of negotiation begins with elders of the two parties. The interest in the continuity of one's matrilineage and the land is so intense and encompassing that they can even convince the deities who rule upon them. It involves a whole transaction of economic, social and spiritual nature between two lineal groups through a series of negotiation. This being unlike the normal ways of establishing conjugal relations between prescribed partners does not require premarital sex with the women to be transmuted however, there are rooms to test the fertility of the women during the process of transmutation. What is most important is to find a family whose parents can bear and afford to part away with a daughter. In four such cases recorded, two males (*Setah* and *Aedusiri*) had no sister to perpetuate the lineage and in other two *(Kasadao* and *Aedusiri)* had sister but for plenty of land unmanageable by them they had to arrange transmutation of women for their wives. Woman for transmutation will be undoubtedly found in a relatively disproportionate family size to the corporate land holdings. Once a family is found, consultation and persuasion through close kin and relatives (especially *Ku*'s role is important), to mediate and bring an agreement. After an agreement is reached with the parents and guardian uncle (*Ku*), a day is decided to take away the girl from her maternal house through rituals. My respondents narrated the whole procedures as follows:

> On an auspicious day, lineal elders of the girl will get together at her natal house when the boy's party along with lineal elders guardian will also come prepared. The determination of wife buyer's party is so strong that it is expressed through a folksong sung on this occasion.[24]
>
> After singing the song, the boy along with his elders will sit together inside the girls house and pay Nama to the mother of the girl. This Nama used to consist of 12 silver coins, one *Gemba* full of fermented millet and grains to be offered to the matrilineal deity. And some such things are also to be carried while taking the girl to offer to the local deities of the residential territory on the way. After paying the Nama they will sit together and drink.

Then they will set out towards the boy's home taking the girl along.

The *Nama* paid on this day is the first installment. After three years from the day-giving enough time to test the fertility of the girl - another Gemba of Yu along with a big pig is given to the girl's parents to be offered to the household deity, lineage deity, the ancestral deity and beg for separation of the girl from her mother's lineage, her ancestral land and spiritual relations whatsoever within which she lived and grew up. This is the second installment of the Nama. The girl thus separated forfeits all the relations whatsoever and would never go back to her natal house even when any members of natal family die. On the other hand the girl has to be accommodated to the husband's matrilineage and to make the local deities accept her so and bestow on her and her offspring the same protection given to all others other husband lineage. The same kind of offerings is to be made to propitiate the local spirits and deities for acceptance and accommodation. After these rituals the girl becomes an inseparable member of the lineage by foregoing her Riih title and taking up that of husband's Riih title for her offspring, and thus she will perpetuate the lineage of her husband's mother's matrilineage.

The third continuing installment of the Nama is given annually at the harvest of local millet *(ewui ka Jarto)* until the lapse of the third year after the death of the woman[25]. In absence of parents the descendant children of the matriliny will continue to pay it without allowing any lapse. For the payment goes directly to the deities any lapse in reaching the annual payment will earn royal indignation of the deities. Misfortunes will befall on the family of the defaulters.

Furthermore, the implications of the matrimonial rules can be manifested in the dynamics of *territorial* group *solidarity* and *social solidarity* of the Doya society. There are certain factors, which allow and limit intra-territorial and inter-territorial matrimonial relations. The aforementioned problem-3 in the maintenance of matrilineage continuity gives leverage to effect intra-and inter-territorial relations and social *solidarity.*

The little room of freedom of choice in the absence of prescribed matrimonial mates allows a matured male or a female to look for his or her mates of choice. Here, also there are certain factors which limit their choices because of the nature of work they do being quite attached to the ancestral land, confines his or her movements within their own territory to allow and also limit his or her choices.

Therefore, the maximum occurrence of intra-Riih (Table 2.4) and intra-territorial conjugal bonds support greater the solidarity of lineal corporate and territorial grouping patterns (Table 2.3).

Nevertheless, the track in the hills taking almost two days with loads involving night halts on the path, every weekend do give an opportunity to ambitious males and females for seeking conjugal partners or otherwise. Rai people are often heard saying; *Orange season is a matrimonial season for* Doya. Indeed, during my four years of stay in the place most of conjugal bonds were formed during November to March but in retrospect it is difficult to comment if the Doya have a matrimonial season.

What emerges out of the analysis is the portrayal of a dynamic and harmonious Doya social organisation through two tenets.

1. Interest in the matrilineage and its consequences in the social relations.
2. Interest in the matrilineal land and its consequences in the formation of the corporate groups.

To further understand the dynamics of Doya society let us discuss some conflicting situations in the society. We have seen how the interest in the matriliny can be maintained in harmony through the 'positive rules' and approved ways and means of matrimonial ties. And also how the solidarity so attained becomes manifest in reality in the execution of 'negative rules' of matrimonial relations with other society.

Situation arose when someone laid claim over some other's authored land and the consequences of it was a cleavage in the territorial solidarity of a village. Payo Setah at Lower Lotukuchu and Jimi, my host at upper Lotukuchu narrated this story.

> Once it so happened that Setah and Geygey both belonging to Namba Riih encroached upon a piece of land authored by Chapey's parents (but remained unused for long time) who belong to Laskey Riih. Setah's parents lived in the middle of Lotukuchu and then shifted down hill at Dillang (lower most residential area in

Lotukuchu) where Chapey had a sizeable land around the place. Chapey lived in upper Lotukuchu. When Setah had risen up a big family he needed more land for cultivation so, he along with Geygey of the same Riih cleared the land around a hill slope, which belonged to Chapey. They used the land and laid claim over it. When Chapey came to know about it he asserted his prerogatives over the land by inherited ownership right. Setah and Geygey objected. A bitter quarrel broke, animosity and hatred doubled up without anyone to mediate. Ultimately, both the parties underwent Nubara[26] and thus committed themselves to socially boycott one another. This created a divide between the two groups that was transmitted down to descendants through generations. Incidentally, most of the Namba people reside in the lower part of Lotukuchu and came to be known with the title Leysand (ley=low) and most Laskey people reside in the upper part of Lotukuchu and they came to be known with the title Rosand (Ro=upper).

After the incident over the land and subsequent Nubara commitment resulted in forming yet another two distinct socially exclusive groups in the same village under two different territorial titles.

Apparent avoidance in interactions and inhibition among the present generation including their children from going to each other's residential areas was observed through my own experiences of living together with both the groups in lower and upper Lotukuchu living evidence to what occurred 40 to 50 years ago.

However, a better comprehension of the dynamics of Doya social organisation is possible only after we have a comprehensive picture of the organisation of the consanguinal family in its stages of development.

Makim and its Developmental Cycle

A consanguinal family here, refers to a family with matured sons and daughters where the mother is in descent line of a primordial matrilineage and occupies an ancestral house Makim with its household and lineage deities and subsists on an authored land which she inherited from her ascendant mother. This consanguinal family members except the father belongs to a particular Riih. We will not proceed anywhere unless we assume another such an ideal consanguinal family co-existing with matured sons and daughters nearby belonging to a different Riih. And also having had already discussed the rules of finding matrimonial mates further discussion here will be confined how such families relate to one another within the positive rules of conjugal relations.

Sons and daughters are considered matured for conjugal ties when they are grown up as normal[27]. The decision to take up conjugal ties mostly depends upon the need of a helping hand in the productive work on the land and also on personal proclivity and curiosity of adolescent adventures on the part of males and females. However, the processes of socialisation in association with Ku's family, own family and among peer groups they get to know the rules and ways of finding their own mates[28]. Deliberate attempts to meet in privacy by the prescribed conjugal mates or they are sometime arranged to meet at home or outside if the parties are not motivated. What goes in such meetings and who goes with whom is an open secret to everyone in the society without any fuss. Once a mutual interaction takes place it is not uncommon for the girl to invite the boy home or anywhere anytime in privacy. Parents of the girl accept the adventures of the boy as a normal behaviour, Generally, when daughters get matured, they are made to sleep separately outside in a small compartment attached to the front side wall of the Makim under the roof falls on a narrow and small bamboo platform raised from the ground. On a particular day when the boy comes at night and joins the girl in her compartment and seen in the morning doing some works at her natal house they announce that the particular boy has *found* his *Me-hin* and the girl has her *Ra-him.* Hereafter, it requires the boy to begin to stay put in the girl's natal house and actively participate in all the household chores and cultivation works in the fields. He becomes an indispensable labour in the household. The boy usually works at his best to show his worth and goes back to his natal house only seldom when required. Some improvements in the girl's improvised compartment is also apparent as they both try to make their sleeping place one of the best in the world[29]. It is then the boy is related and recognised as *Mahnkpa* (resident son-in-law) to everyone in the girl's household. They are often made to cook for themselves using the same *Jikpu* of the house and eat together until they have a separate arrangement if there is more than one daughter. However, legitimisation of this conjugal tie comes much later only when the Mahnkpa succeeds to impregnate his Me-hin.

Over a period of time, the girl one day discloses her pregnancy to her mother and in turn to all concerned. The boy then goes back to his parents to report the same. It requires the couple to prepare lots of Yu from local millet *(ewui ka jarto)* and make ritual offering of the same to the parents and guardians within a period of six months from the day pregnancy of his wife was announced. This present for pregnancy is also called a Nama payment to the girl's parents, uncles and all other related to their household. This payment legitimizes the boy's relation as Ra-him to the girl who in turn relates to the former as his Me-hin i.e. husband and wife. This relation also entitles him to be father *(Payu)* of the future offspring of his Me-hin. Failing to impregnate a woman in such conjugal ties over a period of time often may result in annulling the conjugal ties and dissolving the relationship between them.

When the Me-hin is in her first pregnancy period the Ra-him is seen at his best doing all sorts of works to assist the woman. He would either erect a new hut for delivery of child or further improve on the earlier compartment and make it more broad and comfortable. At the time of delivery he helps his wife, cuts the umbilical chord, washes her clothes, and after he cleans the house, cooks food and washes pots and pans, collects water and all that is required to run the household. He also takes equal part in looking after the baby. Thus, the nuclear family that results over a period of time out of this consociation, later on, takes a shape of an extended household unit under a Kim (a separate house) keeping all the economic and lineal ties with the parent Makim and corporate land ownership

More than one such extended household may come around the Makim if there is more than one daughter in a lineal house. Younger sisters as and when they get their conjugal partners will bud off the Makim like a new shoot bud from a plant *and* establish their own houses at such places to attend to the productive activities on their lands.

The houses where brothers have joined separately or together with different sisters of same parents would also undergo the same processes and separation on their wife's land. These brothers keep paying visits to their mother's house at ritual occasions and to contribute their labour to the matrilineal land and to derive their share of food grains for their own family. He also contributes his labour to wife's matrilineal land for a share of food grains for their family subsistence. At the same time he has to provide a share of food grains to wife's ageing parents who would then be not very active in cultivation works.

As these physically separated conjugal families raise their own consanguinal families their parents also get older. There has to be one daughter to look after[30] the ageing parents in the Makim. There is no hard and fast rule unlike the *Khasis*[31]. One of the favoured daughters with her husband and children will remain in the Makim while others will contribute equal share of grains and other eatables for their ageing parents. The time also comes when the total land of the matrilineage has to be roughly allotted to the consanguinal sons and daughters who now have their own consanguinal families to maintain and also to those who have no family of their own yet.

The decision is that everybody has to have a fair and equal share irrespective of sex. All the brothers and sons join the sisters and parents to discuss and decide as to who would cultivate where and what part of the land. Once, this allotment is done each sister becomes substantially independent with equal obligations to their parents as long as they live. This also is the time they are concerned with the maintenance of the land under the matrilineal ownership and that it does not go in other's hands. The concern becomes more apparently so, when their parents die one after the other. The best solution they find is in MBC-FZC conjugal relations. In that when the brothers re-allot his share of land along with what his wife has inherited from her parents to their children (which would roughly make a proportion of 50:50 of the total land from both mother and father side for their subsistence) at his old age, approximately the same portion of land comes back or re-allotted back to his matrilineage through his sister's sons *(Lhira)* according to the inheritance rule[32]. It all gives a clue to an idea that 'marriage' in Doya social context is a contractual undertaking between two lineal consanguinal families as a means to an end interest where both the parties are regarded as equals to further reciprocal relations in the subsequent generations.

The consanguinal family with which we started has left behind one or more consanguinal families on the matrilineal land distributed independently in land around the residential land but these are all linked to the primary consanguinal household ritually and spiritually through the matrilineal and household deity. They all carry the matrilineal Riih title. However, when the parents especially mother is no more, it becomes brother's duty to keep up the lineal by performing regular worships and offerings to the ancestral deities and by giving necessary guidance to his sister's children for the maintenance of the lineage and the corporate land property intact. In absence of any brother the eldest husband (Mahnkpa) would normally do the service of the brothers in the interest of wife's matrilineage.

These group of consanguinal families which may be called secondary consanguinal families would now have more permanent house like that of Makim but they will not become a Makim as such as long as the original Makim exists and functions as an abode of the ancestress. More or less in the third generation descendants of the secondary consanguinal families will *continue* to inbreed within the lineal group with greater chances of finding preferred mates as the lineage expands horizontally. When the descendants of the third generation children bind themselves in conjugal units and start reproducing further progeny the first generation ascendants of primary consanguinal and secondary families; their roles in the interest of the lineage would be replaced by the subsequent children and grand children. Let some examples of varying types and nature of matrilineal descendant families illustrate the points.

Case Studies

Setah's Matrilineage

Setah (70+) belongs to Namba Riih. He had three sons and seven daughters from his wife Yimjam, who was *transmuted* from her matrilineage in Sanglung, to continue the lineage as all his sisters remained issueless, (2, 3, 4, 5 in G-1). He inherited plenty of land that was again added up as he rose up his family. Most of his productive land was scattered at many different locations in the lower part of Lotukuchu consisting of many Yonk (Jhumming fields), *Ding* (Cultivation land on gentle slopes), Orange orchards and Cardamom fields. He lives in his Makim at Dillang at the lower Lotukuchu where his father shifted from middle Lotukuchu during his parents' time. When his first child, a son called Sakab (8) married a Tamang (Nepali) lady from near Phuntsholing (where he worked as forest guard and later resigned) and brought her home. Sakab was denied any access and right to ancestral land by his enraged parents. Quarrels ensued between father and son. But later he succeeded in getting a piece of residential land to settle then he later managed to buy some land on which he raised paddy, Yonk, orange and cardamom fields. His son

Sakab's is one of the most prosperous families in the whole of Lower Lotukuchu with two daughters (under 14) by sheer hard work. Before he married his Tamang Nepali wife, he had already married two wives one after the other and to the first wife he has a son (now 17 yrs, married to a girl in Satakha) to the second he has none. He had to divorce both of them by paying Nama of *Nu*[33]/Rs. 1200/- to the first as she had a child and *Nu.*/Rs. 600/- to the second for she bore no child. Now his family with his Tamang wife is best maintained unlike any other among his tribe. After him, Setah's 7 daughters got married one after the other, leaving two in between who in absence of prescribed father's sister's children could attract other male's (belonging to different lineage) attractions.

All other sisters have married with men belonging to different lineage carrying different or *same* Riih names. It seemed they did not mind tying conjugal bonds even with their foes (Rosant, two of Setah's *Mahnkpas/resident-son-in-laws* who are Rosant with whom the Setahs had committed Nubara 50 year's ago) Setah's last two sons: Nopchey (17 years) and Norbu (15 years) were not married as they were studying in the school. Setah had an elder brother Muki, aged nearng 80, who also had plenty of land inherited equally from their parents. He remained single without issue and his brother's sons and daughters were subsisting on his share of land, which he was soon going to allot to them, as he was getting senile. Because his brother's sons were the only rightful claimants to his land, Nopchey and Norbu were taking better care of him and help and assisted in his needs whenever they found time out the regular school hours.

When I was staying at Dillang between 1991 and 1992 I noticed 3 of Setah's matured daughters were sleeping in the budded narrow rooms of sidewalls of the Makim separately. Then in 1992 when I came back from home Kongkilang, the last daughter had her husband Zaba and was staying in the same budded narrow sleeping room. All others who were already married or newly married when I came there had extended into small semi-permanent huts (Kim) around the Makim with their husbands forming consanguinal and conjugal families.

During the year 1992 Kongkilang got pregnant and her husband Zaba with the help of other resident-husbands put up a hut near the Makim and moved in along with his wife leaving the budded narrow connubial room vacated. Setah with his wife along with his 3rd daughter and her husband and children (minor) lived together in the

G-I: Setah's Case

Namba Riih

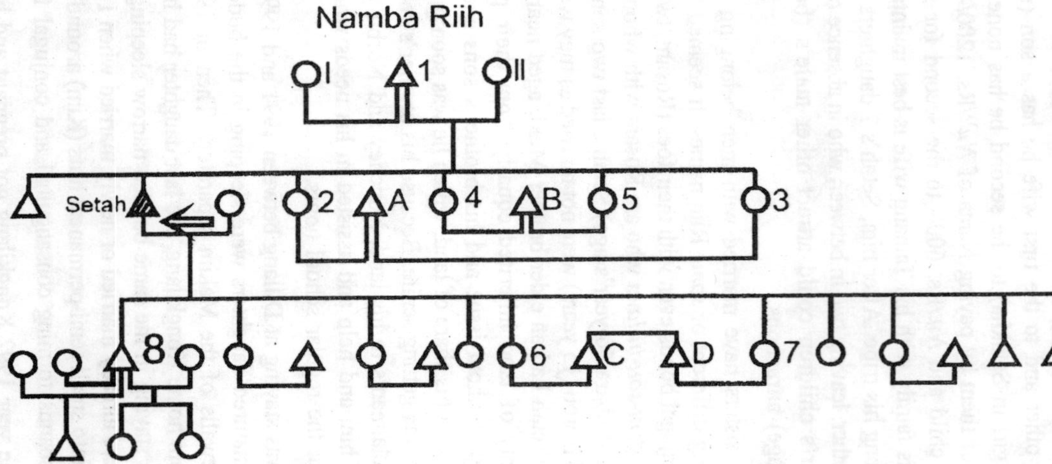

Note: Setah's father had two wives; one was issueless, the second wife (II) gave birth to six children. Setah is the second son. He had to buy a woman for his wife. Between Setah and his wife, they have nine children. Sakab is the eldest of all. Two daughters (6 and 7) got married with two sib brothers.

Makim. This daughter while looking after ageing parents in day-to-day affairs will later inherit the Makim. (Incidentally, the husband of this daughter happens to be the most matured, learned and responsible among his 5 Mahnkpas.) While others will supply equal share of required food grains to the parents and unmarried brothers still continue to share food together with parents. In the Makim there were two Jikpus (fireplace), the other one was for the parents and unmarried ones and the other added one was for his daughter who lived along with them. But there was no restriction in using the parent's Jikpu.

Setahs had already allotted equal share of land to all his married daughters and unmarried sons, too. These daughters along with husbands and children were always on the move working on their allotted lands (Yonk) and orchards and also contributing their labour to the share land kept for unmarried school going brothers in order to help their parents and also to meet their own food grain requirements. Setah had not allotted his paddy fields as it was not enough for allotment and there was hardly any place to raise more paddy fields *(Ding)* as such land was relatively scarce in their territory. So, he allows all his daughters and Mahnkpa(s) to contribute their labour in the paddy fields to extract whatever food grains they could for themselves and a share for him. But to one of his daughters *he had* given his cattle to look after in place of access to the paddy fields. The milk produce from the cattle was shared with her parents and some portion of it she kept for her cash earnings by selling cheese *(Tatsi).* There was also mutual exchange of help to each other among the daughters' families in times of need and also between each and their parents. They all get together in the Makim at the time of annual ancestry and deity worship *(Loh)* and also when important decisions are to be made.

Challamo's Matrilineage

Challamo (60+ years) of Satakha village is married to Chedoji (65+ years). Chedoji is a son of Ya-Chirpey of a neighboring village Sanglung. Challamo is daughter of late Pincho and a Rai Nepali woman. Challamo had one elder brother called Kasadao, one elder sister called Anima and also had one younger brother, Ganesh who died in a mysterious way about eight years ago leaving behind two wives in Sanglung village. The first wife had 5 sons and 3 daughters and second had one young son. The second wife, Chezangmo was Chedoji's younger sister.

G-2: Challamo's Case

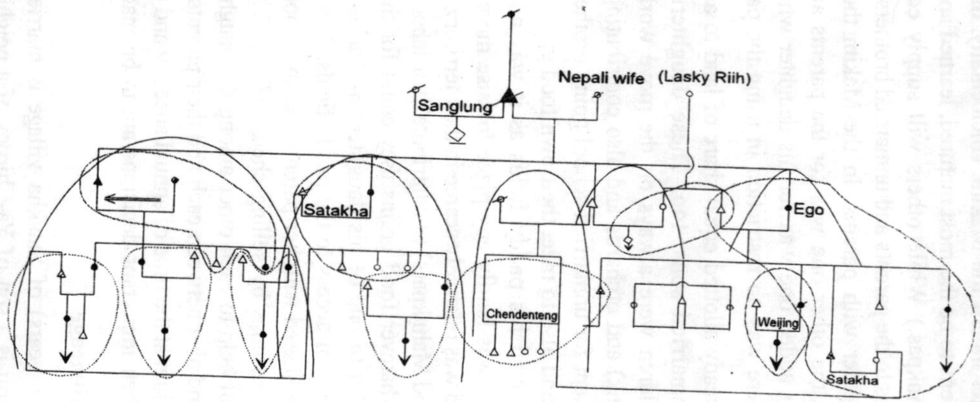

Challamo and Chedoji gave birth to six sons and two daughters out of which the last child, a daughter called Chunglham (18) was studying in Sengten Primary School in class- VI and another son working outside were not married.

Her first daughter, Cha(n)-pem died along with her 4th unborn child during labour. She left behind her widowed husband along with one daughter and two sons in April 1992. Her husband looked after her kids in the house. Challamo's father was an influential man during Penlops time, and was active representative, mediator and an organiser between his tribes and the Penlops in serving the needs of the then rulers. In the whole Satakha village there were just two households and one belonged to her father Pincho's matrilineage with maximum land authored. So among Challamo's brothers and sisters they had a considerable size of land, which was inherited and shared. Challamo's daughters and sons had enough land allotted to them needing no more supplementations from their father's (Chedoji) land from Sanglung, which is adjacent but separated, by a falling ridge and a stream called 'Kamchal'. All her sons are married and established well living in different parts of Satakha with their wives and children raising food crops, orchards, and cardamom fields, wherever they have their allotted lands. When Challamo's daughter died there was a question as to who should take care of the land allotted to her for her family. Long discussion was held with all the consanguinal members, including Challamo's brothers, sisters, resident-husbands and sons. And finally decided to pass the land over to deceased's daughter who was just attaining her teens. On the very day the dead body was to be encased in the Chen. On asking why the land was passed on to a young child when her father was still keeping at home and he had to look after the children, they said that the Mahnkapa was lazy, irresponsible and unreliable man. But the husband had to stay there working on the wife's field for three consecutive years, looking after his children. Then he would be free to decide for himself for his future life. If he so desires, he could always go for a second wife or return to his material household in Lotukuchu to look after their own land and his sister's children.

Challamo has plenty of land still but less manpower. She had the maximum paddy fields also on which sometimes, she engaged/allowed other people (residents of Satakha who were related but do not have the right of access to her land such as her daughter-in-laws, brother's children or sister's sons) to work on her paddy fields. Sometimes, she also engaged hired labour called *Lei-la* for which she had to pay in cash or kind immediately or after the crop yields. If some body asked for use of the land then she gave it on Adhiya (50:50 share basis).

This system got introduced to them with the advent of Nepali community in their neighbourhoods. They did not know it earlier.

Challamo's eldest son got married with her brother's daughter (MBD+FZS) belonging to different Riih, Humchat. Her second son got married with two sisters in Lotukuchu belonging to Dohtag Riih and third son also got married with a woman in Lotukuchu belonging to Metchat Riih (MBD). Since, Challamo's brother, Ganesh was no more and there was no one to look after her daughter-in-law (ED) at her natal home she decided to bring her for his son at her home in consultation with the girls maternal uncles in Sanglung. She said it was quite necessary action as there was no married female at her home to look after her household and that her last daughter Chumlham always kept out of the house for her studies.

Challamo's 4th son's (Jochung's) marriage has a different story. Her son Jochung works in Police department away from the village. However, when he was posted at Sipsoo (a sub-division of Samtse district) he managed to develop a connubial relation with a Laskey girl of upper Lotukuchu during short holidays in the village. In short time he left the girl impregnated in her village. He tried to convince the girl's parents to allow her stay at his posting place for some days. The parents unwillingly allowed *them* against the tradition. After some time when it was known to parents that the girl was fast pregnant and it was time for the man to pay the Nama, the parents sent messages to bring their daughter home but they didn't and time passed without paying the Nama. In the course of time Jochung got posted at Samtse Police Station where the girl gave birth to a child in the district Hospital. It became a social problem for Jochung who neither became a husband nor a father in the society without having paid the Nama during the specified time and the necessary labour services at the girl's matrilineage. He tried to convince the parents but they would not accept him. Lots of unpleasantness came up between the parties. Ultimately the girl was called back home after the childbirth de-recognising her conjugal relation with Jochung. Jochung had to be happy with his job but he didn't give up.

After a long persuasion with the parents through good offices of village elders it was agreed that Jochung should pay a heavier Nama to an elders congregation to get his relation with the girl legitimised. It was done and he was allowed to take his wife to his posting place.

Jochung's, case has set a change in the otherwise static/conservative and traditional society of the Doyas.

Chedoji's Matrilineage

Chedoji belongs to a big consanguinal family in Sanglung village. His mother Ya-Chirpey (116 years old) is the oldest person surviving among the Doyas presents. Her father was a Drukpa from Rangchey - a Drukpa village one and half day walk to the northern hills towards Ha district. Chedoji is the sixth son among the twelve children whom his mother gave birth. Now Chedoji had only four brothers and three sisters. All others died at young age without leaving behind any offspring. They had around 50 acres of land including paddy fields, Yonk, Orange orchards and Cardamom fields among themselves still maintained as a corporate land organised by Chedoji and his elder brothers. His father died 35 years ago. All the brothers and sisters were working at different parts of the land supporting themselves except one of his sisters along with her children who looks after their old mother at then' Makim. Besides working on the land in production works two of the sisters were looking after cattle near the stream called Kampti 30 minutes downhill to supply milk to the Makim and to all brothers and sisters.

Chedoji's Case

Since, all Chedoji' s sons and daughters were well established on their own mother's land in Satakha he was least bothered about them. Most of the time he was found working and tending orchards in his mother's land in Sanglung. He often helped his youngest sister who was widow of his own wife's brother, at Chaplung where she lived in a make-shift hut *looking after cattle* and orchards besides cultivating a piece of land along with her minor children. Chedoji told me that he was helping and doing all he can at his old age for the children of his sisters. Once, when I visited him at Chaplung he was transplanting some orange saplings on a large hill slope. All his elder brothers who were taking residence in their wives, households also often came to see their mother, bring food grains and attended to the household's needs and requirements. The second eldest brother, Kucho (80) was still active and a master of ceremony himself whenever deities were to be worshipped at the Makim. All the brothers come together to organise and perform all the rituals. Husband of two of their sister's were no more so brother's role in the household becomes more than needful.

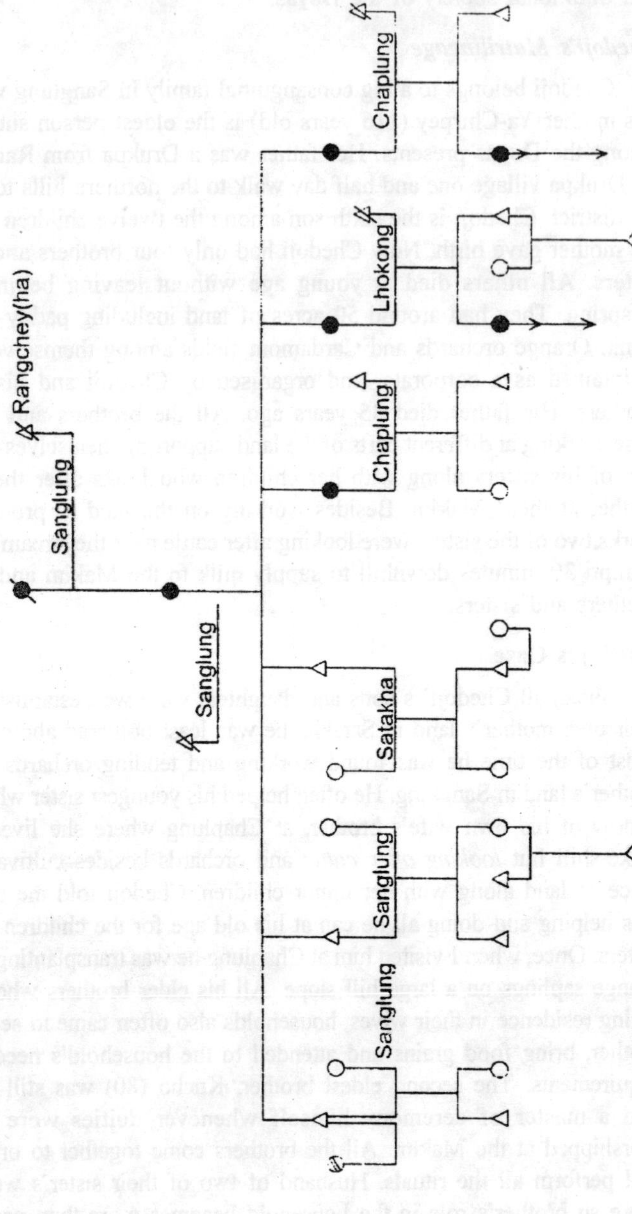

G-3: Chedoji's Case

Samchijem who looked after the aged mother had three grown up sons and a daughter. Two of her sons were out of the house; one had joined Monastery at Samchi and other had married a girl in Satakha. Her only matured daughter was at home to assist and continue the lineage, while the youngest daughters were born *Behpa* (congenital abnormal but physically productive). The whole land after 1965 Land Reformation Act had to be registered under two brother's name Kucho and Passa (Already taken residence in wife's households with grown up sons and daughters in the same village) as Government had put up a land ceiling of 25 acres under a head of household. Kado Tshering, a grandson of Ya-Chirpey studying in class-VI revealed this information.

Summary

Doyas have been able to maintain a distinctive ways of life despite political and cultural dominance of the Drukpas and that of Nepalese in these surroundings. The basic structure of Doya social organisation is based on matrilineality in contrast to the Drukpas and Rais who surround them. This may be one main reason for the Doyas to have been able to maintain their own socio-cultural distinctiveness despite prolonged others' cultural influences they have been exposed while occupying a lower position in the Bhutanese social strata.

Doya society is organised through number of matrilineages (Riih) having distinct titles, origins and associated ancestral deities. Members of a Riih are organised in several extended consanguinal families (Kim) and are linked to one or two main households (Makim) under the eldest female of the line of descent. Each main household is also abode of ancestral and lineal deities. Members of a Riih who may be living scattered at many different places, come together to worship their ancestors once in about three to five years.

There are number of deities who exercise control over health, productivity and climatic conditions of the place. People come together to worship these deities at lineal and territorial levels.

There are four geographically distinct village administrative units for the Doyas. However, Doyas themselves recognise only 3 distinct residential and social units with distinct territorial titles. There may be at least two or three different Riihs descendants residing together in these residential and social units.

There are also further social divisions among themselves based on matrimonial background and residential locations. Descendants of inter-caste marriage are socially segregated and people residing on upper hills are known as Rosants, etc.

A strong tendency of intra-territorial and Riih marriage relations observed among the Doyas seems to support the territorial and matrilineal solidarity of their society where extended families under a Makim form a corporate unit possessing ancestral land. A set of matrimonial rules guides each individual to continue and support the matrilineage.

Land property is inherited through the corporate body of around a female head. Everybody under a corporate body have equal share and access to land and landed property. The set of matrimonial rules ensures that the land remain intact under the corporate body through the children of brothers and sisters. Brother has important roles and responsibilities towards his sister's children in continuance and maintenance of matrilineage households and its land property.

An ethnographic accounts is not complete unless we try to see the social world of other's society through their kin and affinal relations among them through which look at each other in their inter-personal interactions in their day-to-day life. Every society evolves certain terms to denote and refer to one's own kith and kin also those who are related by the way matrimonial ties. It has also been discovered that apparently similar relations between member society have been found to have different in attitudes and behaviour towards one another However, the whole schema of kin terms and relations in a society makes the cosmology of individuals born in the society within which one finds the philosophy of one's life and live wholesomely. Anthropologists, starting from Morgan to Leach in the last two centuries have been studying this diversity of kin terms and relations from different aspects, levels and perspectives to somehow classify them for scientific inquiries. We shall look into the Doya case of kin terms and relations in the following chapter.

NOTES AND REFERENCES

1. Although, the ethnographic studies on many different communities in Bhutan are not to be found the Drukpa society is also generally known to be much influenced by matriliny and matrilocality.

2. *Setah* aged 70+ years belonging to *Namba Riih* narrated the origin of his clan. According to him origin of his clan took place when once God sent a man to earth to fetch a pig for a certain ceremony. The man looked for a pig on the earth and found one. But when he was about to take the pig, it asked if it can get human faces to eat there. The man said no and then the pig refused to go. Fearing the indignations of God in going back without the pig the man stayed back on the earth with the pig. He later married with a local lady and his descendant children; became *Namba.* Another version says that *Namba Riih* originator fell from sky at *Tahlag (Tahlag* is waterlogged place on the upper hill of Sanglung territory still existing. This place considered sacred is under thick forest cover. They believe that a powerful deity resides there). Further, the Doya king who had his palace at Denchukha is said to have belonged to this clan.
3. Talking about their earlier forms of family traditions and ways of life with the local elders in all the villages four different versions emerged:
   (a) Once three brothers came around the region, the youngest brother could not keep pace with his elder brothers. His elder brothers told him to take a rest for sometime while they proceeded ahead looking for better place to settle. They did not come back for days. Later, the youngest brother also followed behind in the direction they went. He went on and on without any trace of his elder brothers. On the way he saw vast area of burnt Jungle with new shoots coming up on the land and he thought it was futile to trail behind his brothers any farther. He decided to settle down there. He married a local woman. It is said that the descendants of this couple became the Doya. Incidentally, this story of origin is quite similar with that of R.Fonig's narration in his book, *"My Vanishing Tribe"* written about the origin of the Lepchas.

   (b) Once there was a big snake in a big pool of water. One day, God came and cut it into three equal parts. From the parts, sprang three men. The first man from the head part went north and became *'Lhakey'* (Tibetan). The man from the middle part remained in the same place and became 'Doya' and the last man from the tail part went southwest and became the Nepali. Some persons criticize this as a concocted story to justify/prove indigenity of the people of Nepali origins in Bhutan.

   (c) There are some elders who bluntly deny the authenticity of this story of origin saying that this is a concoction theory under the influence of migrant Nepalese. They simply say that Doyas originated from this very land and migrated from nowhere. Under-current of this idea came quite explicit in the recent socio-political development of the region, relevance of which will be touched upon in the last chapter.

(d) Another theory, but not the last is very encompassing and has its underpinnings in their belief and knowledge about their natural environment which can also be relegated to the realm of myths. In this theory Doya has been related to certain animals. It says that people are related to tiger *(Kong)* as their Maternal Uncle *(Ku)* and Jaguar (Jig) as their maternal Uncle's wife *(Ni)* who gave birth to a female. On the other hand Bear *(Naisa)* as their Paternal Uncle *(Pang)*, who gave birth to a male. The union of the two female and male resulted in the origin of the Doyas. They say that it is taboo to kill any of these animals and eat their meat. In an interesting incident that occurred with *Yangku's* father Late *Zaba*, who came across a *Jig* (Jaguar) while coming back home through Jungle paths in the evening time. The Jaguar charged and leaped at him and he, in his efforts to save his life caught hold of the animal so firmly that both remained there throughout the night without harming one another. *Zaba's* friend went out looking for him in the morning and found him lying with the Jaguar in the Jungle. After making it sure that the Jaguar was dead, they approached and found that *Zaba* was still alive but badly scratched.

4. Elders in Lotukuchu territory in the course of an informal interview told me that there are nine such deities associated with important *Riih(s)* and that they are brothers amongst who *Tenglha* is the eldest of all.
5. *Kenduma*, a particular deity came to be worshipped after a *Hapa Pau* (another term for Shaman in *Dzongkha* language) who is believed to have influenced the *Satank* people after he had revealed it. The abode of this deity is at *Karmapet* which falls at the vicinity of *Satakha* territory and where the *Hapa* set up their makeshift tent *(Nulak)* in the migration to the south during winter season. Relation between *Hapa* and *Doya* is discussed in Chapter-IV.
6. Please see Table 2.2.
7. Rai people residing adjacent to Sanglung village are also invited to participate and pay respect in the worship of Doya Deity.
8. *Madesi* ox is requisitioned at a time from a family who has committed some social offence in choosing a matrimonial partner.
9. *Chapchu* (24 y) belongs to *Humchat Riih*. He was a temporary cook in the school mess. One day, he came to me asking for some money. I asked the reason why he needed the money. He told me that on 16th of November '92 they were worshipping their *Riih* deity for which they needed to buy a big pig and he had been asked to contribute some money as he was married. A pig has to be procured and fed at home for some days in the name of the deity before the sacrifice at the village *Karbari's* house, where the ancestral deity resides. The *Karbari* of the village, *Senam Dorji* is *Chapchu's* uncle. They live separately. I gave

him the money and he invited me to join the worship.

10. It is prohibited to take the name of such deities. In a flow of conversation once I was able to get some names of clan deity but my informant regretted a moment later to have taken the name. Taking such names is bound to arouse indignation of the deity affecting their general health, and well-being they confided to me.

11. *Adhiya* is a Nepali term referring to a system of land use between two parties. One who has the land owner allows the other to grow crop on the condition that the crop yield at the harvest time will be distributed 1: 1/1:3 according to the extent of labour and resources contribution from the two parties.

12. *Ewui* is relative term like local or locality. One single residential territory with a name such as Lower Lotukuchu may be referred to as *Ewui* with respect to it adjacent upper residential territory at lowest level of reference and then the whole of Lotukuchu Doya territory or the region as compared to other territory far and near may also be referred to as *Ewui* at the higher level reference The term *Ewui* is also used in distinguishing things which are locally available or made as compared to other things which are brought from outside. *For* example, *Ewui to Jarto* = local millet.

13. Residents of Lower Lotukuchu (A) are again distinguished by the term *Leysant* from the residents of Upper Lotukuchu (B) who are known as *Rosant*

14. These names; *Satank, Guchat* and *Binchat* do not refer to any territorial land but to the people who worship different common local deities that control the area where they reside. Further, investigations about these names reveal a particular group i.e. *Binchat* was founded by a *Pama.* My informants said, The Pama belonged to Metchat Riih. He was known for his extraordinary knowledge about esoteric arts and knowledge. He revealed a local deity called Bindin in Lotukuchu. After him his descendants and other people in a Lotukuchu started worshipping the deity and they later came to be known as Binchat. But nothing such could be known about the other two group names in my efforts. They simply say these names refer to people of Satakha and Sanglung.

15. *T*he primary school was established in 1987. It had classes up to V standard 1994-95. There are about 216 students on the roll (1993) age ranging 7 to 29. The total strength comprises of Doya *(Lhopu)* boys and girls with a sex distribution of 101 boys to 29 girls and 50 boys to 32 girls between the *Rai* and minor number of *Lepcha* students. These students come from the surrounding villages (Map-1.2) namely; *Sengten, Satakha, Sanglung, Lumbey, Lapcheygoan, goan,* and *Majuwa(not* shown in the map). The school had boarding facility. Since the year 1991 the boarding started to accommodate only Doya boys and girls.

    Observation of the clustering behavioural pattern of the children in 3 dormitories in Boys' Hostel and one room for girls revealed the following interesting patterns: In the first dormitory some *Leysant-Binchat* (Lower Lotukuchu) along with 1 *Guchat* (Sanglung) and a *Lepcha* boy stayed. In the middle dormitory which is the largest and had *Leysant-Binchat* with three *Satank* staying. Inside each and every room including the girls' shows segregated cluster groups based on the group identity and *Riih* attachment, occupying separate portions and corners of the rooms.

During the school hours when the school is in full strength they get half an hour time of lunch and games, during which time they are left on their own. Lunch was served in exclusive lines of boys and girls, After getting their food they moved out to the playground to eat. During this time pity looking minority group or individual also got their groups to join in. Girls sat at a little distance from the boys group. Doya and Rai girls made their own separate groups in semi-circles. The scattered group comprises of territorial alignments and village groups (for Rai girls). Small minority group often joined friendly groups but what were again apparent among the Doya girls were the *Riih* groupings. The same was true for the boy's pattern of groupings. There was also conspicuous aggregation of groups into sub-groups during playtime among the boys. Here, it must be noted that in general the relation between Doya and Rai at the village level was amicably congenial, which was also reflected in the general behaviour of the school children. But what went on during the playtime is just interesting. Groups of Doya and Rai boys made exclusive teams in the football ground with two local made footballs of plastic rags. They made two exclusive groups of Doya and Rai, which were further divided into 2 Doya opponent teams and 2 Rai opponent teams. One Rai team and one Doya team took to one side of the football field and other two exclusive teams to the other side along common goal posts. In this way, one noticed two goal-keepers (one Doya and one Rai) at each of the goal posts. The play began with two balls at the centre; Doya boys play with their ball with their opposing team and in the same manner Rai boys with their own ball and opposing team played in the same field without any conflict. At first sight, it looked like a total chaos but with a careful observation one could see an order in the disorderly playground. The play went on without any mistakes and mischief between the players of the two groups carefully avoiding obstructions to the other group. They used to get themselves absorbed in carefully tracking their own football and its movements.

16. The four Principles are 1. the women have the children, 2. the men impregnate the women, 3. the men usually exercise control and 4. Primary kin group do not mate (Robin Fox: 1976).

17. *Gon-do-wula is* a term in the national Dzongkha language that refers to a system of free labour services for the state. In this system every household has to provide one person's labour a period of 15 days or more depending upon the nature of work and travelling days involved.

The work generally used to be road and fort construction for the rulers.

18. It is believed that when a woman sing Nangsey keeping her sickle (Goish) with the cutting blade facing upward in the Jhum field to be cleared the song has a magical impact in the work accomplishment. The song goes like this: "Ya Nangsey ya pumo-o-pup cher a . . . Nupchu ya pekpa gu sen ru-a ga tinley ba . . . Ga ugen ya pusem busen ru . . . Ga nangsey pumo popse duna se su o-ya . . . Ga nangsey nalu tin me ba nangsey-ya Ga nabsu ya pepa pupa . . . Gu sin ru pin me banase su . . .". The woman who sang this song for refused to give the meaning of the song while it was being tape recorded and unfortunately later I did not have time to pursue the matter.

19. Folktales often mention of regeneration of the present population from descendant of *Cheli-maiti* (a Nepali term meaning for cross-cousins) conjugation after disastrous population depletion due to war and diseases generations ago. But this term has to be delivered off the Nepali social connotation and articulated into Doyas social milieu to do away with unnecessary confusion, which will be referred in later part of this Chapter. *Cheli* in Nepali society refers to a female who takes residence in the groom's house after marriage and *Maiti* refers to males who bring their wives and stay put in the patrilocal household. Now, in Doya society it is the males to be taken as *Cheli* and not the females as it is a Matrilineal and Matrilocal society.

20. I often ask the question, *who is the most important person in your family among the people.* To the answer they often say, *Mother and then father.* Some important persons in family: *small children say Father and mother.* But elder say: *Father, mother and Maternal Uncle (Ku).*

21. Nama in some kind of ceremonial payment, most often in terms of the local drinks (Yu) done; where a person (s) has to seek social approval or legitimacy.

22. Some of them to name few Late Pincho Ganpa of Satakha married a Rai Nepali lady and settled in his own village, Ujeydema mothered a son to a Gurung Bijuwa Nepali of Bisgoan, Sankonang mothered a son to another Gurung Bijuwa Nepali and Sakab married a Tamang Nepali lady and settled in his ancestral and along with his brothers and sisters.

23. *Matrilineage Transmutation* (according to Oxford Dictionary *Transmute* v. means 1 Change the form, nature, or substance of. 2 hist Change (base metal) into gold refers to a specific case of Doya society wherein a woman from a matrilineage is permanently taken away for procreation of another matrilineage resulting in totally severing any kin or affinal relation between the two lineages. It involves a long process of negotiation and transactions between the two lineages and with the associated deities on both sides during the life time of the woman. Once, this transaction is affected the past of the woman concerned is forgotten

her matrilineage identity gets submerged in that of her husband's matrilineage. This is a rare event in Doya society However, My respondents used the phrase *Wife Buying* for the phenomena. It was understandably for the convenience of communicating to me in Nepali language. In fact the detail description of the whole process as we shall see does not in any way mean commodification of Woman in Doya society.

24. The song goes like this: Ga *choiya-a-bemba !eru-a* Ga *chu!ey-a-mata . . . Ga damba-a-sikti . . .* Ga *doley* ya *mata doji* om *sikti so-oi . . . Ga cha!ey* ya *mat ha chakto sikti so-o-wai . . .Ga !ai* ya *!ada pushochilada . . . gajemo nga yajigobey !ada*-o . . . Ga *!ariya !ada* ya *ika ga . . . sosy ngajemo nga yajigebey- lada-o. . . .* Which briefly means we are taking away the girl after paying the Nama.

    Nothing can stop us from taking you. If the biggest stream obstructs us on the way we will make a bridge over it. If the path is obstructed by biggest rock we will break it with stone. If iron bars block the path we will cut it through with iron. We will find our path. We will take her home.

25. There were occasions when I observed small girls carrying this form of Nama to her mother's natal house in upper Lotukuchu in during 1993.

26. *Nubara* is a term given to swearing in and commitment to mutual social boycott between quarrelling parties. *Nubara Ka* means two parties committed to this act of swearing. The swearing involves drinking a cock's blood. Both the parties chop cock's neck and pass its blood to each other to drink subsequently resulting to severe social ties between the two groups.

27. A normal male or female is the one who is not a deaf, dumb and blind by birth and mentally and physically fit for the productive works. Anybody who has attained the age 14/15 is considered matured for marriage.

28. Finding of conjugal partners: there is no equivalent term for what we generally understand by marriage as associated with certain formal rituals and ceremony. When talking about marital status of people they make use of Nepali term in their language *Biha* and say: *Ka-nga 'Biha' pa-yang* (I *have married).* Ask to avoid the Nepali term they would say: *Ka-nga Me-him long yang. (Ka-nga=I, Me-hin=* wife, *long yang*= found/ male speaking). The same spoken by a female would, be: *Ka-nga ra-him long yang(* ra-him=husband/conjugal male partner).

29. I was witness to one such case during my stay at the lower Lotukuchu in 1992 \when Kougkilang got along with Zaba from middle Lotukuchu. I also saw such cases in different parts of the village.

30. The lineally owned land is located at many different places. Some are at lower hill slopes, some are at upper hill slopes, and some are on

relatively gentle slopes where paddy cultivation can be done. Those fields at the lower hills are relatively fertile and produce number of crops in a seasonal cycle.

31. Pranab Kumar Das Gupta, *Life and culture of matrilineal tribe of Meghalaya,* 1984, p. 94, p. 111.

32. Inheritance Rules:

    I) Parents must allot equal share of land to all their children irrespective of sex.

    II) Sister's brothers must allot an equal share of land to his sister's sons (or other property) while allotting land to his own children.

33. *Nu* stands for the word *Ngultrum.* It is the name of Bhutanese currency, which has money value equivalent to Indian Rupees. Indian currency is also widely used in all transactions in Bhutan.

CHAPTER 3

Kin Terms and Relations

Kinship terminology or relationship terminology (1984:37) which according to Robin Fox (1967) 'makes at least half the anthropological literature' was also seen by Morgan, as 'the royal road to the understanding of Kinship system.'

The proposition that kinship terminology is key to kinship system has been well established in ethnographic studies. Necessary cautions have also been sounded to avoid the tactical use of terms in real social situations and the erroneous abstraction of kinship models by failing to differentiate terms of reference from the terms of address (W.H. Goodenough *et al.,* 1956). Moreover, most of the studies carried out thenceforth, were criticised for male biases *(androcentricism).* Accordingly, I made a conscious attempt to adopt the use of Kin Terms and Relations[1] in this work, also in place of the old use Kinship *Terminology*[2] while keeping in view of the critical review that has been going on in the anthropological literatures on kinship studies.

In the previous chapter I have tried to describe how the matrilineal society of the Doya is organised by forming groups at different levels to facilitate exchange relations of man and materials and how they are also divided along the territorial belongings with shared common titles and allegiance to territorial deities.

In this chapter we look at the terms with which individual sex and age are differentiated and related to all other members and groups in the society. This chapter will further enhance what has been already discussed in the previous chapter. At the end part of this chapter an attempt is also made to compare and contrast Doyas kin terms with some of the communities in Bhutan and other similar systems from the existing anthropological literature.

I shall begin with a consanguinal family with a generation depth of four. Grandparents, parents, sons and daughters, their spouses and children comprise this group of family. Children born irrespective of their sex in this family are generally referred to as *Chu* (CC) by the grandparents (PP). Their parents call them as *Chan* in general but with particular reference to their sexes sons are referred to as *Ra-chan* and daughters as *Met-chan.* Their mother's sisters who share common residence also refer to them as their own children. Father's brothers who may not necessarily share common wife's residence also refer to them as their own children in general while mother's brothers take them differently by referring to them as *Lhi-ra* to the male child and *Lhi-met* to the female child. All the elder generation call the younger by their personal names.

In close society like the Doyas these relations have well defined rules and regulations associated with certain values, attitudes and behaviour in accordance to which they conceive, believe and relate to one another to reproduce their members and sustain the system of relationships through generations. The individuals as they grown up in the system are educated on the terms and relationships through a constant process of socialisation in the families and peer groups. The nature, attitudes and behaviours associated with the interpersonal relations between any two individuals may differ from one society to another. Let us now try to understand how an individual born in a residential unit as children (*chan*) or grandchild (*chu-chan*) grow up and pass through the system of terms and relations within which they find themselves until s/he becomes a grandparent *(Ya/Ta)* themselves and ultimately leaves the society.

Ego's Social Matrix

A new born child who is bestowed with the term Chu or Chan (one's children's children or one's children) not only legitimises the new born as a recruit into the society but also fills in a position in the social matrix of relations already interwoven and passed on to them through generations. A stream of Chu(s) as new recruits into the society continuously flow in through the social matrix from the least differentiated status and roles to greater roles and status as they pass through different stages of their life. In an equalitarian society like the Doyas, a descriptive analysis of the members of household around the female line is the most crucial and important for a better understanding of the structural and functional unit of the society.

The residential group around the descendant females comprising of ego's mother *(Mayu)* mother's mother (Ya) mother's sisters *(Yu)* all brothers and sisters *(Pu, Na, Tsa)* and father *(Payu)* form a segment of one's matrilineal descent and provide and anchorage to many such other lineal groups that inter-linked with each other through consanguinal and affinal relations to make the whole society they live in. Such groups are like pillars of the social matrix whose structure is constantly maintained and reproduced generation after generation indirectly with the help of consanguinal males. The lineal group comprises of consanguinal males *(Ku),* females *(Mayu* and *Yu)* with their children. Thus, for the purpose of our analysis we can extricate one such group, which has an ancestral linearity, and horizontal social link-ups through consanguinal and affinal relations with other such groups and are relatively independent from other such groups under different Riih title.

Ku: Ego's Maternal Uncle

What is apparent here is the position of male siblings (MB), who take position in his wife's residence and yet remain linked with his own natal family. He is referred to as *Ku* (MB) addressed as well differently from that of *Pang* (FB). *Ku* is an important figure in mother's lineage.

He has special relation with his sister's children (Lhi-Ra and Lhi-Met)[3] for different reasons. More so, because Ku is supposed to supply the much needed bone[4] in reproduction and perpetuation of the mother's lineage through his own sons (Ra-chan). He is referred to as Mahnkpa in wife's residential group, Ra-him by his wife (Met-hin) and addressed as Payu by his own children (Chan). It would be helpful to look at the terms of address and reference used by Ego that are relevant to the residential and lineal group with a depth of IV generation, where individuals are positioned and how they identify each other in the group in a reciprocal relationship (Table 3.1).

Ego's Residential and Lineal Group

Resident and lineal unit, which is also a segment of a Matrilineage under a particular Riih title, has an independent physical existence in relation with other such units. They also possess all the attributes and

Table 3.1: Kin Terms

Terms for Alter		Desig-nata	Terms for EGO	
Male	Female		Male	Female
Dug-ta[5]	*Dug-ya*	PPP	*Chu-chan*	*Chu-chan*
Ta	*Ya*	PP	*Chu/Ra-chan*	*Chu/Met-chan*
Payn	*Mayu*	P	*Ra-chan*	*Met-chan*
Dug-ta	*Mug-ya*	EPP	*Chu-chan*	*Chu-chan*
Ta	*Ya*	EP	*Mahnkpa*	*Nama*
Pang	-	FB	*Chan-da*	*Chan-Met*
-	*Nii-me*	FZ	*(Lhi-Ra)*	*(Lhi-Met)*
Ku	-	MB	*(Lhi-Ra)*	*(Lhi-Met)*
-	*Yu*	MZ	*Chan-da*	*Chan-met*
Pu	*Na*	G	*Tsa*	*Tsa*
Pu/Tsa	-	FBS	*PulTsa*	*Na/Tsa*
-	*Na/Tsa*	FBD	*Pu/Tsa*	
(Lhi-ra)	*Na/Tsa*	FZD	*(Lhi-ro)*	*Na/Tsa*
Pu/Tsa-mike	-	MZS	*Pu/Tsa-mike*	*Na/Tsa-mike*
-	*Na/Tsa-mike*	MZD	*Pu/Tsa-mike*	*Na/Tsa-mike*
Pu/Tsa	-	MBS	*Pu/Tsa*	
-	*Na/Tsa*	MBD	-	*Na/Tsa*
Ra-him	*Met-hin*	E	*Ra-him*	*Met-hin*
Mahnkpa	-	ZE	*Kut-pu*	*Na/Tsa*
-	*Nama*	BE	-	*Lung-ma*
Ra-chan	*Met-chan*	C	*Payu*	*Mayu*
-	*Nama*	SW	*Ta*	*Ya*
Mahnka	-	DH	*Ta*	*Ya*
Pu/Tsa	*Na/Tsa*	FBC	*Pu/Tsa*	*Na/Tsa*
Lhira/chan-da	*Lhi-Met/Chan-Met*	ZC	*Ku*	*Yu*
Chan-da/Lhi-Ra	*Chan-Met/Lhi-Met*	BC	*Pang*	*Ni*
Mahnkpa	*Nama*	CE	*Ta*	*Ya*
Chu-chan	*Chu-chan*	CC	*Ta*	*Ya*
Chu-chan	*Chu-chan*	CCC	*Dug-ta*	*Dug-ya*

characteristics of a "Primary group" (Homans: *Groups Theory).* The 'we feeling' *(Rangka)* or the group sentiment becomes an indispensable component of our analysis of the Kin-Group. We look at how and why a particular group is formed, how its individual members are identified and related to each other among themselves through an organisational structure in the group which guides, defines and lays down definite ways of recruiting and recognising its members, allotting them certain positions into the matrix of relationships at different stages of an individual's life as generations pass through as Chu (grand-children) without any importance to their sexes at the entry and exit the structure as sex differentiated Ya and *Ta* (PP/P) with well-defined status and position in the society. An individual member, in the continuous flux of passing generations, knows among many things his/her socially approved possible conjugal partner in relation with some others and with whom she cannot. He is conscious of belonging to his group, in terms of closeness and exclusiveness with other such groups. Individuals in such group feel contained and contented in all matters of life - some degree of certainty in emotional, material and other wants of life - all that is perhaps, comprehensively contained and expressed at large in the local idiom: *Rang yo ka notsum itpo* (we all have common feelings/heart -an expression of resident and lineal group solidarity). This idiom applies to group formation at different stages, i.e. from the smallest residential group to a composite of many such residential groups under one Riih title or more, but it is more suitably applicable to the extended consanguinal family with their affines.

Ego's Group Differentiated

The group thus, connoted by the Idiom, comprises of two descent groups both of which consociate with the eldest women - *Ya/Dugya* (MM/MMM) on certain occasion for one group, and by residing together for the other groups. One group consists of all *Ku* with *Ya* on annual ancestral worship day. The other group has all the residential females of the lineage i.e. *Ya-Mayu-Yu* and their minor children (G-4).

This division in the group is manifested only on a certain occasion by an act of eating together in exclusive groups after worshipping ancestral and Riih deity.

The philosophy of this exclusive group formation is expressed in another local idiom, which says: *Lhu (k) Kek Cha-a-Lhang Tor-ngo,*

G-4 Exclusive Groups in a Matrilineage

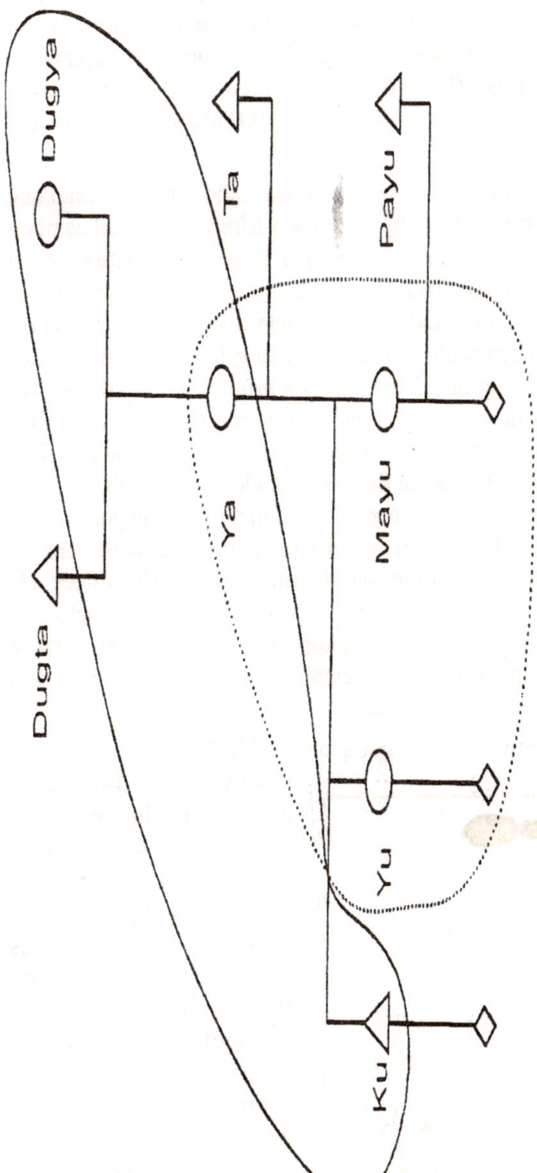

Note. Dotted lines indicate matrilineal resident group of the female descent and their children. Darker lines indicate the matrilineal link with male descendants

Lhang Kek Cha-a Lhu (k) Tor- ngo. (When the jackal eats cock eagles looks on, and when the eagle eats cock jackal looks on). The two groups are commensally exclusive groups at the time of feasting. When two cocks are offered to the deity each group takes one each separately. And if only one cock is offered the group who offered the cock takes it and the other group looks on - they are forbidden to partake the meat together[6].

> *6th March, 1993, Evening*: When I reached Kado's house at Lhokong his second eldest Ku (Passa by name) was trimming a small bamboo branch called *Duishcha* for use in a propitiation ritual to be performed by a Nepali Jhankari that evening for his grandmother. In a short while after Kado's third uncle also came up from his wife's house. Then Kado also came up carrying a branch of a tree called *Chenden sing* and a branch of a broomstick plant. He was a little drunk as he explained to me that he had to take some drinks with his friends on the way home. Kado ushered me inside their house on a small cot near the fire place. Kado's sisters (his mother's sister's daughters) were also there to assist in the evening preparation. Kado's fourth uncle Chedoji was not there at home as he sent his widow sister and her child to join the ritual from *La* at Raibey. He decided to stay back at his sister's *La* to look after the cocks and hens there in their absence. Kangkop, a Doya *Geypa* of Satakha and the Nepali Jhankari from a neighbouring village called Basanti were there to perform the rituals.
>
> Some preparations were also going on outside the house at different places. At a large stone platform in the southwest direction of the house, a tree stump *(Damburr)* with forks on the top was fixed. A blood like sap was coming out from the Phloem of the freshly cut stump of the tree. Passa Ku told me that it was a permanent site for *Zibdag* worship. At another place in the southeasterly direction of the house Ku spread a

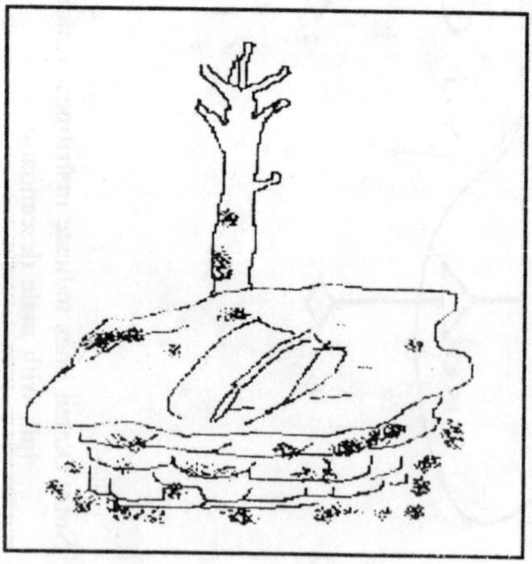

banana leaf on the ground. At the south end of his leaf was fixed a *Duishcha* along with a small branch of Changdon sing and a small model of bow and arrow. Some rice, an egg and stone were placed on the leaf near the Duishcha. A white thread ran three/ four times around this arrangement. I was told that all these arrangements were made for the Nepali Jhankari for Shikari Puja. The Jhankari came out, walked around the spot and began to chant verses with sacred smoke around. A cock was fetched and sacrificed by cutting its neck at the end of the verses. Its blood was dropped on the leaf. The egg was broken and the Jhankari examined its yolk carefully and said there was no bad sign. (The yolk of the egg is used for revealing the cause of any illness or misfortune). The cock and the egg were roasted and offered to the *Shikari* again and after sometime it was removed and cooked for consumption.

On the other hand Passa Ku was giving a final wash and ablution to the stone slab platform with water and Lusing (a herbal plant). Three trident shape figures called *Sebu,* were made of millet dough. A little butter was smeared on pointed ends of the tridents. These trident figures were put on the stump branch angles. The sacred smoke was started. Some fermented Millet (prepared for *Yu*) was put on the middle *of* the *Sebu.* A pot of well-processed *Yu* was kept nearby. As the sacred chanting began a large cock was fetched and given an ablution wash at its feet and mouth and sprinkled with *Yu.* Then the cock was held by the shoulder wings and beaten on the back with the help of chopper until some blood came out of the beak. The blood was put on the middle branch of the stump amidst chanting. Some feathers from tail and wing of the cock were pulled out and put on the *Sebus.* The cock was cleaned off its feather and washed in hot water. After that the chest was cut open and little pieces of all the body parts except for the testicles was taken and offered. All the internal organs of the bird were hung on the forks of the stump. The remaining body was cut into eight parts, put on the platform along with freshly cooked *Chakto.* The meat along with the food was offered to the deity along with sprinkling of Yu and Chanting. The meat and food was taken back home. Passa's sister (Kado's mother) cooked the meat separately. After all the cooking the food was served in two separate groups with each eating two separately cooked meal.

Dogya-Mungya Relation

The presence of Ya/Dugya in the married and unmarried descendant males group is of particular importance as it signifies their link to the common ancestress[7]. The children of descendant males are exclusively kept out from this ritual as they, ideally belong to different Riihs. The consanguinal males are addressed and referred to as Ku/Pu/Tsa and also Ta (MB/eB/By/GF), according to positions they occupy in the social matrix at different stages of their lives. The conjugal units that the descendant females form with their husbands (Ra-him) and children have a structure that is framed by Mayu (M), Payu (F), Pu (eB), Tsa (yB/*Z)* and *Na/*Tsa *(e/y* Z). Mayu is one who gives birth and, Payu is conjugal partner of Mayu. He works together with Mayu. Payu is different from Mayu as he belongs to some other group where his Mayu also resides. He calls Ya and Ta to Mother's Mother and Father. A Makim comprises of many such conjugal units linked with Ya who is a permanent figure for Ego as compared with his own Payu.

Doyas are very sensitive to outsiders. Any conjugal alliance or sexual relation with someone not identifiable in the cosmology of their kin terms and relations and is feared for the indignation of local deity and for the social ostracism[8]. Perhaps, it takes an unconscious and instinctive or emotional move or sometimes force upon on the part of an individual to drive him to the point of committing such an act, which is not approved by the society. Where all the individuals in a group follow the socially approved ways of life and expectation there is everything in the group to satisfy and satiate all the biological, psychological, physical, material drives and aspirations of each and every individual within their society. Just as the "collective conscience" binds individuals in a simple society. The binding power of 'conscience' lies in the nature of the collectiveness of the social collection - the collection of members or the members of a collection have to make up a complete, wholesome cosmology of kin terms and relations for an individual, within which one can live one's life fully. And to achieve such a cohesive, harmonic, and reproductive lineal group, the descent members of both sexes should be capable of reproducing a proportionate number of seedlings (Lhi-Ra and Lhi-Met) to maintain a complete kinship cosmology to guide and propagate the lineage.

Although this number game of sexes lies in God's hand and people accept the realities, which may present many a different situations. When the seedlings of both sexes fall short to the required mates between sexes, the group tries to find other options within the structurally permissible limits of match making as we have discussed in the matrimonial rules.

The matrimonial alliance pattern that emerges from a sample size of 32 couples within a depth of four generations shows a bilateral exchange of sons between two of more segmentary lineage groups (Table 3.2).

Out of the two prescribed choices of mates (FZS/MBS) the frequency of choices for FZS (Ni's sons) is relatively higher than that of MBS (Ku's sons), who should be the first preferred choice for our female ego. But, if we look at the high frequency of occurrence among the prohibited cousins i.e. conjugal union between sisters' children, the higher frequency choices for FZS is overshadowed and needs no further explanation[9] for the society under study. Although, we come to a situation where reality blurs the structural principles of the society.

Table 3.2: Cousins Alliance Pattern[10]

	Cross-cousins		Parallel-cousins			
Generation	MBS-FZD	FZS-MBD	MZC-MZC#	FBC-FBC*	TOTAL	%age
IV	–	–	4	–	4	12.5
III	–	–	8	–	8	25.0
II	2	1	2	1**	6	18.75
I	2	5	7	–	14	43.75
Total	4	6	21	1	32	100.00
Percentage	12.5	18.75	65.625	3.125	100.00	

Doyas also seem to share the problem with that of Khasi's on the question of Patrilineal or Matrilineal classification as reported by Pranab Kumar Das Gupta (1984)[11]. However, Doyas represent a case showing extreme tenacity of group formation deviating from their own structural principles.

G-5: Ego's Collateral Relations

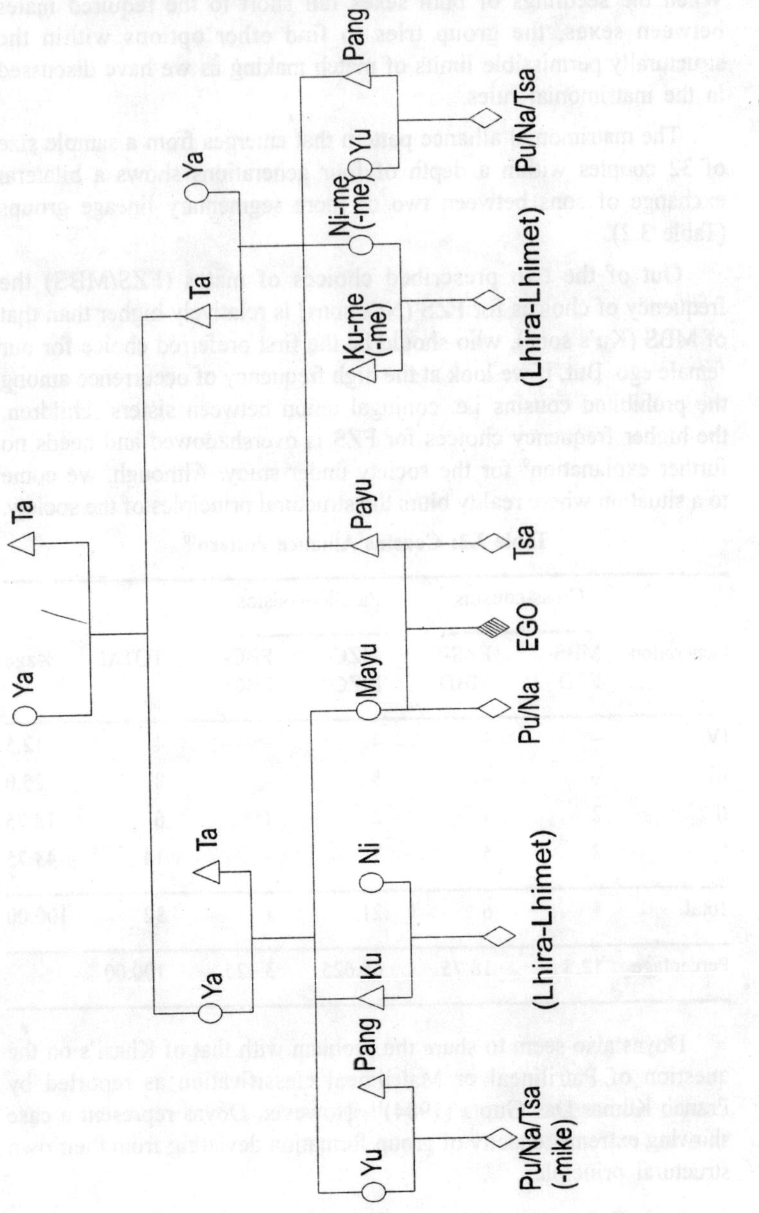

Given the choices of male mates (FZS/MBS), cross-cousin matrimonial alliance help maintain furtherance of at least two parallel segmentary lineal groups under different Riih(s) whereas, the relation between parallel cousins serve the purpose of one's mother's lineage under a Riih only (G-5&6).

Undoubtedly of course, the parallel cousin marriage of consanguinal sisters should positively attribute to the development of an intense in-breeding tendency among the segmentary lineal groups under a Riih although genetically, the intense inbreeding may also prove quite a disadvantage for the survival of the small population of Doya. Nevertheless, the empirical facts seem to support the local history of demographic regeneration of the people, wherein people seemed to have explored all the possible ways of group survival in adverse demographic situation.

This brings us to an interesting aspect of kinship study where we can see how certain structural principles operate under extreme constrains of human resources and how individual members try to adapt to it at the organisational level. But first we see what type of kinship terminology we are dealing with.

Doya System: A Typological Problem

According to the Typological classification of Kirshoff (1931) and Lowie (1928,1929) Doyas case conforms to "Bifurcate collateral"[12] type but according to Murdock's in typology Doyas case closely conforms to Iroquois type[13] in Ego's generation. Yet, Doyas case on one hand, can not be associated with that of Sudanese which is characterised by descriptive terms for all cousins and siblings on the other hand, the Doyas case is not based upon Lowie's "Bifurcate merging"[14] principles also. The problem is further complicated when empirical data show apparent differences between FBC (Pu/Na/Tsa) and MZC (Pu/Na/Tsa-mike). A considerable number of marriages took place involving MZC making a percentage of 65.6 (Table 3.2) in a total sample of 32 married couples taken at random whereas, marriage alliances between FBC was an exception involving strong sanctions against it. This behavioural pattern between MZC makes the Doyas case perplexing to any generally known pattern. These reasons compel one to further consider the Doyas case in particular and see things within its own social, cultural and demographic context.

G-6: Ego's Generational Collateral Cousins

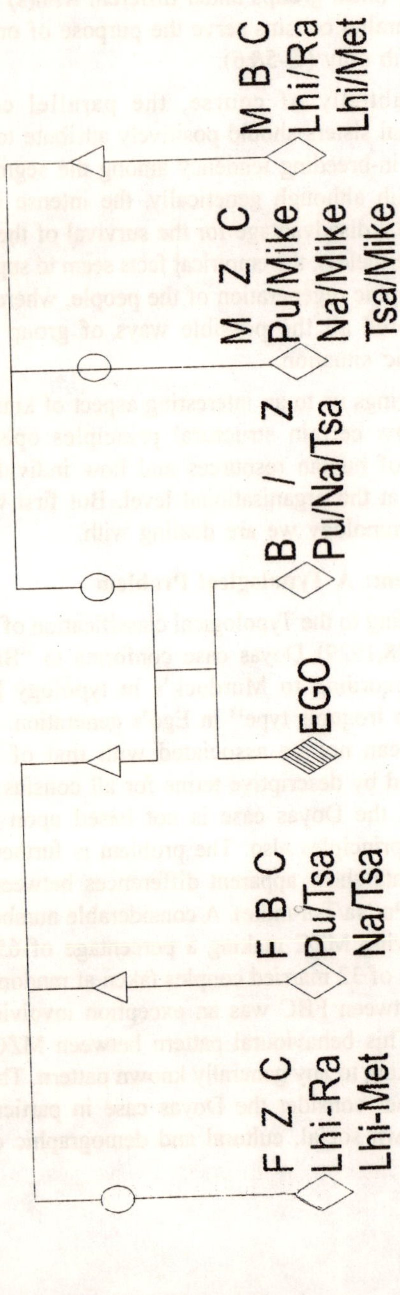

The above genealogy represents the cosmology of kin terms in immediate concern of an Ego. It is apparent that Ego distinguishes FZ (Ni) and FZH (Ku) from that of MB (Ku) and MBW (Ni) by suffixing '-me' and, in Ego's generation MZC from FBC (Pu/Tsa) by suffixing '-mike'. Thus, FZ (Ni) is called as 'Ni-me' and her husband as 'Ku-me', and MZC as 'Pu-mike/Tsa-mike'. The suffix helps in distinguishing real MB (Ku) from FZH (Ku-me) in the same way FBC from MZC. The implication of the distinction can be seen in the distancing order between parallel cousins of opposite sexes in forming a possible conjugal union. It has been shown that in ideal situation parallel cousins on mother's side are forbidden for 3 consecutive generations and on father's side up to 7 generations. In other words we can say that parallel cousins on mother's side are close to Ego's connubia by 3 generations and on father's side far by 7 generations to form conjugal union. And we have seen (Table 3.2) the extent to which the forbidden distance can be reduced to form a conjugal union on mother's side only. Furthermore, in Ego's parental generation we can see the following equations:

M (Mayu) # MBW (Ni-me) # FZ (Ni) # MZ (Yu) = FBW (Yu) # M (Mayu)

F (Payu) # MB (Ku) # FZH (Ku-me) # FB (Pang) = MZH (Pang) # F (Payu)

Now, given the situation where they try to equate parallel and cross-cousins on the maternal side in matrimonial relations where MZ = FBW and FB = MZH and parallel cousin matrimonial relation is prohibited, it is difficult to arrive at any definite conclusion unless we had dealt with 'significata' of the kin terms along with the integral behaviour and attitudes.

Doya System of Kin Terms and Relation

To proceed with we begin with our Ego who enters the matrix of relationship under the cosmology of terms as a Chu (great grand son/ grand son) by a legitimate birth. Chu becomes part of the kinship system the moment she is bestowed with the term Chu. And from this position through a gradual process of education in the residential group Chu gets introduced to all others of his concerned and develops appropriate attitudes and shapes his or her behaviour accordingly towards each and every member associated to him or her with certain terms. Chu remains Chu irrespective of sexes to their grandparents' generation to whom Chu calls Ya and Ta (MM & MF) but to Chu's own parents Chu is Chan and it may be Ra-chan (a son) or Met-chan (a daughter). Both call their parents Mayu and Payu. A conjugal family would comprise of Mayu, Payu with Ego's Na (eZ), Pu (eB) and Tsa (yB & Z). As Ego grows up she comes to know Mayu and Payu very closely. Ego looks upon them as protectors, feeders, comforters and teachers who work together at home and in the fields. Ego also comes to know that their parents expect them to help and assist them at work wherever possible at home or in the fields. Further on, the day Ego discovers itself either as Ra-chan or Met-chan she develops some kind of gender concept and tries to differentiate and associate itself with others in the residential group. Ego as Ra- chan discovers in a gradual process that his Payu who share the same gender with him has no Mayu and Payu in the Makim, that his parents are in some other's household to which he belongs and that he comes to stay with his mother (Mayu). And also that Ego's MB (Ku) also goes to stay with their own woman in some other's house when the time comes -none of the males who are born in the house lives in the house but stay put with their wives in other's house and that he should also follow suit some day because none of the females who are born in his household can be a sex partner. Thus he classifies all females of the residential group i.e. Ya, Mayu, Yu, Na and Tsa in one group and develops a different attitude towards them. He looks at Ya as a kind, benign respectable woman, Yu something like Mayu but not so intimate as she has got her own children to care.

Na and Tsa always remain with Mayu and Payu, to look after them in their old age and he looks at them as woman reserved for some other *Poja* (Boy) but they look at each other with care, affection and confidence. They take it as their moral responsibility and duty to look after Na/Tsa and their children because those males who come to stay with his Na and Tsa as sex partners also feel the same way towards their own Na/ Tsa and their children at their natal homes, as he does. In the same way Met-chan also differentiate and associate themselves with all the females and come to know that women do not leave their ancestral land and lineage and that there are Poja who would come to stay with them from, other's group. They also come to know that it is their duty and responsibility to look after their parents and that there riih title passes through their children only. From the very childhood days they know their Pu/Tsa (B) as most reliable friends at

G-7: Ego's Matrilineage and Connubia

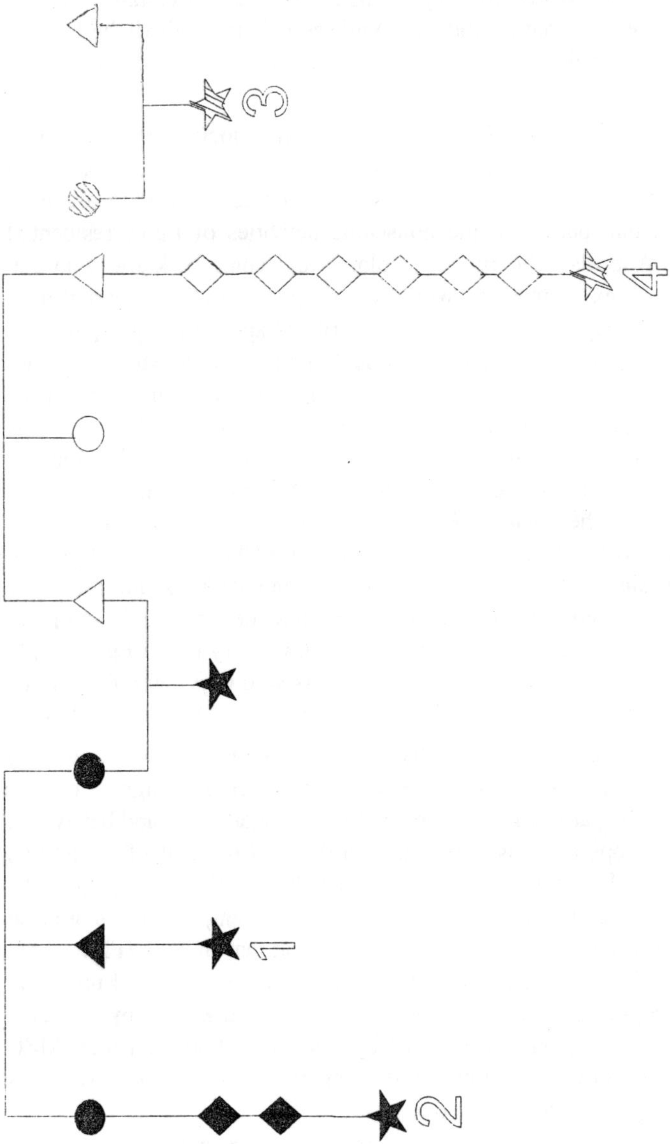

Note: Conjugal relation with 1 is prescribed but with 2 it double ensures the furtherance of the lineage 3 and 4 are alternatives in the absence of 1 and 2.

play and at works. She also slowly discovers that there are certain works that are better done by opposite sex and that certain activities are not done without Pu and Tsa. While associating with all the females and sharing their similarities they are also going to become Mayu one day.

As and when the Ra-chan and Met-chan socially matures along with certain physiological developments in their body their horizon of cosmological knowledge increases to include those who are non-resident but matters in the household activities of Ego's residential group. And also she further explores and come to know who can become a sex partner and who cannot. Ego comes to know that their Ku (MB) plays an important role in rituals and other family matters as he is most confidential and reliable person for Mayu besides her own husband (Ra-him) who is also obliged to his own sisters in the same manner. Ku does not have any term of address for them but calls them by personal names. He refers to Ego and Ego's Pu, Na and Tsa as Lhi-Ra and Lhi-Met (which may literally mean male and female seedling for the lineage). Ego's Mayu also refers to Ku's children as Lhi-Ra and Lhi-Met and do not use the term Chan for them. Ego also realises slowly that there is a special relation with Ku's children. They are not allowed to treat or address them like their own pu/ Tsa or Na/ Tsa. On the other hand, Ego's kinsmen always try to tell Ego directly or indirectly in teasing or playful manners who to go with for her sex partners or life partners to become Ra-him and Met-hin (H&W).

Thus, Ego looks upon their Ku as responsible and resourceful person in man and material needs and behaves obligingly[15] towards them as compared with one's own Payu[16]. The attitudes and behaviour, Ego develops towards Ku is quite different from that of Pang (FB) also. Pang hardly matters in the household organisation of Ego. Like Ego's Payu and Pang are brothers, Mayu and Pang's wife, Yu are also taken as sisters so the children of Pang and that of Yu's (FBW/ MZ) are like Ego's Pu/ Na/ Tsa. They form separate residential units and if Yu happens to be MZ whose husband is also known by the same term, Pang a difference is made by Ego in relation with their MZC (Pu-mike, Na-mike, Tsa-mike). It is this relation which makes Doya's case a specially a curious one.

MB *(Ku)* # FZH *(Ku-me)* # FB *(Pang)* = MZH *(Pang)*

FZ*(Ni)* # MBW *(Ni-me)* # MZ *(Yu)* = FBW *(Yu)*

By the time our Ego attains the age of maturity (13-15) she is quite familiar with all these cosmological kin terms. Our Ego is confronted with a hypothetical equation in which all the consanguinal brothers and sisters of both Mayu and Payu in the same generation could also have conjugal relations like their own Mayu and Payu[17].

This will present a kind of relation between any two connubia in which males are symmetrically exchanged in the same generation. And the first pair of conjugal union will hold a cardinal hinge between the two groups around which rest will fold in to from conjugal union with opposite sexes (G-8). If further throws up many hypothetical situations on the basis of demographic features in times.

If the hypothesis holds true it not only holds the key to the original kinship structure but also brings up many implications. In the first place if mother's brother Ku forms a conjugal union with father's sister Ni there are none other than Ego's own Ku and Ni, and if MZ (Yu) forms a conjugal union with FB (Pang) they are also none other than Ego's own Pang and Yu. The former gives a connubium for Ego or further propagation of the lineage and favours in maintaining the residential matrilineage group while the latter would help in lateral expansion of the matrilineage by segmentation under a particular Riih and would have helped in Matriclan formation by procreating and expanding action of the two conjugal union.

Affines and Kinsmen

What might have gone wrong that the people had to break the traditional prohibited rules and resort to *Bongteng* conjugal formation? The answer may be in the imbalance sex ratio in the residential matrilineage group.

A situation might arise when in conjugal family only male or female children are born. The family in which only male children are born would obviously cease to propagate the matrilineage Riih to which they belong unless resorted to matrilineage transmutation and the family in which only female children are born will not have any connubium for their descending children of the following generation to propagate the matrilineage unless they resort to parallel cousins (Bongteng conjugal formation in the generation) much against the prohibitory rules but perhaps, for the survival of the group if no other options are available. It means, in a residential matrilineage all the members for

G-8: Affines and Kinsmen

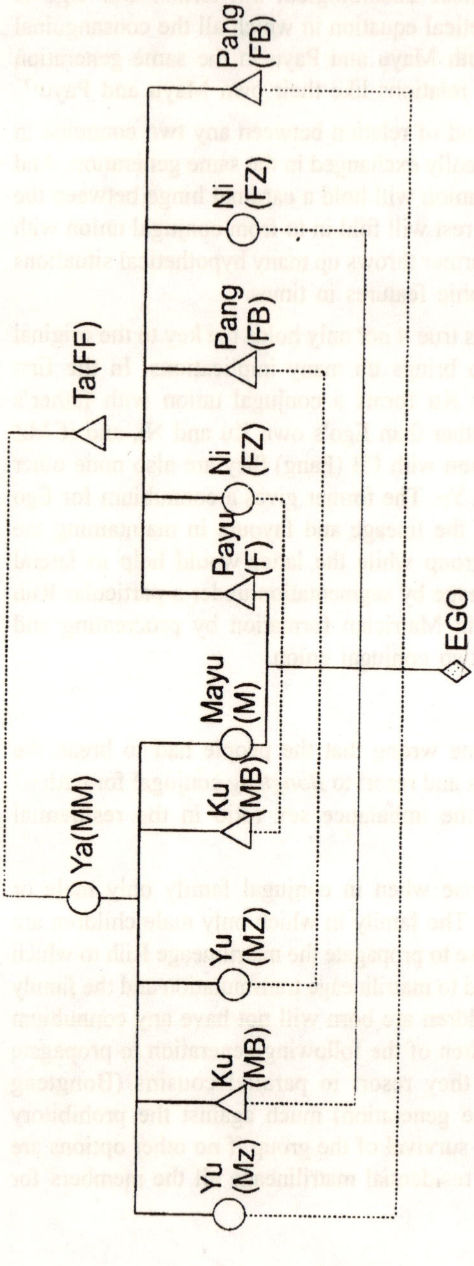

an Ego are all our people as Rangka differentiated from all others such group as Nganka in local terms.

When all the people are our own close kin referred to with certain categorical terms, these terms Ego uses in his/her social environment should have certain definite attitudes associated with which she defines the relations with alters and shapes appropriate behaviour into some order. What was this order? Who brought about this order? R. Fox (1967:31) says, "No Australian aborigine sat down and worked out a blue print for the complicated system of kinship and marriage rules for which he is justly famous, but his ability to conceptualise and classify was as much a factor in this successful development as the claws of a tiger . . . in the survival and success of these species." Or did the order come up because of certain nature of orderliness in the minds of human? And then perhaps, attitude and behaviour also came up by the very nature of the order with which every individual wanted to order his or her own social environment, in the 'our-kin-group' or Rangka. And because the decision on the sex of the unborn child does not lie in the hands of any body, sometimes our group quite possibly must have come across such situation when ratio of sex in children's generation might have failed to support the continuance of 'our-kin-group'. And for the fear of dying out they must have recruited/ contacted/ come by such individual(s) outsiders who could have helped continue the 'our-kin-group'. When such strangers join in the group for reproduction and become a part of household members and grow up in the society the offspring of the strangers need to be accommodated in the same order of society of the Rangka group by the ways of socialisation and education, to develop in them the right attitude and behaviour components towards each and every categorical kin termed individuals.

The order of social environment of our original Rangka group with a set of kin terms makes the complete cosmology of kin terms for the individual members who lived in the group. The larger group grows with the outsiders the greater would be importance of institutionalising and inculcating the basic attitudes of the original kin terms among the members to keep them in the same order.

On attaining the age of maturity our Ego, at any time, when domestic situations are compelling or on one's own motivation on the part of Lhi-Ra or enticed or attracted by Lhi-Met, Ego makes a night visit to his predetermined sex partner much expectedly or receives a night visit. Since that night, Ego either becomes a resident- husband (Mahnkpa) to wife's parents and wife's brothers and sisters and Ra-him to Ego's wife who becomes his Met-hin to the visiting Lhi-Ra. They address each other with the term *O-roh*[18]. The day Lhi-Ra becomes a Mahnkpa in one's Ku's conjugal family, Ku becomes Ta and Ku's wife Ni becomes Ya for the same Ego (Lhi-Ra). On the other hand, to Ego's wife Ego's Mayu and Payu who may be her own Ni (FZ) and Ku (FZH) become Ya and Ta, respectively. Ego's elder brothers who are already settled with their prescribed Lhi-Met become Pang and Yu to Ego.

What is to be noted here is that when Ego gets along with Lhi-Met, Ku gets reliable, faithful and productive person who is also capable of reproducing further progeny and look after the property of wife's residential group at the loss of his sister's household. The only substitute for such a loss of a male is Ku's own son to be taken as a Mahnkpa or husband to Ego's own sister in the natal residential group, even if there are many other options for a substitute (G-7).

Once the Ego is in conjugal relation with the prescribed mates, she gets to know some of his/her affinal relatives. On Ra-him's (H) side, she comes to know her Ra-him's sisters (HZ) whom she calls *Lungma* and she in turn is called *Nama* and between the Ego and all other Ra-him's brothers terms such as Pu/ Na/Tsa are used loosely according to the relative age of Ego and Alter[19]. And on the Met-hin's side, Ra-him gets to know his wife's all the Pu(s) and Tsa(s) who call him Mahnkpa and he in turn refers to them as *Kutpu* (WB) and to all the wife's Na and Tsa (WZ) he uses the same term of reference with a little different attitude towards them from what he would feel with his own Na and Tsa. There can be a joking relation between a Mahnkpa and wife's sisters.

Thus, by the way of becoming Met-hin and Ra-him under certain preconception, our Ego is already well inside the matrix social relationship under the cosmology of kin terms. They are preparing to become more responsible like their own Mayu-Payu and Ya- Ta the day they have their own Chan and begin to take more active roles in the organisational aspects of respective corporate residential and lineal units as they age and have more and more Met-chan and Ra-chan.

The first Chan, Ego gives birth entitles her to be called Mayu by her Chan and Payu to her Ra-him. It is also time the couple are already separated physically from the Makim and settled into their own Kim nearby to form a conjugal family of their own with a separate Jikpu (fire place). And the Mahnkpa enters a testing phase in his life - he takes sole responsibility of organising the small family doing all works himself ranging from manly works to cooking, feeding, washing and even midwifery during the delivery period. His Ya and Ta (WP) guide and supervise and assist if need be. Once this period is passed both the Met-hin and Ra-him take equal share in bringing up the child.

Now, Ego enters into parental generation and by this time all their brothers and sisters are also in their respective conjugal family with one or more Chan. With these developments, our Ego have many Met-chan, Ra-chan (S&D), Chanda and Chand-Met (ZCw.s/BC m.s.), and Lhi-Ra and Lhi-Met (ZC m.s./BC w.s.). And as and when these children mature and become indispensable part of labour force in their respective residential groups our Ego is also continuously concerned about finding substitutes for their Ra-chan who will soon leave the household one day to join his sex partner in a trusted predestined household. And the only substitute he can think of for the loss of his/her own Ra-chan is Lhi-Ra from his/her own sisters/brother's conjugal family. Because, Ego would always look for someone who can be identified and included under the kindred Idiom: *Rang Yo ka no sum itpo* (we all have the same feeling/heart).

When we think of two Egos who are brother and sister the brother becomes Mahnkpa in Ku's conjugal family and the other Ego (sister) is the one who remained as a Lhi-Met in the natal residential group. The descendant children of our Egos would again be Lhi-Ra/Lhi-Met to one another. And for the interest of their own residential group both of our Egos exchanges Lhi-Ra from each other for each other's Lhi-Met.

The day our Egos get into the bond of conjugal union their social positions are further pushed up into the third generation people-they become Ya and Ta to their resident son-in-law (Mahnkpa) and non-residential daughter-in-law (Nama). Once this is over, our Ego in the parental generation and are better served and well looked after by their daughter with the help of their resident husbands. The Ego in consultation with her brothers and sisters and Mayu and Payu and already got a part of the ancestral land allotted equally to her conjugal family and children from which they have to share a certain portion of grain produce towards the maintenance of aging Mayu and Payu. Then there comes a time when one day Ego's sons and daughters give birth to yet another batch of individuals in the continuation of their lineage - a batch of Chu enters into the matrix of relations to replenish the older generation and it is time Ego's generation exit the well-knitted structure of social relations leaving behind their terms and position to the generation following just behind to pass through the way they did.

The cosmology of kin terms and relations associated with that became a part of Doya's life have well-defined ways of conjugal formation, reproducing and recruiting members and disposing off legitimate members in the system. It has its own structural principles *"Dugya-Mungya"* (cross-cousin) conjugal formation.

Matrilateral in filiations and Matriliny in tracing descent and Matrilocality in residence, of the Doyas support the whole relationship structures and have ways and mechanisms of defining an exclusive boundary of its own with respect to other societies.

The Doya structure does not seem to be static and determining but is sensitive to changes and is controlled by the principles of cybernetics where the basic structural principles are not fully executed and adhered to the system in such situation reacts by organising ways of conserving and preserving the system against the affected parts (social ostracism and elders' council): distancing the ordered social body from the deviant group and suppressing deviance by council's admonition and sanction to maintain the commonly shared and accepted/acceptable social ways of life depending on the demographic features of the society.

The ability of the system to accommodate growth in population and, adjust and adapt to changes in the demographic imbalance in sex composition also shows an elastic nature of the kinship structure. In other words, the elasticity of the structure is the function of demographic feature of the society. That is for a given society characterised by 'Elementary structure' (Levi-Strauss), the structural principles (of the people) organised its individual members to form (conjugal) reproductive units in perpetuation of their social tradition not necessarily aware of the laws of genetics. And when the sex composition of the population loses its delicate balance in a particular generation or two, and fails to meet the demands of the social organisation, the kinship structure either stretches to accommodate or gets compressed to find acceptable ways of supporting harmony of the living group.

The Doyas situation shows the limits to which the elasticity of the structure can be compressed to in the times of demographic crisis.

The analyses of empirical facts of the Doya social organisation do not conform to any classified category of kinship system as described by E. R. Leach (1954): Although, Doya case shares certain similarities with that of Kariera type[20] in their marriage pattern but the kin term looks similar with that of Iroquois type. However, the models that can be abstracted from the analysis of empirical data do not qualify entry to any type of system already studied.

The transmission of Riih title exclusively on the female descendants and Matrilocality of female descents manifest a Matrilateral in character where the Doyas society seems to be exchanging sons between any two cross-cousins linked lineal groups to form conjugal units. The exchange can be either symmetrical between any two residential matrilineage group and among many such. Ideally, any two such exchanging groups have to be differentiated and distanced by 'Bongteng' or parallel cousin relations. In other words, Bongteng on maternal side are supposed to act as a wedge to facilitate expansion, exclusion and segmentation of a Riih towards formation of exogamic lineage.

But the tendency of folding-in (Bongteng conjugal formation) among the Matrilateral parallel cousins reduces a group into an intensely endogamous kin group spatially distributed under many Makims with their segmented conjugal units. In such a situation, the only truly exogamous unit in Doya society is the conjugal unit under a Kim and that group of Makims under a particular Riih title does not form a clan at least in its organisational aspects. And it is the extended conjugal unit under a Makim that forms the structural and organisational units and the plurality of which composes the society. The generally accepted norms and ways of life mastered by the individuals and cognisable to other, forms the integral identity of Doya society, and Doya society seems to be losing it by failing to execute the basic structural principles of Kinship.

The absence of hypogamy and hypergamy between any two Lhi-Ra exchanging groups and the sheer lack of political organisation among themselves makes Doya society a homogeneously equalitarian society. There is no hierarchical stratification in the society although it is an ironical situation for Doyas who in their historical antecedence are said to have had developed their own political structure under a king whose palace/fortress still stands in ruins in Denchukha (1980: 17, Vol. II).

The ethnic relation with that of Totos across the border has to be thoroughly explored. B.K. Roy Burman (1956) while talking about close ethnic relations of Totos with that of Doyas gives a detailed description of clan organisation among the Totos but gives a blank sheet on their Kinship organisation and structure which makes it difficult to come up with any concrete conclusion about the ethnic relation at this stage. The problem will become still more difficult in time to come as both the Doyas and Totos are fast getting transformed under cultural and political impact of their respective countries. Further, Doyas may not qualify to be called another 'new tribe' of Bhutanese state-crafty as B. K. Roy Burman talks about Totos who he said were originally inside Bhutan. Doyas has to be seen and understood as an ethnic group or a caste in the Bhutanese context of nation building with its own development of cultural and political history under a legacy of Kingship.

Comparison with other systems

Having said this, let us now present below the kin term of few communities along with that of the Doyas for the purpose of comparison and contrast, thereby initiating the process of better and fuller understanding of some of these lesser-known people. The kin terms of the Nepalese (Lhotshampas) and of a section of the Rais (who are otherwise identified as a section of the large emergent Nepali community, even though they retain now a number of distinctive cultural traits of which kinship is one) locally called Dokhun Rais, possibly because of their residence towards the south (i.e. *Oakshin)* along with those of Lepchas, Doya, Drukpas (the Dogapa community residing at Dorokha Dungkhag H.Q. who are known to have migrated from Ha region in the north.) and Sharcopas are presented in two a comparative tables (Table 3.3). The table shows that Drukpa and Sharcop share number of terms employed in denoting different kin relations.

Lhotsham and Rai share very few terms in common and similarly Lepcha and Lhopu (Doya) have a very few terms in similarities. Geographically, the Drukpas are original inhabitants of northwestern parts of Bhutan popularly known as Ngalom and Sharcops are of eastern Bhutanese. However, there has been strong cultural influence of the

Table 3.3: Comparative Kin Terms

Symbols	Drukpa (Dogapa)	Doya (Lhopu)	Lepcha	Lhotsham (Nepali)	Rai (Dokhun)	Sharcop
FF	Jojo	Ta	thigung	Bajey	Phoba	memey
MF	Jojo	Ta	thigung	Bajey	Phoba	memey
FM	Angey	Ya	nikung	Boju	Moma	abi
MM	angey	Ya	nikung	Baju	Mama	abi
F	*apa*	Payu	abo	*apa/papa*	Papa	*apa*
M	*ama*	Mayu	Ama	*Ama*	*Ama*	*ama*
FB	*aku*	Pang	batim	Barababu	Depa	*aku*
MB	ajang	Ku	*ajang*	Mama	depa/banga	*ajang*
FZ	*ani*	Ni	aniu	Phuphu	nini/dema	*ani*
Mz	amchhum	*Yu*	*mutim*	*asaa/kaki*	*dema/chhenga*	*ajim*
eB	achu	*Pu*	*anum*	*Daju*	*Bubu*	*ata*
eZ	ajim	na	anom	Didi	Nana	ana
yB	nachu	Tsa	ing	Bhai	Yanga	Kata/baning
yZ	sim/num	Tsa	ing	Beheni	Yanga	usa
FBW	achhum/ani	Yu	motim	bariama kaki/asaa	dema/chhenga	ajim
MBW	*ambam/Ani*	Ni	aniu	Maiju	-do-	*ani*
FZH	*ajang/aku*	Ku	batim/aku	Phupaju	pusei/depa	*ajang*
MZH	*aku*	Pang	-do-	barababu/ kaka	depa/banga	*aku*
FBC	*(Pintsa)*	Pu/na/ tsa	anom/lng	daju/bhai/ didi/beheni	bubu/nana/ yanga	*(Yungji)* ata/ano)
MBC	-do-	*(Lhira-Lhimet)*	-do-	bhanja/ bhanij	-do-	*(Khotkir Mathang)*
FZC	-do-	-do-	-do-	Daju/bhai/ didi/beheni	-do-	-do-

(contd. . . .)

Symbols	Drukpa (Dogapa)	Doya (Lhopu)	Lepcha	Lhotsham (Nepali)	Rai (Dokhun)	Sharcop
MZC	-do-	Pu/na/tsa	-do-	-do-	-do-	*(Yungji)* ata/ano
H	phuja	rahim	Abo	Lokney	?	phewaktsa
W	amshu	met-hin	Ayu	Aimei	?	mewoktsa
eBW	nam	*(na)*	Ngiom	Bauju	Namey	
eZH	mak	Mahnk-pa	Ajong	Behena	Maksha	khotkin
yBW	nam	*(tsa)*	?	Buhari	?	mathang
yZH	mak	Mahnkpa	Meok	Juwain	Yangacha	jajamin
BC	?	Chanda/ chanmet	Namkupong	bhatijo/bhatiji	-do-	?
ZC	?	-do-	anom/lng	bhanji/bhanij	?	?
S	bu	Rachan	tugrikap	Chhora	yanga-tsa	ja
B	bum	Metchan	ta-eukup	Chhori	-do-	jamin
SW	nam	nama	ngiom	Buhari	Namey	cheimin
DH	map	Mahnkpa	meok	Juwain	Maksha	map
WM	ani	Ya	aniu	Sasu	Chhadima	ani
HM	jum/ani	Ya	amo	Sasu	-do-	-do-
WF	ajang	Ta	afet	Sasura	Chhadiwa	ajang
HF	ajang	-do-	abo	-do-	-do-	-do-
SS	tshew	Chu-chan	kupjong	Natj	Yangacha	tshew
SD	tshum	-do-	-do-	Natini	-do-	tsham
DS	tshew	-do-	-do-	Natj	-do-	-do-
DD	-do-	-do-	-do-	Natini	-do-	-do-

Note: Italicised words indicate similar use of kin terms among different systems. Terms given under parenthesis are terms of reference.

Table 3.4: Comparative Kin Terms and Relations

Symbols	Drukpa	Doya	Lepcha	Lhotsham	Rai (dokhun)	Sharcop
FB-FBW	aku-amchhum	pang-yu	batim-motim	Barababu-bariama kaka-Kaki	Depa-dema banga-chhenga	aku-ajim
FBC	achu/Ajim-nochu(simnum)	pu/na-tsa	anom-anum/ing	daju/bhai-didi/beheni	Chhogsa	ata/ana-kota/usa
FZ-FZH	ani-aku/ajang	ni-ku	aniu-batim/aku	phuphu-phupaju	nini-pusei	ani-ajang
FZC	Achu-nochu	(Ihira-Ihimet)	anom./anum-ing	daju/bhai-didi/beheni	bubu/nana -yangna	(khotkin-mathang)
F-M	ap-ai	payu-mavu	abo-amo	*papa-ama*	*papa-ama*	apa-ama
EGO	Ego	*Ego*	Ego	Ego	Ego	Eqo
C	achu/ajim-nochu	pu/na-tsa	anom/anum-ing	daju/did-bhai/beheni	bubu/nana-vangna	ata/ana - kota/usa
MB-MBW	ajang-ambom/ani	ku-ni banga-chhenga	ajang-aniu	mama-maiju	depa-dema	Ajang-ani

Symbols	Drukpa	Doya	Lepcha	Lhotsham	Rai (dokhun)	Sharcop
MBC	achu/ajim-nochu(simnum)	(Lhira-Lhimet)	anom/anum-ing	bhanja/bhanij yangna	bubu/nana-Mathang)	(Khotkin-
MZ-MZH	amchumaku	yu-pang	mutim-batim	kaka-kaki	depa-dema/ chhenga-banga	Ajim-aku
MZC	achu/ajimnochu (sim-num)	pu/na/tsa-mike	anom/anum-ing	daju/didi-bhai/ beheni	bubu/nana-yanga	ata/kota-ana/usa

Note: Italicised words indicate similar use of kin terms among different systems. Terms given under parenthesis are terms of reference.

Ngaloms on the Sharcops in the history of Bhutan. It is possible that the Sharcop has popularly picked some of the Drukpa kin terms up. Sharcops have their own mother tongue. The situation between the Lhotsham (Nepali) and that of Rai (Dokhun) systems also seems to have the same history of cultural influence although they seem to belong to quite different linguistic groups and systems of kin terms and relations. Similarly, Lepcha and Lhopu live in the same region as minority groups of people in Bhutan. Local history tells us that they even lived as neighbours long ago. They apparently belong to different linguistic groups and show less mutual influences on one another.

Following the comparisons of Kin terms (Table 3.5) a superficial classification of the six cases based on Lowie and Kirchhoff's system of classification gives us the impression that the Drukpa, Lhopu, Lepcha and Sharcop all together belong to Bifurcate Collateral type, the Lhotsham case being Bifurcate Merging and that of Rai belonging to Lineal system in the first ascending generation.

Yet in another system of classification[22] developed by Murdock there are four main types of Kinship systems (Table 3.6).

It has also been noted that these four types of Murdock's are in general equivalent to that of Lowie-Kirchhoff's types. Murdock's system of classification is based on cousin typology in Ego's own generation. In this system of classification Drukpa and Lepcha system apparently belong to Hawaiian Generational type, Lhotsham and Rai do not seem to match with any of the four typological formulations although Ego in both the system seem to relate with cross-cousins on mother's side in a similar way. Lhopu and Lepcha seem to match well with that of Iroqouis type in their basic features. However, Lhopus case would still be uncomfortable in this type, as they tend to equate cross-cousins with that of parallel cousins on maternal side.

Summary

A consanguinal group comprises of descendant daughters their husband and children. Son takes resident at his wife's household after marriage but he continues to have important roles and responsibilities towards his sister's children and welfare of his matrilineal household. The relations between brothers-sisters, mother-son with respect to mother-daughter and maternal uncle-sister's children have structural importance in Doya social organisation. The relation between sib brother-

Table 3.5: Classification of Kin Terms-1 (Lowie and Kirchhoff[1])

Drukpa	Doya	Lepcha	Lhotsham	Rai (Dokhun)	Sharcop
F#FB#MB	F#FB#MB	F#FB#MB	F=FB#MB	F#FB=MB	F#FB#MB
M#MZ#FZ	M#MZ#FZ	M#MZ#FZ	M=MZ#FZ	M#MZ=FZ	M#MZ#FZ
Bifurcate	Bifurcate	Bifurcate	Bifurcate		Bifurcate
Collateral	Collateral	Collateral	Merging	Lineal	Collateral

Table 3.6: Classification of Kin Terms-II
(Murdock's Cousin Typology Equivalent to Lowie's System.)

Notation	Drukpa	Doya	Lepcha	Lhotsham	Rai	Sharcop
Z	ajim	na	Anum	didi	Nana	Ana
B	achu	pu	Anom	daju	Bubu	Ata
FBD	ajim	na	Anum	didi	Nana	Ana
FBS	achu	pu	Anom	daju	Bubu	Ata
MZD	ajim	na-mike	Anum	didi	Nana	Ana
MZS	achu	pu-mike	Anom	daju	Bubu	Ata
FZD	ajim	Ihi-met	Anum	didi	Nana	mathang
FZS	achu	Ihi-ra	Anom	daju	Bubu	khotkin
MBD	ajim	Ihi-met	Anum	Bhanij	chhogsa	mathang
MBS	achu	Ihi-ra	Anom	Bhanja	chhogsa	khotkin
TYPES	Hawaiian Generational	? Bifurcate Merging.	Iroqouis Generational	Hawaiian ?	Iroqouis ?	i Bifurcatr .Merging

sister is most crucial through which the matrilineal descent lines are perpetuated by an exchange of sons between the consanguinal households of bothers and sisters. In fact the son-exchange groups are also the consanguinal groups. The position of brother is peculiar in the sense that he belongs to wife's natal household by virtue of being a father and a resident-son-law and at the same time he belongs to his own natal house by virtue of being a member of matrilineal descent and corporate group. However, descent groups are formed comprising of son-mother and grandmother on one hand and on the other, mother-daughters and children on the other. This group segregation is expressed in food sharing pattern in the annual ancestral worship day at the matrilineal household. The two groups cook and eat separately where mother has a choice or privilege to join both the groups as point of linkage between the two groups. The groups thus separated ritually facilitate matrimonial exchange of sons between bother and sisters' residential groups marked by strong in-group feeling with respect to one another.

Therefore, all the affinal relatives are also Ego's own kinsmen. When a conjugal alliance takes place between any two cross-cousins they refer to their uncle (MB) and aunty (FZ) as grandparents (ya/ta) clubbing them together with MM, MF, FF and FM. Since the descent is traced through female line with distinct matrilineal (Riih) titles, any two son exchanging groups should ideally have different lineal titles but in Doyas case the two exchanging groups may also have the same title through parallel cousins marriages on the mother's side.

Doya system of kin term and relation show a case of "double cross-cousin" matrimonial relationship pattern wherein at least two matrilineal groups exchange sons instead of sisters as in the case of many other simple societies.

NOTES AND REFERENCES

1. Research Method in Social Anthropology-2, ASA, *Research Practices in the studies of Kinship,* Alan Barnard and Anthony Good, 1984.
2. *Dictionary of Anthropology*, Macmillan, London, 1987.
3. The term *Lhi-Ra* and *Lhi-Met* refers to cross-cousins. There is no term of address among the cross cousins. Lhi-Ra would mean seed/seedling of individuals born by males and Lhi-Met is complimentary to Lhi-Ra born by individuals of opposite sex (met-Ma) and without which an individual cannot be formed through sexual acts. *Ra-Lhi* means maize/paddy seedlings.

Lhi-Ra+Lhi-Met=Chan (children) which can be *Ra-chan (Lhi-ra)* or *Met-chan (Lhi-Met)*.

Natives' elders compare female body with that of soil in their function. And male body with the seed/rain like the way land/soil holds the seed and rain waters to grow crops so do the female body by receiving the bone from males' body.

4. Conception of an individual in human body is taken as a result of a union of *flesh* and *bone* from male's body. Males are supposed to carry the *bone* or *seed* or *bone* and females the *flesh.*
5. Underlined terms are mostly used as terms of reference.
6. Author v.as witness to the ritual ceremony and feastig at *Ya-chirpe's* home in an overe-might stay at satakha.
7. The descendant children within each exclusive eating group are referred to as *Bongteng:* male children will be referred to as *Bongpa* and female children as *Tingma* (FBS/MZS and FBD/MZD). They are forbidden to marry each other. On the other hand, the relation between descendant children of the two exclusive eating groups is referred to as *Dugya-Mungya* who is prescribed to undergo conjugal ties with MBS/D with FZS/D). In other words cross cousins are 'connubium', after Levi-Strauss, to each other's groups.
8. The author had a close relation with a damsel. At one occasion she disclosed this fact after which there was change in my relation with the lady. My close association with the people was attributed to a role of a good father's brother as I was often called Pang.
9. According to Homans and Schneiders's hypothesis "societies in which marriage is allowed/preferred with MBD but prohibited/disapproved with FZD will be societies possessing patrilineal kin-groups, and societies in which marriage is alowed/preferred with FZD but forbidden/disapproved with MBD will be socieites possessing matrilineal kin-groups."
10. The data may not be representative of the population. However, the collection was done at random without any preconceived pattern in mind. #Parallel cousin marriage among sisters' children is formally prohibited up to third generation by descent. *Parallel cousin marriage among brothers' children is strictly prohibited up to seventh generation by direct descent. **This case may be taken as an abnormal occurrence as such this case is extremely rare in the society.
11. Pranab Kumar Das Gupta, *Life & Culture of Matrlineal Tribes of Meghalaya,* 1984, p. 94.
12. F # FB # MB (Doya terms for these notations are Payu, Pang and Ku, respectively for male alters) and M # MZ # Z (Mayu, Yu and Ni respectively for female alters).

13. B=FBS=MZS#FZS=MBS (Doya terms are; Pu, Pu, Pu-mike, Lhi-ra and Lhi-ra respectively for male and Z = FED = MZD # FZD = MBD (Doya terms are; Na, Na, Na-mike, Lhi-met and Lhi-met, respectively for female alters).
14. F = FB # MB: M = MZ # FZ (Doya tenus are; Payu, Pang, Ku and Mayu, Yu, and Ni respectively).
15. It is a matter of prestige and question of additional property for a *Lhi-Ra* if he gets an opportunity to carry Ku's dead body to the burial site. Such opportunity is never allowed to Ku's own sons *(Ra-chan)* if *Lhi-Ra* is there.
16. The relation between *Payu* and Chan can be quite delicate especially with one's own *Ra-chan.* At least three cases of bitter quarrels between *Payu* and *Ra-chan* were recorded during my stay in which *Ra-chan* maltreated or bashed up their own *Payu* in one such case in *Satakha* village elders intervened and got the *Ra-chan* pay a fine of a tumbler (Belheng) of *Yu* to his *Payu.*
17. The empirical data collected during my field studies do not support this hypothesis although in one or two genealogy it has been noticed that consanguinal brothers formed conjugal relation with consaguinal sisters of the same generation (see *Setah's* Matrilineage).
18. *O-roh* is respectable term of address generally used in addressing or calling attention of some one in any inter-personal interactive situation. Junior to senior or to anybody whose personal name has to be avoided in direct address most often uses it or when one does not know other's personal name.
19. Once, a *Mahnkpa* under certain temporary agreement with his wife's parents left her young wife with a kid along with his own parents in his natal house while he went out of station for a year long training. His younger brother (20), a student of mine in class-IV made sexual advances and impregnated her much against his father's disapproval and displeasure. When his father reprimanded the son the latter bashed up the father in an attempt to hush up the matter but it came to the notice of all the people. Soon the elder brother was summoned home and the matter was settled between his elder brother in consultation with village elders. The younger brother had to pay certain Nama/fine to brother and to the village elders after which the elder brother formally severed his conjugal and jural relations with his wife in favour of his younger brother. The younger brother then became the legitimate *Ra-him* and father of the unborn child.
20. Kariera typpe: ". . . man marries a woman who is double cross-cousin (FZD/MBD), . . . simply exchanging women between descent units, . . . it is not necessary that only actual first cross-cousin marry . . . MBD=FZD=MMBDD; FF=MMB" Robin Fox (1967) p. 184-92.

21. Alan Barnard and Anthony Good, 1984, pp. 61-62.
22. Murdock's cousin typology equivalent to Lowie's four types are;

    (i) Hawaiian B=FBS=MZS=FZS=:MBS:
Z=FBD=MZD=FZD=MBD

    (ii) Eskimo B#FBS=MZS=FZS=MBS: Z#FBD=MZD=FZD=MBD

    (iii) Sudanese B#FBS#MZS#FZS#:MBS:
Z#FBD#MZD#FZD#MBD

    Adopted from Alan Bamard and Anthony Good (1984) pp. 61-62.

CHAPTER 4

Doya Response to Questions of Life and Death

Every society with an ethnic identity has certain set of ideas, concepts, ways and beliefs that give meanings to the matters relating to life and death. The society (1973: iii-lv) in their collectivity defines the ways of life and impress upon a set of rules, roles and status in their collective conscience (1963: 85). An individual is born through a physiological process of mating between a male and female does not necessarily become a member of the society. Similarly, when a member of a society dies it is not because of any physiological failures rather some spirits who have been meted with indignities by someone who has done something wrong unto him/her that causes it. And if, the decease carried some hurt feelings against any mortals his spirits will give troubles and more miseries.

There are undisputable ideas and concepts that define birth, death and beyond that facilitate a harmonic life process of the society. These are the ways in which an individual member need to be educated, to sort out problems of life, to take up such roles to relate with other members within which they find themselves, to involve in the activities, to sustain the livelihood of every souls, to meet with their mates to reproduce members of the group in relation with other of their kind, to continue their existence based on the simple fact of life, death, nature and its powers and spirits they know of. Doyas believe that human body is made of flesh and bone. Female and male carry the seeds of flesh and bones, respectively and when they contribute the flesh and bone a child is formed in an act of copulation. However, a member of their society is born only when a pair of prescribed and matured male and female from a well-defined set of group comes together. A social harmony is there when these groups are in full strength to produce enough to eat and drink to reproduce connubial of exchange to sustain and continue the groups with everybody adhering to the set of rules and ways of life. No one can make a mistake, not even the gods and spirits who have made life possible and guarded every mortal. For if ever there be misfortune, death and miseries it is because of a mistake or folly of someone among the mortals. This consciousness of the Doyas make them relent and invent certain ways and means of performing such remedial rituals and reflect on their mistakes or to at least regularly seek grace for the well-being of the member of the society thereby, involving participations of the whole member of the group(s) in offering the best of the things they have to the gods and spirits who must be kept happy. In this chapter, author shall describe how new born become member of the society what are the processes through which the newborn members are educated to further reproduce the society. Who performs what roles to ensure a smooth passage of life in the society? What rituals and performances are involved in legitimising union between reproductive partners, child conception, pregnancy, childbirth and death? What does life of an individual mean? How do they look at a male and a female, father and mother, parenthood in the society? What does death of a male and female member mean to the lineal family, group and the society? These are some of the questions I would try to answer from the ways the Doyas conceive and enact in their society.

Doyas too, have their own ways of interpreting the physiological and morphological change processes of birth, growth, aging and death as it unfolds to them. It is enough for them, to have kids born to every legitimate couple. It is a serious matter if they don't have kids the best one can do is try with some other optional partners. Any child born to legitimate couple is welcomed as a member of the matrilineage and on the third day it is given a personal name. However, personal names have nothing much to do with the kin terms with which she will be related and referred to with other members in the society. The child discovers his or her status, roles and responsibilities as she gradually grows up in the society. Exciting moments and hardship of life unfold as they mature and become responsible for the sustenance of the matrilineage family. They qualify taking responsibilities by practically proving their productive and reproductive capabilities. Slowly and gradually they get educated in life skills and rituals of life. Ultimately, they leave behind rich experiences of having lived through different stages of life. This departure or separation is honoured with elaborate rituals and ceremonies. Life begins small and ends up big.

Birth of a Child

Although Doya say that conception is result of copulation between male and female in which male contribute the bone and female the flesh[1] it does not mean that any male can impregnate a female and the fatherhood or for that matter husband is some one else. There are well-defined categories of males and females with predetermined relations who only can contribute the basic components of conception. Cross-cousins are referred to as *Lhir-ra* and *Lhi-met,* laterally meaning male and female seedling *(Lhi*-seedling, *met*-female, *ra* - male).

Therefore, ideally it is the cross-cousins only who can give birth to a legitimate child in the society. It would be difficult for Doyas to accept a child from a female who has no prescribed partner in the society and also from any other alternative mates arranged by the society under normal circumstances. Once cross-cousins partners are born to siblings their conjugal match and their issues thereon are legitimate member of the society is a foregone conclusion.

The child born to them over a period of time is already member of the lineage and the society. It is just a matter for the cross-cousins to come to their ages and live together in matrilineal household and then one day announce the pregnancy of the women. However it is also not simple process of mechanically fixing a pair of nut and bolt together rather the individuals concerned undergo an educational process of identifying persons around them within one's group and others. They slowly develop the accompanying mindset, attitude and behaviour along with the physiological[2] and social changes occurring with the growing age so that when right time comes individuals beings are self-motivated to execute the conjugal rules and take up such roles in the society[3]. Male partner undergoes a change in his life by taking residence in wife's household that the female partner would find it difficult to understand. On the contrary for the female household to have her a resident husband and become pregnant all means a matter of pride and importance for the household, the matrilineage and partners themselves. It is definitely an occasion to celebrate in the matrilineal household.

Yu-Tungmini

When a woman is conceived the news is announced and shared with all the kith and kin of the lineage. All of them are invited for celebrating the pregnancy by observing the Yu-Tungmini ritual on a particular day. The whole processes are as follow:

> Between 2 to 5 months of the pregnancy the couple prepares *Yu* from *ewui ka Jarto* (brew from local millet). When the Yu is ready, one fine day the resident-husband *(Mahnkpa)* wakes up early in the morning. He takes a *Belheng* (Bamboo Tumbler) full of fermented millet mixed with blood from freshly cut toes of a hen. He goes door to door, leaves a little fermented millet and smears a little blood of the hen at entrance door of all his kith and kin before they wake up. He leaves the following invitation message while leaving everybody's house - *Na mato malo ha ta wei. Ta-hin dak ta wei. Ta-hin na rak an ba wei. Elka ya ta. Ya che yah rang ta wei.*

On discovering this symbolic message of invitation at the doorsteps, all the kith and kin come to the house of the couple. For those who cannot attend the celebration at the house of the couple, the husband reaches a Belheng of Yu at their homes, later. When close kin gather at the house, the husband offers *Yu* to all the brothers-in-law, wife's maternal uncles first (who is most often his own father) by taking the container to their mouths three times and then all other kinsmen. All the kinsmen including children are offered with *Yu* and butter. Then, the brothers-in-law and uncles put *Maika-Tashi* (a mark on the forehead) on the forehead of their resident son-in-law while saying the following words: *Guley tashi tshering ta wei. Mayu ta wei. Lo Ku ta wei. Pu ku ta wei. Sa mei ta wei* (Let good luck be on the mother, brother and maternal uncles). This is a very important stage of transition for the couple and this celebration has several integral meanings to the couple and to the husband in particular, as he would slowly discover in his life.

Ma-mang

When the pregnancy counts nine months they observe another ritual called *Ma-mang* that involves a ritual performance with the help of a Rai Bijuwa or an elderly man. In this ritual performance either a goat or a cock is sacrificed to the household deities by cutting off the head. The head is buried in the earth in front of the house. All others in the household except the expectant mother and her husband consume the meat. It is believed that if this ritual performance is not done, the woman will have difficulties in delivering the child.

Panksang and Mins-tang

The husband is always at a helping hand when the wife is advancing to last stage of pregnancy particularly when it is the first delivery for the couple. His parents-in-law and brothers-in-law give necessary helps and guidance. He erects a small house or improves the room to make it comfortable for delivery and makes all other necessary preparations.

The delivery is done with the help of his mother-in-law and/or wife's sisters who have the experiences. The husband also stands by for his part of role in the delivery and assists the others. Once the child is delivered, the husband is instructed to cut the placenta *(sema)* with a sharp blade of bamboo called *Payung,* wrap it in a piece of cloth/leaf and hang it on a branch of a tree not very far away from the house.

The newborn child is considered defenseless and vulnerable to bad spirits and spells. So it is protected by putting up a branch of a tree called *Changsing* at the entrance right from the day of the birth. It is believed that this branch of tree has the power to ward away evil spirits. The mother and child are kept isolated for three days. The husband takes all care of feeding, washing and cleaning in the house. The mother is given chicken to eat during these days.

On the third day the isolation ends with a ritual called *Panksang.* Any elder male of the household or the husband carries out this ritual. On this day some water *(Moti chio* - water from AmMochhu River) is collected from the AmMochhu river before sunrise. The house is cleaned up and the *Moti chio* is sprinkled inside the house and on the mother and child with the help of a branch of a plant called *Lusing (Antemisic vulgaris).* Matrilineal kin and other in the neighbours turn up including old and young ones for a drink especially prepared for the occasion. On the same day naming of the new born child *Minstang* is done by an elder person of the residential group who may be grandparent or the parents (Ya or Ta or Mayu or Payu) in presence of the kith and kin. All are served with Yu. They take the drink after chanting some words and sprinkling it out three times with their fingers as follows: *Torra tung an. Tahi ahlum Panksang ka yu tung* an.(meaning-let us drink for the naming ceremony of the new born child.)

The mother is also given some drink and meat to take. From this day she and her child are no more isolated. Normally, she is fit for work in 15 days after delivery.

Both the husband and wife take equal responsibility to take care of the child once the mother can be on her feet. There is no fixed day or rituals for giving the first solid food to the child.

Parenthood

Yu-tugmini and *Maika-Tashi* are both very important events in the life of new couple. Having these occurred in the couple's life means; One, it is a matter of great happiness for the couple and the whole matrilineage as it ensures the lineage continuity. Two, it takes the couple to an important transition stage in their lives they would soon become Payu and Mayu (F/M) with great responsibilities of the household, matrilineage and the lineal properties. The husband in particular raises his status from being a resident-husband by qualifying to be a father of the future child and then as time passes he shall also become a Ku (maternal Uncle) with the responsibilities towards his own sister's children and wife's brother's children for the furtherance of the both the matrilineage. An issueless couple fails to take these responsibilities adequately and they live a handicapped life. Therefore, having this *Yu-tungmini* ceremony is a matter of social pride and status. The biological proof of fatherhood is not necessarily important to Doya society as usual in all the traditional societies. A legitimate male becomes a legitimate father of a conceived child by the act of offering *Yu* to his wife's parents, as the relationship is already predetermined by the fate of having born cross-cousins.

Children born to legitimate couples are usually incorporated as Chu/Chan (grandchildren/children) in a matrilineage as bonafide members of the society. As the chu/chan grows into Lhi-ra and Lhi-met their parents would have greater responsibilities and after carrying all the duties in their life when they die they are given an elaborate send off with full honour and respects. Individuals dying even before getting conjugal relations in young age are not given any ceremonial rites.

Death and Funeral Rites

No other event of life is so pronounced as the death and funeral is in Doya Society as well. An individual below age of 12 is considered to be still a child though she may be very helpful or productive at work. So, the death of a child is not given a formal funeral ceremony. They are simply buried in the earth without giving a ceremonial expression to the feelings of the parents and matrilineage group. If a women dies in labour without delivering the child, her husband cuts open the abdomen with an attempt to rescue the child. If the child is found alive the father and close kin take responsibility to bring up the child and if the child is found dead inside the womb, the fetus is taken out and buried separately without any funeral ceremony. On the other hand, mother's dead body receives elaborate funeral rites, little different from that of father or a resident husband.

The Death

Death is taken as the end of the physical life. They seem to believe in the duality of existence. They say, at the death of a person *Sehok* leaves the body continues the journey without in the open space. And finally at the end of the journey beyond the *Sehok* joins another world of "*Simpu'*. Unnatural, death is most feared and taken seriously, as it is often believed to have been caused by some evil spirits or bad spells from somebody or by having caused indignities to some deities. In the case of such unnatural death, the' Sehok' of the death is believed to trouble those who are believed to have been behind the death of the person. The bereaved kith and kin seem to mind their guardian deities for not preventing the untimely death. They appeal the decease with food and drinks not to cause troubles to the surviving kinsmen before removing the body to the burial site.

Funeral Rites

When death occurs, the dead body is kept in the house for 3 days. During these three days the deceased is given elaborate treatment. Much care is taken in feeding and looking after the deceased body. It all looks as though the deceased would take grudge against the survivors for allowing the death to come.

Dead body of a woman is kept inside the inner room of the house while that of a man who is often the Mahnkpa (residential husband) is kept in the entrance room of the house. Funeral rites of a married man are normally carried out at the wife's house but this can also be done at his own natal house. A woman's funeral must be carried out only at the natal household. She must also take her eternal rest in the ancestral land.

When a person breathes his or her last, the body is folded and tied in the fetal position. After that the body is rolled up in a bamboo mat, tied round by three strong strings of cane *(Lising)* running parallel. Tying up the body reduces the length of the body under 4 ft in any case. The food that is offered to the deceased is dropped at the head side of the body that is already rolled up inside the bamboo matting. The dead body is kept inside the house for two nights guarded by at least one person who would also take the body to the burial site. The person who sits guard is not allowed to leave the body except for natural calls. She also feeds the deceased. The food for death of a man is prepared outside the house by his niece or grandson/daughter. And that for the deceased who is a female the food is prepared inside the house by her own kin but not belonging to her household. These persons can be the deceased's sisters, sons, daughters who are already separated from the household. The preparation of the food is done separately for the deceased and is elaborate with Yu, meat, butter and cereals. When the food is offered all the kin of the segmentary matrilineages join together. The food is offered amidst sympathising wails and chanting - pleading the deceased to accept the food good or bad for that is what they could offer to him/her. The deceased is also pleaded not to mind or take any grudge on anybody while leaving for the death that has seized upon him/her-*Go happily, they say in chorus. It is not only you to leave the living world. We all have to follow you behind one or the day, etc. to the dead one*[4].

During these three days of mourning, relatives from both the mother's matrilineage and father's matrilineage pour in with packets of fermented millets and uncooked cereals.

On the third day also all the relatives comprising almost the whole of residential territory come with gifts of unprocessed fermented millet and uncooked cereals packed in leaves. This is also the day the dead body is to be finally laid at the burial site.

Preparation starts early in the morning at the selected site[5] that is at least 30 metres away from the house towards the north direction. A day earlier, some kinsmen would have already fetched enough planks[6] from a freshly cut *Kimbur' (Moracease-morus levigata)* tree.

A small area next to the earlier burial is cleared and made even while all others engage themselves in finding and collecting stones from all around the fields surrounding the house. On the piece of land cleared, a horizontal stone foundation is erected just above the ground. On this plinth of stone, the planks which are cut to standard sizes are arranged to form a cuboidal box measuring 3 × 2 × 4 ft. Around this arrangement stones are piled up to hold the planks in position to form a coffin/box in place. While the stone level around the box comes up to the height of the box, others erect a small hut to house the whole stone mound that would finally come up. The lifted ridge of the hut runs almost northeasterly direction and is roofed with leaves. And around the hut a pole fencing is erected. But before enclosing the arrangement inside the fence the dead body has to be laid. There are gaps and holes between the planks, these gaps and holes are filled with especially collected gray clay from a sacred stream[7]. This is done to prevent any insect inside the box where the deceased would lie. The person who stands guard to the deceased and none others does the filling work. Once this is done, it is time for the same person to bring the body to the site after the last meal is served at home.

The body rolled up and wrapped in the bamboo matting is taken out from the house by the bearer and carried on the back with rope harness supported by his forehead and shoulders.

No one else should help him. He should complete to carry at one go and not in stages. An unmarried daughter of the matrilineage carrying a basket (Wank) containing crockery, knife and other articles of day-to-day use of the deceased, leads the procession to the burial site. In the meantime, other kinsmen prepare food, Yu and flat bread for funeral feasting of all those who are gathered. Many men and women get engaged in cooking and preparation.

When the dead body is brought to the burial mound others help to lift the body above the box with the head to the north and the face looking upward. The body is swung up and down 3 times over the burial box and then lowered into the box for the final rest. All his belongings especially his/her valuables[8] including money and knives are also kept beside the body in the box while vocally informing the dead one each time that nothing of him/her is being held back by anybody, when all his articles are being kept in the box. After this the box, is closed with the remaining planks and the gaps on the covering planks are filled up with the same clay. Soon after many hands come together to pile up stones over and around the box and finally it takes the shape of a pyramidal stone mound over the ground inside which the body is encased in an insect proof closed box. A pointed stone is put on the top of the mound as the last piece of stone under the hut. This stone mound with the dead body is called a *Chen.* On the mound the dead one's crockery are mounted and his household items like baskets, bamboo containers are hung below the ridge of the burial hut. Around the hut at the feet of the fencing poles, the girl who led the procession sows some food grain and cottonseeds in three circumbulations around the hut. When everything is kept inside the hut the fencing is completed by thickly pegging pointed logs all round the hut. Finally long cane strings running three times around bind the fencing. And then the roof of the hut is also bound by running three strings across from side to side over the ridge and tied to the fencing poles. Lastly, a tall bamboo pole is put up near the Chen with a spear shaped wood cut out and a piece of white clothe on the top[9]. This completes the work of burial into the Chen.

Now, the lineage people along with the bearer of the dead body offer the last meal of the day (Lipto) near the Chen. After this, a ritual feasting of specially prepared food and drink takes place at the burial site. The food is to be taken in a different manner. No one should eat the food with bare hands. They have to take it with the help of a piece of hard leaf to pick the food and throw it into the mouth without touching the lips. The drink is taken as usual in bowls or leaf pouches.

The funeral food should not be thrown away. It can be taken home and consumed. Small children are closely guided in this matter. After the food and drinks, people start moving home after paying condolences leaving behind the bereaved family near the Chen. If any relative of the family stays back on this day she has to stay continuously for another three days at the deceased's home.

When all these works are completed and people leave for their home, it is taken that half of the day is over. Because they believe that in the next half of the day the dead man will do his share of work. There is a division of distributing working days between the death and living.

Division of Working Days

The disruption caused by death of a person takes several days of mourning, restricted activities and heavy drain on resources, all of which is made possible with cooperation of several kinsmen and relatives, to finally restore things into normal order.

The first three and half days until the dead body is finally laid to rest in the chen are taken to be the working days for the survivors. In the second half of the third day the bereaved family would just sit and mourn - no one should do any work. Any non-resident kinsmen cook their food. The fourth day, following the disposal day is again working day for the survivors. The fifth day is again for the death. And from the sixth day onwards, the surviving members of the lineage can resume their normal works at home and in fields, if the deceased is a female. For male's death up to the seventh day is for the deceased and from the eighth day the living can resume their normal works (Table 4.1).

The offering of food and drink to the deceased at regular intervals however, has to be continued till the 15th day when final ritual feast is offered to the death in the presence of all the kinsmen. A cow for females or an ox for male's death is slaughtered on the 15th day for the feast. All those who attended the 3rd day ritual have to join in this feast.

The cooked meat along with food (Chakto and Kersey roti) and drink (Yu) are offered to the deceased first in the same manner near the Chen. After this all partake the meat, food and drink. The Sehok of the death is believed to be leaving the body and household on this day to join the others at Simpu (world of the death). It is believed that the Sehok hovers around jungles and streams within the residential territory after this ritual.

Every three years, the deceased's Sehok is offered with Yu in the first harvest of Jarto, which coincides with the yearly Loh celebration. Most often, people believed that most of the common sicknesses and illnesses are caused by one of these Sehoks of the death persons who may have been neglected or disregarded. The witch doctors help them identify the particular spirits through oracles. So whenever anything, food or drink is offered to a deceased she is requested not to harm or curse any of the poor living kinsmen. They say while offering, please, accept whatsoever we could manage to offer to you and stay *happy and contented wherever you are.*

Table 4.1: Division of Working Days[10]

Elhni (Good) days	Ritual Activities	*Zehni* (Bad) days	Ritual activities
Day- 1 to 2	Death occurs. Kinsmen go around to make necessary arrangements for the dead body.	Day-3	In the second half of the day after burial rites, kinsmen keep away from normal works.
Day-3	The first half of the day (when all the burial rites are accomplished with feasting and last offerings of the day at the burial site) is for the kinsmen. The third day kinsmen cannot take food with bare hands.	Day-5	Special offering of Honey, Fish, and butter along with elaborate meal is made to the death twice a day at the burial site.
Day-4	Kinsmen go out for normal works.	Day-9	Kinsmen keep away from normal works.
Day-6	Kinsmen can take food with bare hands from this day. Normal work resumes in case of female death.	Day-12	Non-working day for the kinsmen.
Day- 7 and 8	Normal working days for the kinsmen resumes after 8th.	Day-15	Non-working day for the kinsmen.

(cont. . . .)

Table 4.1: *(cont. . . .)*

Elhni (Good) days	Ritual Activities	*Zehni* (Bad) days	Ritual activities
Day- 10 and 11	Normal working days for the Kinsmen.	Day-18	Non-working day for the kinsmen.
Day- 13 and 14	Normal working days for the 13 and 14	Day-21 kinsmen.	As above
Day- 16 and 17	As above	Day-24	Observed as *Dalhni* for female deceased. Elaborate feasting and offering is made to the decease. A cow is slaughtered for the female. For female deceased *Dalhni* is observed on the 27th day. An ox is slaughtered for the purpose.
Day- 19 and 20	Normal working days for the kinsmen.		
Day- 22 and 23	-do-		

Beliefs, Restlictions and Austerity

For the first three days after the death, the dead person's guard is isolated untouchably from other resident or non-resident people. Other bereaved members of the household do not touch any pots and pans of the household and do any work. They observe austerity and mourn the death. Non-resident matrilineage people come to help in cooking and doing all the household chores. The bereaved members of the household cannot touch their mouth with their hands while eating; they have to eat with the help of leaf spoon without touching their mouth for the first three mourning days after the death. All the resident husbands (Mahnkpa) also observe all the restrictions when death occurs in his wife's household. Meat and fried food is strictly avoided for the first 3 days.

In case of resident husband's death a set of crockery which includes, a pot, a pan, a plate, a bowl, a Yu tumbler (Belheng), a bamboo basket (Wank), a Ladle (kulik) and other articles are separated and kept outside the house. A hanging fire place (Jikpu) is made along the front side of the house to prepare food for the deceased husband. For females these things are kept inside the house and cooking is also done inside the same house.

When a husband dies, the bereaved wife has to observe austerity for a period of 3 years during which she should not enter into anybody's house and also look for another husband. And if a wife dies; the bereaved husband has to observe austerity for a period of 3 years if he has fathered kids to look after or otherwise for one year if he hasn't fathered any children. He is restrained from cutting his hair for the austerity period. So, it is very easy to find out a widower in a village by looking at the long hair, he keeps.

During this austerity period bereaved ones cannot enter into anybody's house. And if any body is found doing so she is hit with dead charcoal and residue of *Yu*. If a bereaved one comes in another's house, she is believed to bring misfortunes in the household. So hitting with charcoal and residue of *Yu* is to ward off or neutralise and a way of showing the disapproval to the defaulter.

The Matrilineage in which a death occurs does not worship any deities or celebrate Loh for the following austerity period of 3 years.

Summary

Life is a fact. Its passage is also a predetermined fact as the flesh and bone of human body. Likewise, childbirth is also a matter of fact as the seed with the rain from the sky fall on the earth sprouts to grow to fruit plenty of seeds for consumption, sharing and exchange between own groups for further reproduction. All these are made possible by the grace of gods and spirits who control over all the facts of life and nature.

Individuals follow well-defined set of rules in executing the roles in one's life and any deviation from it or mistake out of ignorance causes indignities to the gods and spirits who can in turn cause death and miseries to life.

Life and birth is desirable death is not. Life after death joins the realm of the spirits. Their spirits must be pleased and kept happy by all the kinsmen together for the well-=being of all the members of the society.

For all these reasons relations between males and females should be discreet, sacred and predetermined. Doya society also accepts the child born out of this sacred relationship without having to solemnize with ceremonial rituals at the time of physical union. The child that is conceived as an outcome of the sacred relation between them is a matter of great pride and happiness for the kinsmen and the household. This occasion is marked by ritual offering of *Yu* to the members of matrilineal household including the father of the husband to bestow the couple's roles of father and mother.

Sex is secret acts. Out of this secret acts when a child is finally born the mother and child have to be looked after, protected and guarded against anything evil by the husband in isolation for three days. On the third day with an ablutionary ritual the elders give the child personal identity. They celebrate this occasion with drinks and the kinsmen.

The child grows in the close company of the mother's matrilineage group, educated in sorting out things and people around him/her in discreet categories to differentiate people around. The child observes the reproductive behaviours of the man and animals around, enacts them in the role-plays and games while still young. F...ally when the child matures they follow the ways of the social life to take up different roles to execute rules of the society.

For the lineage to continue, the land is to be kept intact, the member of the matrilineage need to work together for the livelihood, the women needs to be respected in her own place. Men can be mobile like seeds and rain. When women dies it is an irreparable loss but when men dies the matrilineage loses only a resource of the exchange groups of the lineage and there can be alternatives, although men in matrilineage do have important roles to play in the rituals of life.

Death as such is not desirable for both. The spirits after life still rules the well-being of the surviving kinsmen of a lineage. They should be pleased while leaving the surviving group. The separation of the soul (Sehok) from the physical body after death takes three days of consoling and pleading with gifts and offerings of food and drinks. The death is sent off with all the basic commodities of livelihood with the hope that she would continue to live happily even after. She is contacted at regular intervals through elaborate offerings of food and drinks to assure the linkage and ensure continued well being for the surviving kinsmen and their descendants. The Doyas live in the past and present. Future is not theirs.

NOTES AND REFERENCES

1. They say that human body like animal is also a combination of flesh *(Sa)* and bone *(Ruish)*. Also in the conception of child male is like that of seed *(lhi)* and rain *(wai)* and the female is like that of land or soil *(boh)*. The soil holds the seed and rain waters to gerrninate and grow so does the combination of bone and flesh from a male and female give rise to an individual. I asked Ap Yallgku what Would happen if few males have sex with a woman. He said that it would not make the woman conceive any child because the bone from the other male will spoil the bone from the first male as a result no child will be born to the woman. On the other hand, if a male has sex with two different women they will conceive children.
2. The anxieties associated with the physiological changes from childhood to adulthood remains with the peer groups and family circles. Certain rituals and restrictions mark puberty and menstrual cycle in the case of women Manipem, mother of two kids says that the first menstruation comes between 12-14 years During the period a woman is neither allowed to serve drinks to other nor take drink herself. She is also not allowed to go near any blooming crops. However, she does not observe isolation in the family. She can do all other household chores as usual.
3. Van Gennep (1960) has coined the term *'Rites-de-passage* ' to describe the *'ceremonies accompanying an individual crisis'*, . . . activities

associated by distinguishing three separate rituals; *'separation'*, *'transitions'* and *'incorporation'* of the individual in the society.

4. The exact Lhokpu wordings of the chanting could not be recorded, as it was very difficult to catch the words from the chorus amidst wailings of many kinsmen. However one of my informants gave me the meaning at a later time.
5. A site is selected next to the last burial sites of the kin towards the north direction. The next burial (Chen) is to come up farther towards the north direction away from the house.
6. The mastery of cutting out planks from a tree is worth mentioning. They do not use any saw but they manage to chop out fairly uniform and smooth planks with the help of choppers and axes only.
7. The clay *(Buh)* is to be collected by kinswomen only. There are only few places wherefrom the clay can be collected and not from any other places. The one in Lotukuchu is called *'Geyti'* and *Kamti* at Sataklla. They think that the clay from these places have special property of keeping away from insects.
8. In earlier times, they said that they used to keep personal valuables like precious stones and gems in the coffin(Chen) of the decease. There were curious incidents of breaking open some of the very old chens in Lotukuchu suspected to be works of treasure hunters in the region. The matter was being reported to the sub-divisional authority and it was being investigated during my stay.
9. This pole is put up only at Man's *Chen*.
10. As part of ritual observance after a death has occurred, days are divided as *Elhni* and *Zehni,* alternatively, between the deceased and surviving kinsmen. *Elhni* days are considered good for the survivors to do normal works and *Zehni* days are considered bad for the survivors to do normal works. They keep away from normal works.

CHAPTER 5

Economy and Livelihood Pattern

Economy and livelihood activities of the Doyas are closely linked with their natural environment and are "embedded" in their Kin relationship. It is difficult to distinguish the economic activities as defined in the modern economy from their social ways of life and beliefs.

Doyas live under the power of supernatural forces that rule their lives in interactions with their immediate physical environment: land, water, rain, forests, plants and animals all of which belong to their omnipotent and unseen powers. For them the "force of production" *per se* would also include the unseen forces who they have to always communicate with time and again for their agricultural productivity, to seek a permit to work on the lands and appease them for good crops through rituals of food and drinks offering and sacrifices of animals and birds. For them the unseen powers are beyond their controls and they have no technology to supercede the whims and designs of the supernatural beings.

The whole of their social productive activities are in the first place governed by and organised under the whims and fancies of the omnipotent powers and is limited by the physical aspects of the natural environment within which they find themselves and the people who affect their livelihood in their immediate social environment. We shall try to see how the Doyas organize themselves for their production, distribution and consumption activities within their close kin groups and maintain a pattern of livelihood under the constraints of their natural environment and the domain of their supernatural forces. Secondly, how the people in their immediate surrounding affect their economy and livelihood pattern and thirdly, how the market economy is impacting on their traditional livelihood pattern.

Traditional Subsistent Economy

The richness of the natural forest resources in the sub-tropical junction of lower and middle Himalayas seems to have always nurtured the Doyas also in abundance of food grains and animals with simple tools and techniques known to them best. To continuously ensure this abundant livelihood out of their environment, they keep their supernatural lords who control over all the resources and live informed and pleased through ritual offerings from time to time.

All the materials required for housing are derived from the forests. Logs, poles, planks, bamboo, fastening strings, stones, roofing grass and leaves are all that are required to erect a house for them. Members of a consanguinal household participate in making the houses. The art and skills of erecting a house is a general capability of every able body. Almost all the matured men know the art of erecting a house and females do the supporting work in the house construction.

They had nothing much to depend on outside their society for their living if they had not been conquered and enslaved by the Drukpas and if Nepalese had not immigrated into their territory and shared their natural resources. Except for a few essential commodities that they get in exchange. But perhaps, the human society would not leave anyone community in isolation.

Extended consanguinal families moved freely in the vast expanse of the hills, along with cattle and ponies, authored land by slash and burn methods, forecast cereal seeds and produced enough food grains to store in the granaries (Tokim) at different places away from the main houses (Makim). The food grains produced were much more than enough to run the whole seasons round for each and every household. They also produced plenty of dairy products but not all for themselves. It belonged to the rulers. They used to barter certain essential commodities such as cooking pots, salt and implements, etc. with some of their forest products.

Makim: A Unit of Household Production

The land being Matrilinealy owned around a Makim, consanguinal families under a particular Riih[1] and the extended consanguinal families of daughters with their husbands and children work on different parts of the land growing food grains, grazing animals, hunting and gathering wild animals, roots and plants. Each and every individual born in the matrilineage has equal access to any part of the land possessed. At times the whole matrilineal work force may be working together at a particular field with mutual arrangement according to the labour requirements. There is no specialisation in any production activities. Thus each extended consanguinal family under a Makim is capable of self-subsistence in the basic material aspects of living. Such a "primary group" of consanguinal family forms a unit of production and reproduction of a matrilineage.

Distribution Pattern

All the consanguinal units produce enough food grains to support themselves; a part of the total produce, according to their capacity is shared with their old parents in the Makim. They also contribute equal amount of food grains and other products at the time of ritual feastings and worship of ancestral and territorial deities. There is also mutual sharing of food grains among the extended families and also with brothers of consanguinal families. The close relation between mother's brothers and father's sisters come to the fore for all the rituals and material (food grain) needs and requirements in the matrilineals extended families and Makim.

Matrilineal males not only contribute their labour in their mother's and sister's work in the fields but also provide food grains at times of need from the produce of wife's matrilineal lands. This brings a close relation between the matrilineages. There is an element of reinforcing matrilineal (male) exchange with material exchange relation between the collateral kin of brothers and sisters. In this kind of production and distribution system of the Doyas, ideally they can either only be equally well off or equally poor, which is expressed in the kinship idiom: *Rang Yo Ka Not Sum Itpo* (we all have one feeling/sentiment).

Consumption Pattern

Consumption of food grain is done separately in each extended family. In the Makim, the parents, unmarried children or a married daughter along with husband and children eat together. Huge amount of food grain and meat is consumed in the annual or occasional deity worship and at the time of Death. All people in a particular village along with close kin residing at different villages come together for ritual and feasting. Considerable amount of grain is utilised (Jar to) in making Yu (local drink). Buckwheat (Kersey) is grounded into flour and made into Roti (flatbread). Their main food at the time of ritual feasting is Sorghum. Rice is supplementary. Maize is roasted and beaten flat and is taken with little cinder mixed with it.

Exchange and use of Currency

The surplus food grains used to be either just wasted or eaten up by animals. Later, when they also began to keep their own cattle the dairy produces were used as means of exchange for procuring essential commodities like salt, cloth, iron implements and pots and pans from the border market place (Chamurchi near Samchi district gate). Use of currency, as medium of exchange was not appreciated till early twentieth century although British Indian silver coins were in currency in the Indian plains, then.

When the coins appeared in the weekly markets it seemed to have become another attractive and precious item to be possessed in exchange of what they produced. The coins they came to possess were very rarely used in procuring essential commodities from the exchange markets. Rather they became a valued precious property of females in a matrilineage. These coins dating back to 19th century became as precious beads far necklaces and chains[2]. Such necklaces passed through the descendant females. They also became a precious property to be paid in the form of Nama in the rituals of female transmutation. Most of the elder ladies today possess these coins chains as a passive but long-term saving. People have now begun to dispose these valuable possessions at times of hardship[3].

Agriculture and Technology

Doyas grow buckwheat, maize, millet, sorghum in their shifting fields and paddy in their terrace fields. Some of them grow varieties of seasonal vegetables such as beans and creeper, squash, pumpkin *(Jungka),* gourds *(Jopsey)* near their houses. They also collect and cultivate varieties of rhizomes roots and tubers for their food all round the seasonal cycle (Table 5.1).

Most of them do not maintain a proper kitchen garden like the Nepalese in the neighbourhood do. The Nepalese grow mainly maize, millet, paddy and tapioca along with varieties of leafy vegetables, beans, pulses and creeper vegetables following a similar seasonal cycle.

Table 5.1: Seasons and Crop Cycle

Months	Local Seasons	Agri. works and Crops grown	Crop harvested	Other activities
Dec. Jan. Feb.	*GUNSUM*	Slashing and burning (in the upper hills) for Maize, Millet and Sorghum	Buckwheat	
Mar. Apr. May	*SOH-KA*	Field preparation and paddy plantation.		
June July Aug.	*JA-SUM*	Paddy millet and Sorghum	Cardamom,	
Sep. Oct. Nov.	*SHE-KA*	Slashing and burning in the lower hills for Buckwheat and Sorghum.	Maize, Paddy and Orange	Loh: The new year festivity. Maniage season

Besides the rudimentary agricultural activities for the main food grains they also catch animals like wild boars, wild goat, deer, wild buffalo, varieties of rodents, porcupines, monkeys, wild cats, birds and fowls, frogs, fish and varieties of insects. In addition they collect tubers, rhizomes, roots, leafy wild vegetables and Fruits to supplement their nutritional requirements.

It seemed that shifting cultivation and hunting and gathering activities were the mainstay of Doya economy and livelihood pattern in earlier times while cattle herding as an occupation was forced upon them. The sedentary way of life with settled form of agriculture is relatively a new development in the Doya ways of life.

Tools and Implements

Chopper *(Chabu),* Sickle *(Goish),* along with locally fabricated wooden hoe and pecker are some of the indispensable agricultural implements (Fig-16). Chopper and sickle are procured from markets while the other local implements are made from hard logs and branches of tree. Hunting implements like bows and arrows, and Snares are still in use. Few families have shot guns but not many can afford such expensive tools. Nevertheless, most of the other household articles and some agricultural implements are indigenously made and used still today.

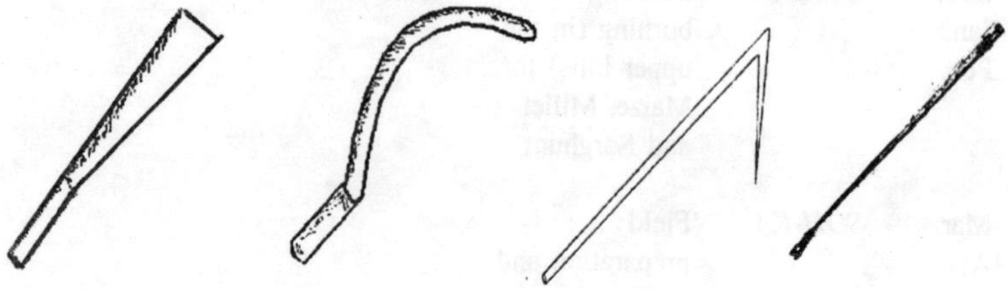

(a) (b) (c) (d)

Fig 16: Some agricultural implements[4]

It is also said that Doyas knew the art of weaving their own traditional clothes. They still use a fine bamboo spindle *(Rim)* and a fine plant fibre *(Jin)* to do rough stitching on their torn clothing. These indigenous implements are also being fast replaced by the steel needles and mill threads.

Livelihood Situation

In a village census conducted in 1994 on size of household, land holding, livestock, food crop production, annual income and period of food sufficiency from a sample size of 74 registered land-holder households including a neighbouring *Rai* village called *Lapcheygoan* between *Lotukuchu* and *Sanglung* villages. The following results are drawn in simple mathematical analysis of the data (Annexure 5.1-5.5).

Sharing of Resources

Many Rai families of the neighbouring Nepali villages have temporary land use agreements through the ritual friendship ties or otherwise with mutual consent for cultivation of food grain at many different locations in the Doyas land. Rais grow their food grain in under-utilised and difficult shifting fields of the Doyas and pay back in cash or in kind at the time of harvest in the ratio of 1:3. However, if the land owning Doyas also work together with the Rais, the ratio of sharing the product is 1: 1. This system of land use is gaining popularity among the people as it reduces the hardship and labour problems. However, it is a matter of speculation as to the implications that be in the simple corporate land use system and society of the Doyas. They have Adhiya system of land use with many people including the Hapas who seasonally migrate into the region.

Land Holding Pattern

In an economic and statistical survey conducted during the field there were at an average about 15 households with 186 populations to 274 acres of land in each village (Table 5.2).

Table 5.2: Land Holding Pattern

Sl. No.	Name of villages	No. of Households	Total household members	Total landholding (acres)
1	Lotok	8	132 (16.50)	102.90 (12.863)
2&3	Lotukuchu (A & B)	34	445 (13.08)	443.20 (13.04)
4	Sanglung	23	204 (8.87)	636.96 (27.69)
5	Satakha	9	151 (16.77)	188.17 (20.9)
	Grand Total Average Lapchey goan	74 (14.8) 14	932 (186.4) 121 (8.64)	1371.06 (274.21) 118.19 (8.44)

Note: Figures in parentheses show average of respective villages and of the total.

The population and land ratio in each Doya villages works little different from one another. Lotok has, for every household of 16 to 17 persons approximately to 12 to 13 acres of land at an average (man-land ratio being 0.75). Lotukuchu A&B together have at an average, 13 acres of land for every 13 members households (man -land ratio being 1 : 1). Sanglung has, for every 8 to 9 members household to 70 to 79 acres of land making a land-man ratio of 1 : 3.1 and Satakha has 11 to 11.7 acres of land to every 16 to 17 members household making a land-man ration of 1 : 1.24, approximately. On the other hand, average land holding in Rai Nepali village (Lapcheygoan) was 8 acres of land for every 8 to 9 members household (land-man ratio being 1 : 1). The difference in the overall population-land ratio between Sanglung and Lapcheygoan (Rai village) and the physical proximity of the two (see Map 1.2) give room for sharing of land resources between the two communities.

Local Production and Shortages

The total annual production of food grain in all the four Doya villages was 112.4 metric tons of cereals[5] and 28.85 tons of rhizomes, roots and tubers (Table 5.3). The neighbouring Rai villages produced a total of 11.24 metric tons of food grain and 1 quintal of roots and tubers (Annexure 5.5). That means 1512 kg of food grain and 340 kg of roots and tubers were available to each Doya household of 10 to 12 members at an average and in 14 Nepali households of 8 to 9 members 803 Kg of food grains and 7 Kg of roots and tubers along with other vegetables and pulses are available in a year.

Table 5.3: Annual Food Production and Shortage Period

Name of village	Buckwheat (Pathi*)	Maze (Pathi)	Paddy (Pathi)	Millet (Pathi)	Sorghum (Pathi)	Roots (kg)	Shortage period
Lotok	140	640	150	445	675	930	4
Average	(17.5)	(80.0)	(18.7)	(65.0)	(84.4)	(11.6)	
Lotukuchu (A&B)	695	3560	2060	2685	3680	23880	5
Average	(20.4)	(104.7)	(60.6)	(78.9)	(108.3)	(702.4)	
Sanglung	1420	1265	2830	760	2480	3030	5
Average	(61.7)	(55.0)	(125.2)	(33.1)	(107.8)	(131.7)	
Satakha	640	1030	1270	630	000	1010	5
Average	(71.1)	(114.4)	(141.1)	(70.0)	(000.0)	(112.2)	
Grand Total	2875	6495	6360	5520	6835	28850	5
Average	38.8	87.8	86.0	76.0	92.4	389.8	

* Pathi is a local unit of measurement. Pathi is a Nepali term. Doyas do not have this unit however, they have another smaller unit called *Pul* according to which 1 Pathi = 8 Pul, 1 Pul = 7 Chola (handful). Further, 20 (ltkal) Pathi = 1 Muri (Doya term) = 80 kg = 2 Mounds.

This also means that in Doya household with 10 members had 151.2 kg of food grains and 32 kg of roots and tubers are available to an individual in a year and Rai family of 8 members only around 100 kg of food grain and less than a kg of roots and tubers in a year for consumption.

The situation is alarming but these figures indicate a declining crop production in the region (Table 5.4) and also show the growing importance of raising cash crop that has become the main source of income for the people to supplement the shortage of food crops.

Table 5.4: Productivity[6] at Different Locations

Crops	Lumbey	Lapchey -gaon	Lotok	Dam-bey	Seng-ten	Sata-kha	Sang-lung
Paddy	01:25	01:25	01:20	00:00	01:18	01:20	01:25
Maize	01:30	01:60	01:25	01:60	01:70	01:20	01:60
Millet	01:80	01:60	01:80	01:25	01:70	01:20	01:80
Sorghum	01:35	00:00	01:80	01:90	00:00	01:20	01:90
Buck-wheat	01:80	01:80	00:00	00:00	01:40	01:20	01:80
Wheat	00:00	00:00	00:00	00:00	00:00	10:01	01:10

Livestock

Livestock as usual is an essential part of life for the Doyas, also. Most of the livestock are kept for ritual purposes, common feasting and for milk products. They depended on the wild animals and birds for all their flesh requirements in earlier times. Now, they depend on domesticated livestock for meeting not only domestic meat requirements but also for earning some cash by selling meat locally. The food situation now in the village is that those who can afford to keep livestock can only have the meat and money while the wild life in the degraded forest is getting scarce day by day.

Doyas keep some cattle *(Pink),* goat *(Rha),* pig *(Pank)* and hens and cocks *(Kek)* in almost all the house. Keeping ponies and horses for transportation of goods is a recent development associated with the cash crop trading activities.

Table 5.5: Livestock

Villages	Ox	Cow	Goat	Birds	Pig	Pony
Lotok	13	46	10	46	5	2
	(2.7)	(5.7)	(1.6)	(5.6)	(0.2)	(0.3)
Lotukuchu	53	116	35	168	11	2
(A&B)	(1.6)	(3.4)	(1.1)	(5.0)	90.1)	(0.1)
Sanglung	26	61	4	86	8	7
	(1.2)	(2.6)	(0.2)	(3.7)	(0.4)	(0.3)
Satakha	16	34	7	50	9	23
	(1.8)	(3.8)	90.8)	(5.6)	(2.0)	(2.6)
GRAND	108	257	56	350	32	35
TOTAL	(27.0)	(64.3)	(14.0)	(87.5)	(8.0)	(8.7)

Data available from the five administrative residential units revealed that there were around a thousand livestock with an average of 27 oxen, 65 cows, 14 goats and 88 birds, 8 pigs and 8 ponies in the four Doya villages (Table 5.5). This makes an average of 14 oxen, 35 cows, 7 goats, 47 birds, 4 pigs and 5 ponies to every 10 households compared to 10 oxen, 23 cows, 18 goats, 35 birds, 15 pigs and no pony to every 10 Doya households in Lapcheygoan (Rai village/ Annexure 5.5). Sanglung, Satakha and Lotukuchu villages have the maximum livestock. Satakha village alone has the maximum number of ponies. This difference with the rest of the Doya villages has an impact on the living standards and ways of life of the Satakha people from the rest of the Doya people altogether, there are 838 livestock in the whole of Doya villages and every two animals have little more than 3 acres of land for grazing.

Cash Crop and Annual Income

Seventy-four households in four Doya villages produce a total of 178 mounds of cardamom and 12,870 ponds of oranges valued approximately around (market rate, in 1993 Samchi) more than Rs. 1.26 Million, approximately (Tables 5.3 and 5.6 Sources of Family income). This gives an annual income of Rs. 17,000 roughly to a household but the annual income data collected during the field works does not tally with the calculated figures.

Table 5.6: Sources of Family Income

SI. No.	Sources	Units	Rates
01.	Oranges	Pon (80 Pcs.)	Nu/Rs. 60 to 70/ pond.
02.	Cardamom	Mound (40 Kg.)	Nu/Rs. 2400/mound.
03.	Portage	4-5 pond/80 Kg.	Nu/Rs.150/trip
04.	Pon carriage charge	6-8 pond/80 Kg.	Nu/Rs. 200/trip.
05.	Butter	Kg.	Nu/Rs. 70 to 80/ Kg.
06.	Cheese	Balls	Nu/Rs. 5/ball
07.	Hen & Cock	Whole	Nu/Rs. 70 to 80/pc.
08.	Beef	Kg.	Nu/Rs.35/Kg.
09.	Pork	Kg.	Nu/Rs. 40 to 50.Kg.
10.	Mutton	Kg.	Nu/Rs.60/Kg.

The field data based on house-to-house survey, on annual income, gives a figure of Rs. 5,32,000 for 74 households making an average of Rs. 7,190 (appx.) annual income per household (Table 5.7). The difference in the two figures is a glaring indication of Doya people's indebtedness to others. The minimum annual income among the Doya household is Rs. 2000 per annum and a maximum of Rs. 25,000 per annum in Lotukuchu village and in the neighbouring village the annual income range between minimum of Rs. 1000 to maximum of Rs. 20,000 (Table 5.7). The average income in the Lotok, Lotukuchu, Sanglung and Satakha villages are Rs.1100, Rs.7088, Rs.5609, and Rs.8222, respectively. Most of the lower income group lives in Sanglung village, Lotok village with just 8 households ranks the top in the average annual income (Rs. 11000) and Satakha village with 9 households ranks the second (Rs. 8222).

Impacts on the Doya Economy and Livelihood Pattern

Actually, the Doyas had only access to the land they authored and lived making their livelihood out of it. But legal ownership right as such did not exist until the middle of 20th century. By the turn of 20th century when the country became a sovereign Kingdom under a single line of hereditary Kingship, the first hereditary King took up major political, administrative and revenue reforms in the country. Slavery was abolished. At a later stage, Wage Labour was introduced and Land Reformation and Revenue Act, 1956 came into force. Doyas began to lead a dignified and settled way of life. But the introduction of Land Revenue Act also began to put pressure to set a structural change in their traditional system of matrilineal corporate system of Land ownership and inheritance. Land authored by each household at many different places was registered in the name of eldest man in the matrilineage or in absence of the lineal man, the eldest resident husband of a household and very rarely in the name of the eldest female of a household (Annexure 5.1 to 5.5) giving rise to considerable importance to male heads in the traditional matrilineal households and the society at large. This was perhaps done quite ignorant of the traditional cultural values of the Doyas to establish the commonly accepted male supremacy cultural values of the national cultural mainstream.

Table 5.7: Cash Crop and Annual Income

Sl. No.	Village Names	No. of Household	Annual income (Rs./Nu.)	Cardamom (40 kg/Md)	Oranges 80%/pon[7])
1	Lotok	8	88,000	21	1,850
		Average	(11,000)	(2.60)	(231.25)
2	Lotukuchu	34	2,41,000	83	5,270
&3	A&B	Average	(7,088)	2.44)	(155.00)
4	Sanglung	23	1,29,000	48	4,060
	Average	(5,609)	(2.09)	(176.52)	
5	Satakha	9	74,000	27	1,690
		Average	(8,222)	(3.0)	(187.77)
Total		74	5,32,000	178	12,870
Average			(1,06,200)	(35.8)	(2,574)

A land ceiling of 25 acres also restricted them from taking on fresh land within their territory. Land Registration Cards *(Thram)* were issued to each main household recording land specifications, usages and sizes of pieces of land they possessed at different places. Then they began to pay annual land revenue and property taxes to the Royal Government of Bhutan (Table 5.8).

Table 5.8: Land and Revenue Taxes[8]

SI. No.	Land and Property	Tax Rates (per annum)
01.	Houses	@ Nu (Rs.) 10/- per house.
02.	Livestock.	@ Nu (Rs.) 3/- per house.
03.	Shifting/ Jhum Field.	@ Nu (Rs.) 10/- per field.
04.	Cardamom field.	@ Nu (Rs.) 300 to 500/- per field.
05.	Orange field.	@ Nu (Rs.) 12/- per field.
	Total Range	@ Nu (Rs) 335 to 535 per annum

Matrilineal corporate households with land in excess of 25 acres were distributed among the consanguinal elder males and formally registered in their names.

Impacts of the Drukpas

Folktales of the Doyas tell us that they evidently had their own form of self-rule with a King or a Chief *(Pon)* in a stone built palace at *Denchukha*[9] before the Drukpas incursion. Folktales reveal that Drukpa Lamas with magical powers came down, captivated, killed and devastated them and their palaces. The remaining of the people was then enslaved. They had to take refuge in deep jungles and made their living in the wilderness and abundance of the forest resources. And whenever called for they in all their strength (men and women) used to be engaged in building fortresses and palaces, making bamboo baskets and carrying loads for the rulers who had seasonal trade between Chamurchi in Indian plains and Denchukha involving days of trekking in the hills and Jungle paths[10]. The Drukpas used to come down along with their sepoys, fleets of ponies and horses.

In the non-trading season Doyas used to be left alone with most of the ponies and horses for grazing in their territories. They were also made to look after hundreds of cattle for the supply of milk products and meat to the rulers[11].

> 2nd *March* 1993: After a brief morning meal and a starter drink at Challamo's house, in Satakha Chedoji and I went down to Raibey where Chedoji's sister live in a *La (hut)*. On my query about their past he narrated the following story as we were walking

down. In earlier times Doyas used to be keeping large flocks of cattle, practice shifting cultivation widely in a large territory of land. We never used to tether the cattle. They used to graze freely in the Jungle. There was abundance of milk and its products. Oxen used to be much larger and stronger. We did not know how to yoke an ox. Oxen used to be kept for meat only. Paro Raja used to routinely come down and they were required to give free labour service for carrying goods. We used to carry huge loads on our own expenses for days together to reach a godown at Denchukha. From thereon, Hapas used to carry the loads in relay to Paro. We were also made to look after large flocks of cattle for the *Ranis* (Queens). If anyone of us was found reluctant or disobedient in complying with the orders we used to be physically abused and chased by large dogs. In return to our services to the Rajas we were given free hand to exploit resources in vast area of forest for our livelihood.

Doyas looked after the ponies and horses, and cattle in makeshift huts in different corners of their territory. They milked the cows; processed cheese and butter, slaughtered aged cattle and prepared meat to be lifted for Kings. All of these used to be collected by Sepoys (who used to periodically come down for the purpose) and nothing used to be left behind for the Doyas who toiled in hardship.

Doyas had no direct gain from all these works but in return they were allowed, free access to the resources of the region to make their living. When they carried loads for the rulers for days together they had to carry their own ration and nothing was paid in return. It was Royal service to the rulers called *Gondo-wula.* At times they were also heavily engaged in opening up new trade routes to India and other important places in the country for which they had to keep away from their homes for months together.

This system of forced labour kept most of the able bodied away from their villages for days and months at times. It also widely dispersed the conjugal families within the territory away from their main households and residential areas. They made their living wherever they moved with their simple traditional tools and techniques of cultivating food grains in shifting fields, hunting animals and gathering food to meet their nutritional requirements.

Living with the Rais

Nepalese who are mainly Rai occupying lower ranks in the Nepali caste hierarchy had begun to immigrate into the Doya territory in the earlier part of 19th century. Warrior castes; the Gurungs and Kshetris had already established themselves forming a powerful community involved in trade and commerce between India and Bhutan contributing to the economic development of the country.

The Gurungs in particular, established their power centre at Samchi and nearly ruled the economic and socio-political affairs of this part of Southern Bhutan with tacit approval of the then King of Bhutan. This is a different story but the presence of Nepalese[12] in and around the region greatly influenced Doya ways of life.

Doyas were small in number living amidst abundant natural resources in the interior of the southern hills. The Rais slowly moved in, in search of green pastures and forest resources in the vicinity of the former. The Rais carried a superior socio-cultural technology in regard to agriculture and associated community labour organisation. They made friends with the kind Doyas and took possession of land in exchange of nominal cash or kind without any resistance even from the Royal Government. The kings of Bhutan then, seemed to require more labour force to exploit rich natural forest resources for the socio-economic development of the country and Doyas needed a reliable and friendly neighbour to live with. In the quest of better living Rais seems to have exploited the situation to their advantage. They established inseparable social friendships through rituals and mutual consent popularly called *Mit*[13] and helped the Doya brethren in many ways in an intense socio-cultural intercourse between the two communities over the years. Rais brought in more advanced cultural traits, agricultural knowledge, techniques and trading practices including growing of cash crops. Some of the cultural traits among the Doyas that are apparently of Nepali origins are as follows:

- Knowledge and techniques of making plough
- Turning terrace fields out of hill slopes and Jhuming fields
- Vegetable Gardening
- Nepali language as means of oral and written medium of communication
- Building houses with stone and mud

- Preparation of variety of drinks through crude distillation processes
- Social festivities and new form of games and entertainment
- Nepali Folksongs, ladies dress, costume and ornamentations
- Adoption of Nepali names
- Raising of Cash crops
- Trading activities and practices
- Standard of measurements
- Production and distribution practices
- New forms of labour organisation
- Personal and Household ornamentation and decoration
- Some social beliefs and practices.

In the earlier days when both the communities began to exploit the natural environment shoulder to shoulder through shifting agricultural practices with simple technologies, it mounted pressure on the local resource base. Vast tracts and areas of hill began to look worn out exposing naked earth. Nepali community then began to become a competitor in the same resource base using better technology.

To meet the increasing foodgrain demands of growing population Nepalese began to change over to the settled form of agricultural practices with their advanced technologies. They made terrace fields, raised orange orchards in the lower hills and cardamom fields along the upper steams and gorges, while Doyas, given to their old habits and traditional practices, took time to adapt to the emerging environmental constraints until the *Jhum* cycle dropped down to 4/5 years and even less duration with lowering productivity and limiting territorial areas.

Slowly and gradually, Doyas began to take up the new technologies and cash crops cultivation and related trading activities. They began to have terrace fields wherever possible, fashioned ploughs and used oxen to till the land resulting to far reaching implications to their traditional ways of life, social organisation and general attitudes towards the material aspects of life. Processes of monitisation, sense of private land ownership, differences in living standards among themselves and emergence of new social categories pertaining to inter-marriages in the otherwise homogenous society mark the changes occurring among the Doyas due to the close social interaction with the Rai communities in their vicinity.

Impacts of the Migrating Hapas

Hapas, seasonally come down towards Samchi passing through the Doya region. They fix up their make shift huts all along the hill tracts between Dorokha and Samchi. As usual in their nomadic ways of life, they come down with fleets of ponies and horses and cattle for grazing and earning out of their livestock. People of one whole village in *Ha* Damthang District under a *Mandal* (block level leader) temporarily settle here for about 7 to 8 months between October-November and April-May every year trekking down for about 15 days from their settlement areas in Ha. They stay in 30 to 40 *Nulaks* set-up at certain points all along the path to Samchi in the hills. They possess some pasture land also in the region from their forefather's time and own some orange orchards and cardamom fields. These are left under the care of some Doyas or Rais on certain terms of contract like Adhiya from which they are always known to make the better deal out the produce for themselves. Similarly, they also leave behind most of their cattle at times with either Doya families or Nepalese to look after until their next seasonal return. Their Nulaks on the paths also serve as Inns for travellers providing food, drinks and a shelter. Their ponies, altogether around 150 to 200 strong fleet are pressed into active transportation of oranges and cardamom. On the return trips from the market they bring bags of food grains and sell at the doors of Doyas and Nepalese. They transport maximum loads of oranges and cardamom from the whole of Dorokha sub-division. Their benefits from these business earnings are more than those others can do in the whole region.

Relations between the Doya and Hapa in general are of suspicious nature where the Hapas are known for their thrift and cunning nature and the Doya for their nature of gullibility and simplicity. In the past Hapa were known to have forcibly taken away Doya children to take care of their cattle. For long time since the incidents took place Hapas movements the Doya residential areas remained restricted.

When Hapas come down they bring dried needles of Blue Pines *(Dupa:* used as incense smoking) from the north. This is an essential ritual article, which is used at the time of ritual performance and worship. Blue pines are not grown in southern Bhutan and hence it is a scarce commodity for many in the south. Hapas drop in each and every Nepali and Doya households give them some handful of Dupa as a gift to every household get some food grains in exchange.

Thus, they try to make best of their 6 to 7 months stay in the south through collection and earnings and go back with enough money and food grains to spend the rest of the year in peace and comfort in their villages in the high and cold north. Some Hapas have become very prosperous dealing in orange and cardamom and have permanent export business establishments at Samchi owning huge buildings and assets.

Impacts of the Market Economy

Growing cash crops, transportation and trading activities associated with the use of currency have brought in considerable prosperity among the Doyas on one hand. On the other hand, it has also cast adverse impacts on the social structure and organisation of the Doyas society. Some Doyas have made good fortunes in these activities and many others have brought improvement in their living standards by their earnings. Monitisation processes have considerably affected simple ways of life. On the contrary, the concept of rich and poor is emerging among the people in an otherwise equalitarian society. Male importance and dominance is being emphasised in the changing livelihood pattern, to mention few.

Every year during the months from November till late March, many of them can be seen moving up and down the hills in groups of men, women and children with baskets of oranges and cardamom on their backs to Samchi market. An adult person can make an average of ten thousand in several trips of orange loads on the back in a season. Others make in term of thousands and lakhs of rupees by selling the oranges for those who have orchards.

Samchi has now developed into a proper market with regular shops and weekly markets on Sundays. There are around 30 to 40 permanent shops, stalls and small bars built by the Royal Government selling all sorts of commodities including varieties of bottled drinks, luxury items, ornaments, cloth, iron implements, pots and pans, modern kitchen ware, electronic gadgets, food grain and a variety of vegetables, meat and eatables. Indian businessmen from the erstwhile Chamurchi market have moved into this growing township at Samchi running shops and canteens. There is also a Cinema hall in the market place.

Out of curiosity, most of the Doya spend out their hard earnings in seeing cinema and purchasing ornaments, shoes, eatables and luxury items in the markets. Considerable amount of income go out in procuring millet for keeping stock local brew for local brew. Many of them spend heavily on drinks including women. Responsible persons buy enough food grain to meet the shortages, but only very few persons have some money for the rest of the year.

Most of the Doyas have close relations with one or other businessman in the market from whom they take food grains on credit promising certain amount of oranges or cardamom in the next season. Only very few of them mainly from Satakha and Lutukuchu villages have emerged rich dealing in the orange and cardamom trades directly. (See Appendix II: Some Persons and Personalities.) Some of them have stonewalled and corrugated Tin roofed -double -Storehouses in the villages. Some people in Satakha have bought ponies worth thousands of rupees to improve on their earnings. Doyas in general could have benefited much more from trading activities had it not been partly for their own ignorance and simplicity partly because the migrating people take a major share of the local business.

Changing Pattern of Livelihood

Under the environmental constraints and dwindling resource base and increasing population pressure of both the communities, Doyas had to adopt new means and ways of production techniques and practices for raising resources and earning. Certain cultural traits and values associated with the new techniques and practices were also absorbed in the Doya way of life, from the neighbouring Rai communities.

When they had to turn their barren sloping fields into terrace fields and grow food grain it required more labour and intensive labour organisation and use of different techniques and implements. Techniques and practices such as use of *Kodal* (Spade), *Halu'* (Plough), making of water channels *Kulo* from nearby streams, raising nursery fields for seedling *(Ra-Ihing),* transplanting in the terrace fields, Manuring and weeding, raising cash crops, fencing and related trade practices imparted considerably on their traditional organisation and way of life, making for a change.

The use of plough brought in a cultural value associated with gender. Women are prohibited to plough in Nepali society. The plough brought in an idea of gender specific form of labour division in the agricultural activities among the Doya. Paddy cultivation requires well-organised skilled labour in a society. Doyas had simple technology for shifting cultivation with their labour organised in small relatively autonomous consanguinal groups. When they had to adapt to the permanent form of cultivation they had to adopt the labour contract/ exchange system of labour organisation and also the associated techniques.

Terrace field owners needed to have some resources already to organise extra labour. These imperatives brought about labour dependence to other groups, among themselves and to the Rai neighbours. Since paddy fields are continuously used year after year with limited scope for further expansion or shifting, whichever consanguinal family group of matrilineage created and maintained it over a period of time, a sense of attachment or private ownership also developed quite contrary to the corporateness and free access to all the land under a matrilineage. (See Challamo and Setah in Chapter 2). Oranges and cardamom brought in considerable amount of cash by direct transportation and selling at the Samchi market. More and more Doya began to raise cardamom fields and in the gorges along the streamlines. They began to take direct part in trading activities bringing them in closer interaction with business communities from the Indian plains. Since this is an activity only men do, their importance in the matrilineal Doya society grew. More and more men began to keep away from their family fields leaving behind women and children to take care of children and production activities. Doyas became more and more market oriented for all sorts of commodities. More of them including women and children are getting increasingly exposed to the market every orange season.

Summary

The Doyas have lived in closely knit kin groups in the wilderness of sub-Himalayan tropical forest with simple technology of shifting cultivation and hunting and gathering practices to supplement their nutritional and cultural needs. They are not pastoral people although circumstances under the rule of the Ngalom forced upon them to be engaged in the occupation in earlier times. Their labour were also cheaply exploited by enslaving them to menial works of porterage, domestic services and free labour to the service of the Rajas. This seems to have brought about some disruptions in the normal ways of life in Doya society.

They had sufficient economy. The system of kinship organisation is related with their mode of production. Each consanguinal unit of a matrilineage forms a production unit and they in turn form connubium of man and material exchanges and sharing amongst them. These production units around a female line moved from place to place on their shifting fields. They had simple technology of production for their living in the vast territory abundant in natural forest resources since time immemorial. However, with the changing time, heavy migration of people from the south and north began to put pressure on the local resources and soon their simple technology became almost outdated.

The people who came nearest to them and influenced the most were the Rais who migrated in the interior of southern hills of Bhutan in the nineteenth and twentieth centuries. The Rais considered low caste people in Nepali society also have distinctive cultural tradition of ethnic nature as different from that of Hindu ways of life.

The Doyas adopted new technologies of settled agricultural traditions, some other cultural traits and language to adapt to the changing livelihood situation as, the productivity fell.

Their livelihood pattern is not only closely linked to their traditional kinship and relations but it is also greatly influenced by the surrounding socio-cultural and political environment. Powerful Drukpas on one hand exploited their simple ways of life and status. The Hapas seasonally migrate into their life and exploit their labour and economic opportunities. Nepalese on the other hand affected them greatly by settling into their proximity and co-sharing the same resource base in an intense socio-cultural intercourse causing a considerable change in their ways of life and attitudes. Their direct participation in the trading and business of cash crops has enhanced the influence of money in their day-to-day life breaking up the traditional system of corporation in the Matrilocal residential organisation of labour, production and self-subsistence.

With the coming of modern education among the younger generations and emergence of male importance in the changing socio-economic scenario. Doyas are all set for a change with increasing exposure to outside world and modern technological development under the patronage of Royal Government for the upliftment of disadvantage communities in the kingdom. Efforts are on to open a motorable road passing through the Doya villages to improve communication and exploit resource potentials of the region. Moreover, a serious effort is also being made to bring up the Doyas to the national cultural mainstream. Doyas are at a crossroad. They are at a tri-junction where they are exposed to cultural influences of the Nepalese, the national cultural mainstream and the market oriented modern culture.

Environmentally, the increasing pressure of population had brought down the natural vegetation at an alarming situation with the continuation of shifting cultivation but on the other hand, increasing expansion of cardamom fields all along the streamlines with tall trees deliberately allowed to grow for a cool shady shelter to the cash crops below and the thick and spread orange orchards all along the hotter foothills are ensuring water and soil conservation to certain extent. This pattern of local resource regeneration seems to ensue a new ecological set-up in the region for future economic securities.

NOTES AND REFERENCES

1. The whole of Doya land registered under many households can be identified fewer than 10 to 20 Riih matrilineage groups. A Riih with larger descendant females would tend to have large areas of land in their possession.
2. The coin chains used to be made by Nepali Goldsmiths. The coins are chained in a beautiful thread work by making holes at the borders of the coins. Sixty to seventy coins are linked in a beautifully woven thread work and the long chains of silver coins adorn ladies across their shoulders.
3. At many instances, men and women used to come to the teachers at the school and others to sell off their silver coins at rates ranging between Rs. 10 and 100 per coin in the time of distress.
4. Starting from left Fig. 15 (a) at page 170 is a chopper locally known as *Patang,* Fig. 15(b) is a sickle known as *Goish,* Fig. 15(c) is a hoe used for loosening the soil before sowing seeds and Fig. 15(d) is pecker used for putting maize seeds by pecking on the soil.
5. Please see Table 5.3: The sum total of buckwheat (2875 pathi = 11500 kg), Maize (6495 pathi = 25980 kg), paddy (6360 pathi = 25440 kg), Millet (5520 pathi = 22080 kg) and Sorghum (6835 pathi = 27340 kg) is taken as the total cereal production, which is approximately 112,340 kg or 112 metric tons.

6. This ratio indicates the quantity of food grain production to one *pathi* of seed sown at different locations in the Doya territory.
7. One Pon = 80 pieces of orange.
8. These rates of Revenue and Taxes are based on the field *Survey* conducted in 1993.
9. The author visited the ruins of the Doya palace in 1994, April.
10. The rulers of Paro had their regular trade passing through Ha, Denchukha and Samchi to Indian plains. Commodities procured from Chamurchi in India used to reach Paro in 20 to 30 days in a relay transportation involving many groups of people inhabiting the region. Doyas used to lift the loads till Denchukha and from there Hapas used to lift it to Paro in a relay.
11. Elders aged between 80 and 100 years say that there used to be flocks of cattle belonging to different Ranis and Rajas that they used to look after to supply dairy products and meat whenever asked for.
12. Nepalese who began to inhabit the Southern part of Bhutan in great numbers contributing their might towards the development of Bhutan came to be known as Lhotshampa (meaning the Southern dwellers) in Bhutanese parlance differentiating them from Ngalom (mainly the Drukpa, the Northern dwellers of Bhutan), the Sharcopa (Eastern dwellers) and the Lhop/Lhopu (Doya of the South Bhutan). They became part of Bhutanese Human Geography.
13. *Mit* relation is affected between any two individuals of usually same age and sex group after having mutually and consciously agreed. It involves a ceremonial oath taking between the two partners in presence of elders and family members of both the parties on an auspicious day. The two persons sit together in front of a lamp and take oath of mutual faithfulness, co-operation and also to maintain and observe certain moral obligations and social relations towards each others kith and kin in the name of God and mutual welfare. It entails adopting each other's family socially in the capacity of each other's social role and status. This relation contracted once passes down the families through several generations. The two persons address each other, as *Mitsaheb* - it is taboo to take each other's personal names. They address all other family members like one's own mother, father, brother, sister, son and daughter, and grand-children by prefixing the *Mit* to the kin terms.

ANNEXURE 5.1: STATISTICAL DATA OF LOTOK

5.1.1 Household-wise Statistical Data

Sl. No.	Head of Household	Family members	Land holding (in acreage)	Annual income Nu./Rs.	Annual food grain sufficiency period
1	Chitchema (F)	06	9.00	20,000	12 Months.
2	Ajijem (F)	11	10.00	8,000	7 Months.
3	Chungsey	10	16.00	10,000	12 Months.
4	Aedu Tshering	05	11.60	10,000	7 Months.
5	Gyen Tshering	42	27.25	20,000	8 Months.
6	Uley Tshering	35	11.76	10,000	6 Months.
7	Sebab	10	8.48	5,000	6 Months.
8	Lebda	13	9.10	5,000	7 Months.
	Total	132	102.90	88,000	65 Months
	Average	16.5	12.8625	11,000	8 Months

5.1.2: Household-wise Production Data

	Cereal Crops						Cash crops	
HH No.	Buck-wheat (Pathi)	Maize (Pathi)	Paddy (Pathi)	Millet (Pathi)	Sorghum (Pathi)	Roots (kg)	Cardamom (Mound)	Orange (Pound)
01-01	20	80	0	25	20	90	7	500
02-02	60	60	90	50	70	150	1	100
03-03	0	100	0	10	25	120	0	300
04-04	0	50	30	20	80	60	1	200
05-05	0	120	30	140	140	30	5	600
06-06	60	150	0	80	240	200	0	100
07-07	0	20	0	40	40	100	3	50
08-08	0	60	0	80	60	180	4	0
Total	140	640	150	445	675	930	21	1850
Average	17.50	80	18.75	65	84.375	11.625	2.33	205.56

5.1.3: Livestock

House-hold Nos.	Ox	Cow	Goat	Hens & Cocks	Pig	Horse	Total
01-01	02	7	–	3	–	–	12
02-02	3	3	2	4	–	1	13
03-03	4	15	–	6	–	–	25
04-04	2	1	1	6	–	–	10
05-05	4	10	2	10	2	–	28
06-06	3	6	3	10	2	1	25
07-07	1	1	–	3	1	–	6
08-08	–	3	2	4	–	–	9
Total	19	46	10	46	5	2	158
Average	2.11	5.75	1.25	5.75	–	–	19.75

ANNEXURE 5.2: STATISTICAL DATA OF LOTUKUCHU

5.2.1 Household-wise Statistical Data of Lotukuchu A & B

Sl. Nos.	Head of Household	Family members	Land holding (acreas)	Annual Income (Rs)	Food grain sufficiency (months)
09-01.	Pento	15	6.50	15,000	5
10-02.	Yangku	10	19.00	15,000	6
11-03.	Namjey	18	13.25	15,000	5
12-04.	Kinja	16	7.61	2,000	8
13-05.	Tompa	9	40.33	3,000	7
14-06.	Toksey	29	9.17	8,000	5
15-07.	Pudum Tshering	20	11.55	5,000	6
16-08.	Chencho	17	13.90	6,000	6
17-09.	Muki	3	11.50	3,000	9
18-10.	Gomchey	15	8.20	5,000	6
19-11.	Tashi Tajey	3	5.50	2,000	9
20.12.	Setah	31	25.00	12,000	9
21.13.	Meley	25	21.85	25,000	7
22.14.	Duri	34	23.45	5,000	7
23.15.	Dodnam	3	13.50	5,000	5
24.16.	Chitenji	18	7.09	5,000	5
25.17.	Pema	8	11.40	3,000	7
26.18.	Jimi	2	3.40	5,000	6
27.19.	Tanjidok	2	8.10	5,000	6
28.20.	Jimi dorji	13	6.31	10,000	8
29.21.	Tanjey	24	5.38	4,000	6
30.22.	Chiptenji	27	13.21	3,000	9
31.23.	KKuchutenji	12	23.90	10,000	8
32.24.	Diri	13	11.55	7,000	8
33.25.	Thering pau	13	28.45	3,000	7
34.26.	Dankachen	5	10.13	5,000	6
35.27.	Damey	25	19.40	7,000	6
36.28	Im tashi	18	17.52	5,000	6

Sl. Nos.	Head of Household	Family members	Land holding (acreas)	Annual Income (Rs)	Food grain sufficiency (months)
37.29	Kejon	20	6.90	2,000	6
38.30.	Daupalak	6	12.08	6,000	6
39.31.	Rinchey	50	15.00	15,000	8
40-32.	Nado	20	9.79	6,000	6
41-33.	Chenjo	18	6.88	6,000	6
42-34.	Pemo (F)	3	7.90	8,000	5
	Total	545	454.7	241.000	225
	Average	16.03	13.37	7,088.24	6.62

5.2.2 Household-wise Production Data

HH Nos.	Buck-wheat (pathi)	Maize (pathi)	Paddy (pathi)	Millet (pathi)	Sorghum (pathi)	Roots (kg)	Cardamom (Mound)	Orange (pond)
09-01	0	150	80	80	80	150	0	30
10-02	0	100	0	40	100	100	5	400
11-03	80	180	160	160	160	180	0	300
12-04	200	80	150	40	40	100	0	50
13-05	20	60	40	30	40	130	3	60
14-06	0	80	100	160	40	150	3	500
15-07	0	30	0	100	200	200	0	100
16-08	0	100	100	40	100	150	0	300
17-09	0	60	60	0	40	50	6	150
18-10	0	60	0	40	0	160	0	400
19-11	105	100	50	50	80	60	1	0
20-12	0	150	150	60	60	100	2	500
21-13	0	200	0	160	80	150	0	0
22-14	0	40	80	240	160	170	2	50
23-15	0	80	100	50	240	100	0	200

(contd. . . .)

(*contd. . . .*)

HH Nos.	Buck-wheat (pathi)	Maize (pathi)	Paddy (pathi)	Millet (pathi)	Sorghum (pathi)	Roots (kg)	Cardamom (Mound)	Orange (pond)
24-16	0	60	0	80	80	100	11	100
25-17	0	50	60	80	80	80	1	0
26-18	0	60	0	50	80	100	1	100
27-19	0	150	0	5	520	80	1	0
28-20	0	100	130	80	240	30	2	500
29-21	0	40	0	200	80	100	2	0
30-22	80	100	50	50	80	180	2	0
31-23	0	150	0	160	200	100	1	300
32-24	0	160	0	80	120	100	3	100
33-25	60	100	100	80	50	130	3	0
34-26	100	80	200	60	60	100	3	100
35-27	50	90	0	60	60	120	2	30
36-28	0	100	100	60	160	160	1	0
37-29	0	80	150	30	80	20060	2	0
38-30	0	350	0	100	400	150	1	300
39-31	0	300	0	240	100	150	20	500
40-32	0	120	150	60	100	100	3	100
41-33	0	0	50	60	0	80	0	100
42-34	0	0	0	0	0	10	2	0
Total	695	3560	2060	2675	3910	23880	83	5270
Avg.	20.44	104.71	60.59	78.97	111.71	702.35	2.44	155

5.2.3 Livestock

House-holds	Ox	Cow	Goat	Hens & Cocks	Pig	Horse	Total
09-01	2	4	0	6	0	0	12
10-02	2	5	0	6	0	0	13
11-03	2	6	3	10	1	0	22
12-04	2	2	1	0	1	0	6
13-05	0	0	0	6	0	0	6
14-06	2	7	2	6	0	0	17
15-07	2	3	3	4	0	0	12
16-08	1	3	0	4	0	0	8
17-09	2	2	0	0	0	0	4
18-10	0	0	3	0	0	0	3
19-11	2	7	0	4	0	0	13
20-12	1	0	1	3	0	0	19
21-13	0	0	1	3	0	0	4
22-14	4	8	0	9	1	2	24
23-15	1	3	0	4	0	0	8
24-16	1	1	0	3	0	0	5
25-17	0	2	0	3	0	0	5
26-18	2	2	0	4	0	0	8
27-19	0	0	2	4	1	0	7
28-20	2	2	1	4	1	0	10
29-21	2	10	0	3	0	0	15
30-22	4	5	2	6	1	0	18
31-23	2	7	0	4	0	0	13
32-24	0	3	2	5	0	0	10
33-25	0	3	0	4	0	0	7
34-26	2	2	3	4	1	0	12
35-27	2	0	2	5	1	0	10
36-28	2	1	0	6	0	0	9

(*cont.* . . .)

(*cont. . . .*)

House-holds	Ox	Cow	Goat	Hens & Cocks	Pig	Horse	Total
37-29	3	3	0	4	0	0	10
38-30	2	1	0	6	0	0	9
39-31	2	10	0	15	1	0	28
40-32	2	5	1	5	0	0	13
41-33	2	3	3	6	1	0	15
42-34	0	2	3	5	0	0	10
Total	53	116	35	168	11	2	385
Average	1.56	3.41	1.03	4.94	0.32	0.06	11.32

ANNEXURE 5.3: STATISTICAL DATA OF SANGLUNG

5.3.1 Household-wise Statistical Data

Sl. No.	Head of Household	Family Members	Land Holding (Acreage)	Annual Income (Rs)	Foodgrain Sufficiency (Month)
44-01.	Dugjon	8	19.00	5,000	6
45-02.	Dugjey	5	33.44	5,000	6
46-03.	Matob	5	13.72	6,000	5
47-04.	Chimidoji	4	18.60	3,000	5
48-05.	Punah	7	25.40	2,000	7
49-06.	Sakezang	4	12.40	10,000	5
50-07.	Hidoji	3	29.46	4,000	6
51-08.	Pento	3	23.48	5,000	6
52-09.	Tashi penjo	11	15.75	4,000	2
53-10.	Chentob	1	22.39	2,000	6
54-11.	Pedo	39	47.72	5,000	7
55-12.	Tshering aedu	9	45.80	7,000	6
56-13.	Sarshopkota	22	2.49	6,000	7
57-14.	Dankachen	11	17.62	7,000	4
58-15.	Imbo	13	25.99	4,000	6
59-16.	Nam Tshering	14	29.80	6,000	6
60-17.	Gampu	9	20.59	6,000	6
61.18.	Saridoji	4	22.79	6,000	9
62.19.	Yesheydoji	1	22.41	9,000	7
63.20.	Passa	11	23.34	7,000	7
64.21.	Kuchu	7	28.45	7,000	7
65-22.	Kangkop	2	41.08	8,000	8
66-23.	Dungchap	11	89.54	6,000	6
	Total	2167	631.26	130,000	141
	Average	94.22	27.45	5,652.17	6.13

5.3.2 Household-wise Production Data

House-hold Nos.	Buckwheat (pathi)	Paddy (pathi)	Maize (pathi)	Millet (pathi)	Sorghum (pathi)	Roots (Kg)	Cardamom (Mound)	Orange (pond)
43-01	160	0	40	40	90	180	3	150
44-02	0	0	120	80	150	120	0	250
45-03	0	0	70	0	50	90	0	30
46-04	80	60	60	0	360	180	0	0
47-05	0	100	120	40	40	120	2	500
48-06	0	0	40	0	90	60	3	50
49-07	200	0	40	40	180	70	0	300
50-08	240	0	180	40	90	200	2	50
51-09	80	0	90	0	130	30	0	100
52-10	0	0	360	120	270	250	4	200
53-11	0	130	180	80	90	210	3	60
54-12	0	160	180	0	90	230	1	50
55-13	0	250	60	40	0	60	4	200
56-14	0	0	40	0	140	200	4	20
57-15	0	150	120	40	90	250	4	50
58-16	0	125	60	40	50	90	6	500
59-17	0	130	120	80	90	100	1	50
60-18	100	0	120	40	50	60	1	100
61-19	0	160	300	0	90	10	7	50
62-20	240	0	180	0	80	120	0	0
63-21	0	0	100	40	80	120	3	0
64-22	160	0	120	0	90	80	0	400
65-23	160	0	180	40	90	200	0	500
Total	1420	1265	2880	760	2480	3030	48	4060
Avg.	61.74	55	125.22	33.04	107.83	131.74	2.09	176.52

5.3.3 Livestock

House-holds	Ox	Cow	Goat	Hens & Cocks	Pig	Horse	Total
43-01	0	0	0	6	0	0	6
44-02	0	0	0	4	0	0	4
45-03	0	0	0	3	0	0	3
46-04	2	1	0	3	0	0	6
47-05	2	6	0	3	0	0	11
48-06	2	0	0	3	0	0	5
49-07	0	10	0	4	0	4	18
50-08	4	0	0	4	1	1	10
51-09	2	1	0	3	0	0	6
52-10	0	0	0	3	0	0	3
53-11	0	5	0	3	1	0	9
54-12	2	2	0	6	0	1	11
55-13	3	7	0	4	0	1	15
56-14	0	4	0	3	2	0	9
57-15	0	4	2	4	0	0	10
58-16	2	5	0	3	0	1	11
59-17	1	3	0	3	0	0	7
60-18	1	0	0	3	0	0	4
61-19	0	5	2	4	0	0	11
62-20	1	5	0	4	2	0	12
63-21	2	0	0	4	0	0	6
64-22	0	3	0	5	1	0	9
65-23	2	0	0	4	0	0	6
Total	26	61	4	86	7	8	192
Average	1.13	2.65	0.17	3.74	0.3	0.35	8.35

ANNEXURE 5.4: STATISTICAL DATA OF SATAKHA

5.4.1 Household-wise Statistical Data

Sl. Nos.	Head of Household	Family members	Land holding (acreas)	Annual Income (Rs)	Food grain sufficiency (months)
66-01	Daw Tshering	6	16.45	2,000	5
67-02	Himtenji	6	13.25	3,000	6
68-03	Nando	27	28.77	7,000	8
69-04	Pudum Tshering	13	0	6,000	6
70-05	Pa Tshering	10	9.20	6,000	6
71-06	Namajey doji	14	34.10	8,000	8
72-07	Jep Tshering	7	29.60	5,000	7
73-08	Senam doji	45	61.05	25,000	7
74-09	Kasadau	23	12.20	12,000	8
	Total	151	188.17	74,000	61
	Average	16.78	17.69	8,222.22	6.78

5.4.2 Household-wise Production Data

HH No.	Buck-wheat (Pathi)	Maize (Pathi)	Paddy (Pathi)	Millet (Pathi)	Sorghum (Pathi)	Roots (kg)	Cardamom (Mound)	Orange (Pound)
66-01	0	80	120	60	0	80	0	100
67-02	80	160	100	0	0	180	1	0
68-03	80	140	180	30	0	100	15	50
69-04	0	100	120	160	0	140	1	0
70-05	80	120	0	80	0	150	1	20
71-06	200	150	140	50	0	160	1	350
72-07	60	60	60	50	0	60	1	20
73-08	100	200	350	150	0	60	6	800
74-09	40	20	200	50	0	80	1	350
Total	640	1030	1270	630	0	1010	27	1690
Avg.	71.11	114.44	141.11	70	0.0	112.22	3	187.78

5.4.3 Livestock

House-hold Nos.	Ox	Cow	Goat	Hens & Cocks	Pig	Horse	Total
66-01	2	0	0	3	0	6	11
67-02	2	0	0	4	0	2	8
68-03	0	3	0	6	1	0	10
69-04	0	1	1	5	1	0	8
70-05	2	1	0	4	1	2	10
71-06	0	7	0	4	1	4	16
72-07	2	0	0	20	1	1	24
73-08	6	20	0	3	3	6	38
74-09	2	2	6	1	1	2	14
Total	16	34	7	50	9	23	139
Average	1.78	3.78	0.78	5.56	1	2.56	15.44

ANNEXURE 5.5: STATISTICAL DATA OF LAPCHEYGOAN (RAI VILLAGE)

5.5.1 Lapcheygoan (Rai-Nepali) Village

Sl. No.	Head of Household	Family Members	Land Holding (Acreage)	Annual Income (Rs)	Foodgrain Sufficiency (Month)
75-01	Misraj	11	8.32	7,000	8
76-02	Tikadhan	7	39.00	8,000	5
77-03	Dhan Bahadur	8	5.39	15,000	7
78-04	Purnadoj	16	13.02	6,000	6
79-05	Bartalal	10	10.18	6,000	5
80-06	Suk Bahadur	8	3.05	3,000	5
81-07	Judabir	7	7.55	2,000	12
82-08	Rtnadoj	4	1.40	2,000	8
83-09	Amrit	1	7.54	3,000	4
84-10	Roopdoj	6	1.65	2,000	3
85-11	Dhan Bahadur	8	8.55	1,000	6
86-12	Prithidoj	9	4.30	2,000	5
87-13	Jangadoj	18	2.49	20,000	4
88-14	Manbir	8	5.75	5,000	7
	Total	121	i18.19	82,000	84
	Average	8.64	8.44	5,857.14	6

5.5.2 Household-wise Production Data

HH No.	Buck-wheat (Pathi)	Paddy (Pathi)	Maize (Pathi)	Millet (Pathi)	Sorghum (Pathi)	Roots (kg)	Cardamom (Mound)	Orange (Pound)
75-01	0	150	120	120	0	0	2	70
76-02	0	0	60	50	0	0	3	200
77-03	120	200	40	0	0	60	0	1000
78-04	80	0	70	50	0	0	0	0
79-05	-	-	70	50	0	0	0	0
80-06	0	0	0	0	0	0	0	0
81-07	100	50	90	160	10	0	0	50
82-08	0	0	40	0	0	0	0	20
83-09	0	0	0	0	0	0	0	0
84-10	0	0	80	0	0	0	0	100
85-11	20	0	240	40	10	0	0	50
86-12	100	0	240	100	40	0	1	50
87-13	200	50	120	0	40	0	2	150
88-14	0	0	0	0	0	0	0	0
Total	620	450	1170	570	100	60	8	1690
Avg.	44.29	32.14	83.57	40.71	7.14	4.29	0.57	120.71

5.5.3 Livestock

House-hold Nos.	Ox	Cow	Goat	Hens & Cocks	Pig	Horse	Total
75-01	2	1	2	5	2	0	12
76-02	3	1	0	3	1	0	7
77-03	2	3	3	4	1	0	13
78-04	2	2	0	4	1	0	8
79-05	1	2	2	4	0	0	9
80-06	2	2	1	3	1	0	19
81-07	0	6	1	3	3	0	13
82-08	3	0	2	3	1	0	9
83-09	0	6	0	6	1	0	13
84-10	0	1	6	0	5	0	12
85-11	0	2	0	3	1	0	6
86-12	0	2	1	4	1	0	8
87-13	0	4	1	3	2	0	10
88-14	0	0	6	5	1	0	12
Total	14		32	49	21	0	141
Aerage	1	2.29	1.79	3.5	1.5	0.0	10.07

CHAPTER 6

Summary and Conclusion

Doyas are an indigenous and socially distinct group of mongoloid people in Bhutan. They have been existent in the southern Bhutan as *Kepoti* (Nepali term meaning 'original inhabitants') since time immemorial.

There are various myths regarding the origin of Doya people and their relation with other groups of people in their surroundings. Some of these myths share similarities with the Monpas and many other indigenous people in the Himalayan region. There are many factual and oral traditions which tell that Doyas lived in a vast area between south-western hills of Bhutan and adjacent plains of North Bengal under their domain. They claim to have their affinity with that of Totos in Totapara in North Bengal but any physical and social relation between the two communities had been cut off from each other for long enough now to find it difficult for the people to relate among themselves. A recent linguistic studies has shown that the Doya language is more closer to the Monpas, Lepchas, Rai and Newaris spoken in the Himalayan region.

Socio-cultural and political history of the east Himalayan region amply prove that Doyas are a segmented group from a large ethnic background whose identities seem to have disintegrated in obscurity.

Doyas are today a predominantly mixed population. Genealogical studies of the people have shown various instances where the Drukpas and Nepalese men married some of the Doya women in the past and present generations. Progenies of such inter-community marriages comprise a considerable proportion of the present population. Such marriages seem to have helped continuation of Doya society from total disorganisation and the problem of near extinction sometime in their memorable past although; the descendants of these inter-marriages are not fully accepted in their traditional society.

Descendants of Doya-Nepali conjugations are labeled as Danchat and they are kept socially segregated from the rest of the conservative society. However, the descendants of Drukpa-Doya women are accommodated without any much discrimination.

Controversies over the name of this group of people itself are an indication of the current socio-political dynamics to which the people are being exposed. It is enough to highlight the facts that the different names employed to call the people originate from different cultural perspectives through which the people have been known and interpreted from time to time. Lhop (Lhops used in plural sense) is a Dzongkha term for the south. The Drukpas who inhabit the northern highlands employ this term for the people dwelling in the south. Doya seem to a derivative of a Sanskrit word *daya,* which is commonly used in Nepali language also. Nepalese who migrated into the region accorded this term for the generous and kind people who welcomed them to settle in south Bhutan as neighbours. Lhopu, is also a Tibeto-Burman term, meaning *southern dwellers*. The people, however, prefer to be known as Lhopu. Nevertheless, these names are geo-specific and interpreted from different cultural perspectives. Hence, none of these names can be said to be ethnonym of the people. Prominence of any of these names of the people at a particular time in the past also speaks much about the cultural influence on these people. The people are predisposed to an identity crisis whether they realise it or not the future generation will research for themselves.

There have been disruptions in Doya people's way of life affecting their physical, social and cultural aspects in coping with many a crisis situation in the past which resulted in assimilation of many cultural traits and practices from others and corruptions in traditional social norms and practices. Nevertheless, the distinctive nature of their cultural tradition persists with a distinct language still spoken even against strong currents of acculturation processes from the national mainstream in the country and current of Hindu cultural traditions from the southern Nepali migrants. There are indications that some sort of cultural revivalism will ensue among the Doyas in near future to assert their distinctive cultural identity and redefine their ethnic relations with others.

The first batch of people who went to school in 1960s are retiring in their villages after getting exposed many different communities in

Bhutan while serving the Royal Government at different places. These retired people vocally take pride in being Lhopu and the Lhopu-ness in their ways of life as compared to others. This is quite contrary to the general impression and feelings about the people of being lowly and unworthy among the older generation of people themselves.

The Satakha or Satank group of people who are mostly Danchats are making a lead by becoming an influential and dominant section of people in Lhopus affairs despite social discrimination they suffer from the rest of their society.

Lhopu society is organised along matrilineal descent groups or Riihs wherein descendant females are permanent resident of matrilineal households, Makim. Males take resident in wife's household after marriage. The Makim is a centre around which males assume important roles to maintain and continue the matrilineage and the society at large. The Riih title is transmitted through female lines only. A consanguinal unit of at least a son and daughter is the ideal unit of the society which can reproduce only when the son and daughter find their conjugal partners to reproduce children who would in turn undergo preferred conjugal relations among themselves to reproduce and form a society of their kind. In absence of such prescribed conjugal partners on the cross cousin's sides the continuation of the lineage is affected by either bringing a male of any other matrilineage home or in case there is no young female in a household, any marriageable male in the household get a woman for his wife from another matrilineage through a process of transmutation to continue the matrilineage. There are several Riihs with different titles. Each Riih has its origin and associated deities. These deities are worshipped at regular intervals to express lineal solidarity and seek blessings for general well-being of all under a Riih. There may be one or more segments of a single Riih located at different territories or at different places within the same territory all of who can be linked to one or several Makims under the same Riih title.

Although, Doya society is supposed to be exogamous matrilineages (Riih) society intra-matrilineage marriages have also been observed. This makes us surmise if the society is also organised along segmentary intra-matrilineage system with a specific generational spacing among the descendant generations. However, imbalance in the sex ratio among the lineages and disproportionate population situation for the execution of ideal rules of marriages also seem to have forced upon frequent lineage endogamy under a single Riih title even among parallel cousins of mothers side to somehow continue the lineage groups in adverse demographic situation.

Although, Riih endogamy seems to have become necessary for the survival and continuity of matrilineage, the unfavourable demographic situation seems to have also caused aberrations and corruptions in the traditional norms of conjugal relations among the people.

Each descent group under a Makim possesses certain area of land scattered at several places. Each member of the descent group irrespective sex has equal access and usufruct right of the land according to an agreed allocation arrangement among the descendant consanguinal families. Decisions relating to lineal properties are taken mainly among the adult members of matrilineage comprising of mother, sons and daughters under a Makim. Production is shared between extended consanguinal families and Makim. Married sons also contribute their share of labour and food grain to the Makim or seek help at times of hardship. Land is inherited through the consanguinal group and distributed among the segmentary lineages of sisters.

The intense intra-territorial and intra-Riih marriages among the segmentary groups seem to support the corporate nature of social organisation and its management of land and members of descent groups closely around themselves, at different levels. Solidarity in such group levels is expressed in the household ancestral deities, lineal and territorial deities. The group sentiment at different spatial and lineal levels is also expressed in the local idiom, *Rang* yo *ka notsum itpo.* Elders including women in a congregation such group acts as social control device at times of social crises. Thus, territorial groups comprising of many lineal and sub-lineal descent groups have different titles by the virtue of their residence in different villages and geographical locations. Further, these territorial groups under different common titles are not exclusive groups as one or two segments of Riihs may be found commonly in two or all the villages under different territorial titles but they would have their allegiance to their own lineal solidarity. Moreover, inter-territorial matrimonial ties among these territorial groups are also observed. Each level of group division on different criteria is associated with strong sense of 'we' and 'they' feeling and antagonism of varying degree at various social occasions.

It is often said among the people themselves that they are quarrelsome people. Here it may be said that the very dynamics of Lhopu society is the active division of people for different reason on one hand and on the other active consolidation and solidarity of descent groups round a matrilineage Makim for its control over the resources and interest in the perpetuity of the corporate group. Hence, the annual ancestral and deities worship around a Makim holds its own importance. A Makim with its resident-husband and matrilineal female is the structural and functional unit of Lhopu society under the prescription of matrimonial rules. This close group is also the group among whom the males are exchanged. Lhopu society does not have distinct marriage exchange groups as in the case of other simple society.

The inheritance of property through the members of this group ensures conservation of resources and a relative economic independence and mutual cooperation among the extended consanguinal units under a Makim.

Lhopu type of kin terms and relation is special requiring further field and academic inquiries. According to the Lowie and Kirchhoff system of classification Doya cases sounds like Bifurcate Collateral but when the same case is seen through the Murdock's cousin typology it matches with the Iroqouis type in their basic features. However, the tendency to equate cross-cousins with that of parallel cousins on the maternal side makes the Doya case uncomfortable in both the systems of classifications.

Doya response to the questions of life and death is based on simple facts of life experiences. Anything beyond the simple facts of life and their logic of similarities and association is relegated to the realm of supernatural powers to whom they trust their lives and sustenance.

Male and female are indispensable parts of the facts of life. Male is compared with the seed or rain for their mobility and potent, and female is compared with soil, the of basis life on the mundane world. Conception and birth of a child are as natural as pollination and fruiting of seeds on the plants but they are very important events or the driving force in their social and individual life. Death is a painful separation between the known ways of life and unknown. The unknown is to the super natural as death is to the unknown. The question: why does death come at all in their life scares the concern surviving individuals, humbles them for moments of reflection on the questions of death and integration of what is known and the unknown for all the explanations and answers to carry forth the life in their society.

The economy of the region is fast being overtaken by Market economy from subsistence livelihood pattern of exchange and barter system. The traditional technology and attitudes do not match the deteriorating environmental situation and increasing demands from the growing population with the improvements in the health situation of the people. Average annual food sufficiency for each household has gone to a low of only six months a year. People are getting tempted to possess more and more manufactured household articles from the markets right from building materials to day-to-day use commodities including food luxurious items. There is an increasing tendency of people turning to cash crop cultivation and private ownership of such assets. Those people who have no suitable land for developing cash crops are finding lots of difficulties in their livelihood. People in general are indulging in living on credits of the business community and better offs among themselves to meet their basic needs of food and drinks. Resultantly more and more people are getting caught into a debt chain, giving rise to a peculiar situation of acute indebtedness among the people. Today, Lhopu people are exposed to many a disturbing factors that might have far reaching social consequences even before they realise it themselves.

Lhopus need an enabling environment for their development without any cultural prejudices from outside. They need to be treated as equals to recognise and appreciate their distinct cultural identity. Holistic educational and development approach and facilities aimed at ennobling and enabling them develop scientific temperament and human capabilities and sensitivity to others in their surrounding and natural environment will greatly help in the development processes of the people.

Glossary

Adhiya	A system of distribution on 50:50 basis (Nepali term)
AmMochu	River Toorsa in Dzongkha language
Ba-sing	Bamboo
Bee	Flour
Behpa	Idiot
Belheng	A bamboo tumbler for drinking local brew
Binchat	A title for the residents of Lotukuchu and Lotok among the Doyas
Bindin	*Riih* deity of *Binchat* lineage
Boh	Soil
Bongpa/Tingma	Parallel cousin brother and sister who get into conjugal relation. This is a term for reference
Bongteng	Parallel cousin relationship
Bupsop	Land dwelling snail
Burr	An esculent root
Chabu	A cutting knife
Chachang	A sieve made of fine bamboo strips
Chakto	Sorghum
Changsing	A medicinal shrub used for ritual ablution purposes
Chatub	A stirrer made from twigs of a tree. It is used for processing food.
Chen/Rombu	Burial mound
Chiptok and tumbu	A pestle and mortar

Chu/chan	Grandchildren
Chuisey	Squash
Chutek	Measles
Da-hol	A pestle made of wood for churning milk
Danchat	Offspring of Nepali and Doya inter-marriages
Dasho Dzongdag	Head of district administration equivalent to district collector (DC) in Indian Administration
Denchukha	A block under Dorokha subdivision
Dharam raja	Religious head of the dual administrative system of Bhutan
Dii	Salt
Dillang	Name of a residential site in lower Lotukuchu
Ding	A term for plain land
Dokhun	An ethnic community among the Rais
Dorokha	Name of a sub-division under Samchi/Samtse district
Doya bura	A Nepali term for an old Doya man
Doya juwain	A Nepali term for a resident-husband in a Doya family
Dugya-Mungya	A term for cross-cousin matrimonial relationship
Dungkhang	Sub-divisional Headquarters in the national language
Drukpa Kague	A sect of Mahayana Buddhism in Bhutan established by Phajo-Drukgon-Shigpo (1232AD)
Dzongkha/Zhungkha	The national language of Bhutan.
Dzongkhag	District administrative office
Eechan/Geynea	A term for household deities
Elhni	Good/working day for survivors of deceased family.
Ewui	A residential unit /local/locality with indigenous connotation
ewui ka jarlo	Local food grains

Gelong	Junior lama
Gaada	A traditional dress of Doyas
Gemba	A term for large earthen pot
Geypa	Witch doctor/Sorcerer in Dzongkha language
Gho/Kyira	National dress of Bhutan. *Gho* is for man and *Kyira* for woman
Goish	Sickle
Gomchen	Name of the *Namba* clan deity
Gondo-wu-la	Free labour service for the state
Gonkey	A title used by Taba-Ramteykha group of Doyas for the Lotukuchu group of Doyas
Guchat	A title for the Doyas residents of Sanglung
Gumba Gurubabu	A term for teacher in Nepali language
Ha	Name of a district to the North of Samchi/Samtse in Bhutan
Halum and tok	A term for milk churning cylinder
Hapa	People of Ha district in Bhutan
Hatt	A weekly market
Hinto	Evening meal
Jaadan	A title for the Bengalis living in the Indian plains adjacent to Bhutan
Jaldhaka	A river that flow between Sikkim and Bhutan border. It is called *Jiti* in Doya
Jarto	Millet
Jaru	A service spoon made of bamboo
Jikpu	Fireplace in a household
Jimpey	Lineage deity of *kordang*
Jin	A string/thread for stitching
Jiten	A carrying basket
Jiti	River Jaldhaka in Lhokpu/Doya language
Jig	Jaguar

Jopsey Jungka	A bitter-gourd shell used for storing seeds and fermentation Pumpkin
Kamchal	A stream flowing between Satakha and Sanglung
Karbari	Village head nominated by administration
Kek	A cock
Kenduma	Local deity in Satakha
Kersey	Buckwheat
Kheng	Another ethnic community in Bhutan
Kim	A house
Kimbur	*Moracease-mores levigata:* a timber tree
Kong	Tiger
Ku	Maternal uncle
Kuensel	A weekly newsletter
Kulik	A bamboo ladle
Ku-me/Ni-me	Father's sister and her husband
La	A makeshift house
Lama	Monk in Dzongkha language
Laskey, Namba, Himajang, Humchat, Metchat Dohtak, Ruischat, Binchat, Kordang, Dingchat Dupsont, Konsiring, Asonk,	Names different lineage among the Doyas
Lehdan	A title for plain dwellers on the Indian side
Lei-la	Wage labour
Lhang	Eagle
Lhokong	Name of a hillock in the Doya territory
Lepcha	Ethnic group of people residing in Bhutan and Sikkim
Leysant	Residents of lower Lotukuchu village among the Doyas

Lha	High god
Lhakey	A name for the Drukpas and Tibetans given by the Doyas
Lhira/Lhimet	A term of reference for cross-cousins on mother's side
Lhokpu	Doya language
Lhopu/Lhop	Another name for the Doyas in Bhutan
Lhotsham	Nepali language in Dzongkha
Lhotshampa	Nepali migrants in the south of Bhutan in Drukpa language
Lhuk	Fox
Lipto	Night meal
Li-sing	Cane
Lo	A new year
Loha	Frying pan made of pig iron
Lohbol	Tapioca
Lotok	An extension of Lotukuchu residential territory in the east
Lotukuchu	Name of a residential territory
Lungma	Husband's sister/sister-in-law
Lusing	An aromatic plant with *(Antemisic vulgaris)*
Madesi	A name for tea garden labourers
Mahnkpa	A resident-husband
Makim	The main household
Mamang	Rituals related with birth of a child
Mayu/Payu	Mother/father
Maika-Tashi	Mark put on the forehead in ritual occasions *(Tikka* in Nepali).
Metchan	Daughter
Met-hin	Wife
Mihgoe	A mythical figure/humanlike giant creature popularly known as Yeti in English

Minstang	Naming ceremony of newborn child
Mitchi	A time span of a generation
Monpa	Another ethnic group of people in eastern Bhutan
Moti	River Toorsa/AmMochhu
Moti-chio	Toorsa river water used essentially for rituals
Murris	Chili
Nama	Son's wife/daughter-in-law
Namba	Name of a lineage *(Riih)*
Nangsey	A folk song sung during slash and burn activities
Nehdag	A local deity in Sanglung
Newari	A dialect of *Newari community* in Nepal
Nganka	Others
Nubara	A *ritual* of mutual *exclusion* in a quarrel between two groups.
Orlhung/Lhungma	Local deity in Lotukuchu
O-roh	Term of address to one's husband/others with respect
Pa-chi/Ga-da	Doya traditional dress *Pa-em* Bamboo shoots
Pama/Geypa	Local witch doctor
Pang	Paternal uncle
Pank	A pig
Panksang	Ablution rite on the naming ceremony of child
Payung	Bamboo blade used for cutting umbilical cord
Penlop	Political head of a region nominated by religious head
Peychop	A land dwelling Snell
Phuntsholing	A commercial town-gateway to Bhutan
Poja	Boy
Porr	A bowl
Pu/na	Elder brother/sister
Pu-mike/Tsa-mike	Cross-cousin brothers on father's side

Ra-am	Rice
Ra-chan	Son
Ra-him	Husband
Rai	A low caste community of Nepali society
Rangka	Ours
Rihto	Night meal
Riih	A lineage
Rim	A needle made of bamboo
Rog	A cooking pot
Rosant	Residents of upper Lotukuchu village among the Doyas
Roung	A standard measuring basket
Ruish	Bone
Sa	Meat
Sa-(n)g	Green leafy vegetable
Sa-em	Edible variety of ferns
Sama	Placenta
Samchi/Samtse	Name of a district in the southwest of Bhutan
Sanglung	A residential territory next to Satakha
Sarmi	A title for the Taba-Ramteykha group of Doyas given by the Lotukuchu group
Satakha	A Doya village in the extreme west
Satank	A title/name for the residents of Satakha
Se-hok	Soul of a person
Selen	A flat tray made of bamboo
Sengsey	Beans
Sengten/Sengdhyen	Name of a block under Dorokha subdivision
Sharcop	Eastern Bhutanese people
Simpu	Another world after death
Simteng	A mortar of cylindrical log for pounding
Sing	Wood/tree

Sipsoo	Another subdivision under Samchi district in the southwest corner of Bhutan
Taba-Ramteykha	Another Doya residential site near Phuntsholing.
Tal	An eating plate
Tehphoo	A section of people originating from the Duars who once ruled Bhutan before the advent of the Drukpas
Tenglha	*Namba* and *Kordang* lineage deity
Tibuk	A bamboo cylinder for carrying water
Todey tanka	Name of a place in south of the present Doyas
To-kim	A high granary
Tol	A cradle/baby carrier
Tonk	A raised sleeping platform
Toorsa	A popular name among the Nepalese for AmMochhu or Moti river in the south-west of Bhutan.
Tra	A winnow
Tsa	Younger brother and sisters
Uripemo/Uripudal Yuhma/Chohminh	Local deities in Sanglung territory
Wank	Carrying basket made of cane and bamboo
Ya/Ta	Grandma and grandpa
Yonk	A shifting field
Yu	A local brew/drinks
Yu-tungmini	Ritual drinking on the naming ceremony of a newborn child
Zehni	Bad/nonworking day for the survivors of a deceased family
Zibdag	*Laskey* lineage deity

Select Bibliography

Books and Articles

Alan Barnard and Anthony, Good (1984), *Research Practices in the Study* of *Kinship,* as a Research Methods in Social Anthropology-2, Academic Press, London.

Aris, Michael (1980), *Bhutan: The Early History* of *A Himalayan Kingdom,* Vikas Publishing House, Ghaziabad.

Bose, K. K. (1815), An Account of Bootan. In: *Political Mission to Bootan,* Ashley Eden, H.K. Kuloy (ed.), Manjusri, New Delhi (1864).

Burling, Robbins (1956), Garo Kinship Terminology. In: *man in India,* Vol. 36, No.3, pp. 203-218.

Cantlie, Keith Sir (1974), *Notes on Khasi Law,* A.S. Khongphai, B.L. (Ed.), Aberdeen, Printed by Henry Munro Ltd. Privately distributed, 192 pp. Appendices.

Chakravarti, B (1980), *A Cultural History* of *Bhutan,* Chitaranjan, Hilltop Pubis. Calcutta.

Chattapadhyay, K.P. (1941), Khasi Kinship and Social Organisation. In: *University* of *Calcutta Anthropological Papers.* New Series, No.6, pp. 1-39.

Dalton, G (1965), Primitive Money, *Amestlan Anthropologist,* 67: 44-65.

Das Gupta, P. K. (1984), *Life and Culture* of *Matrinlineal Tribe* of *Meghalaya,* Inter-India Publications, New Delhi.

Das, Nirmala (1974), *Dragon Country: The General History* of *Bhutan.* Orient Longman, Bombay.

Dorji, C.T. (Dr) (1995), *A Political* and *Religious History* of *Bhutan* (1951-1906), Prominent Publishers, Delhi.

Durkheim, E. (1973), *On Morality and Society: Selected Writings,* ed. and with an introduction by Robert N. Bellah, Chicago Univ.

Durkheim, E. (1963), *Primitive Classification,* tran. from French and ed. with an Introduction by Rodney Needham, Cohen and West, London.

Eden, A (1864), *Political Mission to Bootan* H. Ko Kuloy (ed.), Manjusri, New Delhi.

Evans Pritchard, (1940), *The Nuer,* Oxford E.E.

Foning, R (1987), *Lepcha: My Vanishing Tribe,* Sterling Publishers, New Delhi.

Fortes, Meyer (1953), The Structure of Unilineal Descent Group. In: *American Anthropologist,* Vol. 59, No.1, pp. 17-41.

Fox, R (1974), *Kinship and Marriage: An Anthropological, Perspective,* Penguin, Harmondsworth, England.

Gordon, P.R.T. (1914), *The Khasis,* London.

Hasrat, Bikrama Jit (1980), *History of Bhutan,* Education Department, Royal Government of Bhutan, Thimphu.

Homans, G.C and (1955), *Marriage, Authority and Final Causes: A Study of Unilateral Cross-Cousin Marriage,* Glencoe, Free Press.

Hutton, J.H (1963), *Caste in India, its Nature, Function and Origin.* 4th Edition Univ. Press, London.

Karan, P. P. (1990), *Bhutan Environment, Culture and Development Strategy,* Intellectual Pubishing House, New Delhi.

Kirchhoff, P. (1931), Die Verwandtschaffsorganisation der Urwaldstamme Sudamerikas. z. *fur Ethnol.* 63, 85-193.

Leach, E.R (1954), The Structural Implications of Matrilateral Cross-cousin marriage, *J.R. anthrop. Inst.* 8(1 (also in Leach (1961a), pp. 54-104.

Levi-strauss, C. (1969), *The Elementary Structure* of *Kinship* (1949) English *trans.,* London.

Lowie, R.H. (1920), *Primitive Society,* New York: Horace Liveright - A Note on Relationship Terminologies.

Lowie, R.H. (1928), *American Anthropology,* 30, 263-268 - Relationship terms, *Encyclopedia Britanica* (14th edn.) 19, 84-86.

Maine, H.S. (1861), *Ancient Law,* London.

Majumdar, B. (1991), *The Doyas: A Small Community in Bhutan.* In: *Religion and Society in the Himalayas,* Tanka S. Subba and Karubaki Dutta (ed.), New Delhi.

Malinowski, B.K. (1922), *Argonauts of the Western Pacific,* New York.

Mehra, Dutton G.N. (1973), *Bhutan:Land of the Peaceful Dragon,* Vikas Publishing House, Pvt. Ltd. Delhi.

Mitchell, J.C. (1956), *The Yao Village,* Manchester University Press for the Rhodes-Livingstone Institute.

Morgan, L.H. (1870), *League* of *Iraquois* (1851): *Systems of Consanguinity and Affinity,* Washington, DC.

Murdock, G.P. (1949), *Social Structure,* New York, Macmillan.

Nakane, Chie (1961), *Garo and Khasi: A Comparative Study in Matrilineal Systems,* Mouton and Co. Paris.

Playfair, A. (1909), *The Garos,* London.

Polanyi, K. (1957), *Trade, Market in Early Empires,* Boston.

Roy Burman, B.K. (1958), *Dynamics* of *Persistence and Change of a Small Community - The Toto.* Unpublished Thesis, Calcutta Univ.

Roy, Sarat Chandra (1921 Khasi Kinship Terms. In: *Man in India,* Vol. I, pp. 233-238.

Sanyal, C.C. (1973), *Meches and Totos: Two sub Himalayan Tribes* of *north Bengal,* North Bengal University.

Schneider, D.M and Gough Kathleen (1961), *Matrilineal Kinship* (ed.), University of California Press, California.

Singh, Nagendra (1988), *Bhutan: A Kingdom in the Himalayas,* S. Chand and Co. Ltd., New Delhi.

Sunder, D.H.E. (1895), *Survey and Settlement* of *Western Duar in the District* of *Jalpaiguri,* Culcutta.

Van Gennep, Arnold (1960), *Rites-de-passage:* trans. from the French by Monika B. Vizedon and Gabriella L. Caffee, Chicago Univ.

Other Publications

Bhutan. *A Geography of Bhutan, Class-VI,* Education Department, Royal.

Bhutan. *A History of Bhutan: An Introductory Course for Class VI,* Department of Education, Royal Govt. of Bhutan, Thmiphu.

Bhutan. *Encyclopedia of SAARC Nations* (6), *Bhutan,* Verinder Grover (ed.), Deep and Deep Publication, New Delhi, 1997.

Bhutan. *Kuensel,* A Weekly Newsmagazine, Thimphu.

Bhutan. *The Southern Bhutan Problem: Threat to National Survival,* Ministry of Home Affairs, Royal Government of Bhutan, Thimphu, 1993.

Dictionary of Anthropology, Macmillan, London, 1987.

Government of Bhutan, Thimphu.

Himal Association, Nepal. *Himal,* a bimonthly magazine.

North and Northeastern Frontier Tribes, Intelligence Branch Division, Chief of Army Staff, H.Q., India, 1983.

Appendices

APPENDIX I

(i)

Ref No. DPS/DK/93/30D6

To

The Dzongkhag Education Officer

Dzongkhag Administration

Samtse, Bhutan

Dated: 19th September,1993

Sub: Submission of Article for N.I.E. Silver Jubilee celebration.

Dear sir,

I am herewith, forwarding an Article entitled, "**A report on Lhosu: Past and present**." Written by Mr. B. Deben Sharma, a teacher of this school. The matter in the article is authentic and original in itself

Please kindly go through the matter and do the needful.

Thanking you.

Enclosed: A copy of the Article.

Faithfully yours,

-sd -

(K. Chophel.)

Head teacher

Sengdhjyen Pry. School

Sengten, Dorokha Dungkhang.

(ii)

FAX No. 23550, 22578, 22627

Telephone. 22252, 22724, 22713

Gram: EDUCATION, TIMPHU

ROYAL GOVERNMENT OF BHUTAN

MINISTRY OF SOCIAL SERVICE

DEPARTMENT OF EDUCATION

Ref No. CAPSS/EDN/53/93/-5765 Date 30-9-93

Dear Mr. Sharma,

I am in receipt of your article on the Doyas for the NIE magazine (Silver Jubilee) sent to us by DEO, Samtse. In the Silver Jubilee magazine we were going to publish mainly the articles on pedagogical issues and experiences. so your article will not be published in that magazine.

However, I have found your account of the Doyas very interesting and I am certainly thinking of a possibility of publishing it separately. In fact, I was ordered to make a study on the same people and put it on record for future for which I intended to visit the area some time during the dry seasons. I am glad that you have done most of the works. Still, I think we will need to clarify a lot of points in this article and I will need your help. I will be keeping in touch with you on this matter.

Regards.

Yours sincerely,

Mr. Deben Sharma

Sengdhen Pry. School -sd -

Samtse Dzongkhong (Jagar DoIji)

Director, CAPSS

Copy to:-

1. DEO, Dzongkhag Administration, Samtse, for his kind information
2. O/C

APPENDIX II

SOME PERSONS AND PERSONALITIES

In the following pages I would introduce some persons and personalities, whom I know very well and with some of whom I stayed and had close association and interaction. They were my guides, friends and company throughout my stay among the Doyas. This is however, not an exclusive list of personalities I was associated with some of these persons will be often found referred to during the course of the text.

1. Tshering

Tshering (18 years) was a friendly, polite and obedient ex-student from Satakha. My first contact with him came when he was one of the six porters carrying Headmaster's and my luggage from Samchi (Samtse). He guided me on the way and brought me to the school safely on my first reporting. That year, in 1990 he was a student of mine in class-III. His father, Ngitenji (56 yr.) has 3 horses and he often earns by carrying things on the horses on holidays. Tshering has been very responsible student in the school. He was a captain of the school when we managed to bring him up to class-V in 1992. The same year he joined Samtse Primary School for the class-VI common exams but he could not pull on and dropped out from the school on Headmaster's warnings.

He then started looking after his father's horses and started earning by carrying loads from Samtse. Sometimes, when engaged he carries school supplies, too.

In the December vacation of the same year, he eloped with a Rai girl who was then in class-IV in the school. These, two had developed an affair while they were in the school. People often say Tshering would not have gone for a Nepali girl if he were not a student in the school. He had to face a tough time of social sanctions by his own parents and society. In the course of it, once, he had a quarrel with his father.

The girl's father, who was a popular Rai Bijuwa particularly among the Doyas as he treated the Doyas like equals and spoke some Doya language.

2. Po Tshering

Po Tshering (18 yr.) was another student in the school. Drukpa teachers in our school did not like to call him by this name because the word *'Po'* is a word for male sex organ in the national language, Dzongkha. So, they changed his name in the school to Phub Tshering. Po was also another obedient student in the school. My teacher colleague Mr. Karma Chophel with whom I shared quarter and kitchen, made Po to stay in our quarter to help us in our kitchen and maintenance of the quarter. Po liked staying and serving the teachers. To be with teachers he seems to find himself different from the rest of his friends. Once he found no vegetable to cook except some bulbs of ginger in the kitchen, so he gave us a ginger curry with lots of gravy. He was very curious about everything in the quarter we possessed so he used to amuse himself with each and every household article and clothes and other electronic gadgets, etc. Nothing escapes his curiosity in the quarter.

After having stayed with us for about a year, one day he asked me Sir, why do teachers always engage us in some personal works in a very thoughtful mood while we were cooking together. I said, that most often teachers are not able to do all their works themselves so they have to depend on their students. And who else would help them? He silently listened to it but did not further pursue the question. He is curious and an open-minded person if not treated strictly and sternly.

Po likes to lead a saintly life. He liked the daily prayers and takes special interest in it unlike many others. He passed class-V in 1992 and joined another Primary school at Dorokha sub-division for doing class-VI. In the same year, he also bashed up his own father due to certain differences. His father has two wives and he was Karbari of Satakha village till 1993. Po Tshering is second son of the first wife, he and his mother do not like his father always running to Lotukuchu and staying there off and on at his second wife's house. Po Tshering was doing class-VIII in Drugyal school in Paro. He often keeps in touch with me through letters.

3. Chhumlham

Chhumlham (14 years) was also a student who passed out from the school in 1992. She was in Tshering's batch who all went to join the Samchi Primary School for class-VI studies at the Dzongkhag H.Q. Samtse after passing out class V from Sengten primary school. She was the only girl among the Doyas who made to this standard. She was doing class-VII in Tseerang (Chirang) when I left Bhutan in 1995. Her father, Chedoji is a Doya but her mother Challamo is a daughter of a Rai woman who was also married to a Doya man. They were outcaste from the rest of the society for a long time till her mother's time. Chhumlham was sometimes, jeered by others calling her 'Danchat' (son and daughters of other Rai). She is the second daughter to her mother. She was good at studies unlike others. She is smart and intelligent. Like Chhumlham, all her brothers and sisters were better off and enterprising than anybody among the Doyas.

4. Kasadau

Kasadau (65 yr.) was Chhumlham's maternal uncle, who is also another Danchat. He brought Jengcha home for wife from Lotukuchu by paying for heavy ritual transaction with his wife's matrilineage household (female transmutation). He still, sent his married daughter to pay the triennial payment *(Nama)* for having bought his wife from her matrilineage. Kasadau has a brother and sister, Ganesh and Anima respectively. Kasadau was quite a respectable figure in Satakha village.

5. Sarsopkota

Sarsopkota (50 yr.) from Sanglung was married to Kopen of Satakha. He was proud father of 10 children. He owned a shop (sort of an inn) on the path to Samchi, 1 hour walk from the school. We used to make a stop-over at his shop every time went pass by while going to district HQ.

6. Chapchu

Chapchu (24 yr.) was the eldest son of Sarsopkota and Kopen. He was class-11 passed and married to Nimlham in the same village, Satakha. His wife's father Dung chap from Lotukuchu worked in the school as a cook. He did a Militia training course for six month during the 1991 Nepali uprisings in southern Bhutan. Later, he was absorbed as another temporary cook in the school on the behest of his father-in-law (Dung chap). He was one of my companion and an informant. He liked telling about his people's traditions and village. He often takes me to his village.

7. Lobey Tshering

Lobey Tshering (29 yr.) was Chhumlham's mother's brother's son. He married a lady in Satakha, (Manipem). He was also a source of information for a trusted friend and me. I carried a census survey with him. He works as peon in the school.

8. Kado Tshering

Kado Tshering (18 yr.) from Sanglung was a student of mine. He had many Ku(s) and Ni(s) who were all well known to me. One of his Ku(s), Chedoji was Chhumlham's father at Satakha. I stayed at Kado's house at many occasions. I did a biography of his grandma (Ya) who is reckoned to be around 120 years old and was the oldest living person among the Doyas. Kado was a good student, at times he tried to over smart his teachers so teachers used to find him quite a hard nut and challenging lad to deal with. He stood at odd among many who are generally submissive characters in the school. One of Kado's aunts was Chhumlham's mother's brother's wife.

9. Ujey Tshering

Ujey Tshering (40 yr.) was a militiaman, and generally popular as troubleshooter in the community. He became more so when he got trained himself as a militiaman in 1992 batch. He originally belongs to Lotukuchu but he is married to a lady in Sanglung. He was bold, a bit high handed, loyalist and native in character. He took pride in being Lhopu rather than to be called 'Doya' by other people. He had a lecherous tongue and can pick up trouble with anybody. He liked to be a militia leader so he does not leave the army dress all the time. In a couple of visits to his house he gave me some information about some local deities and rituals. He was good at performing rituals. But he is a difficult person at times he used to make me feel quite foreign and at time he shows submissive character. He liked talking about his people's culture and tradition. His role in the community along with some other militiamen was the main cause of inter-community tension after 1990 in the region. Because of his high handedness and over smartness in matters where he should not involve, he has had his share of bad impression in the locality.

10. Kangkop

Kangkop (70 yr.) was a Doya *Pama* (Shaman) but almost non-performing. He lived in Sanglung near Kado's house. He is believed to possess some antiques of magical paraphernalia. He was respectable figure for his knowledge about his people.

11. Madhubabu

Madhubabu (60 yr.) was a Rai Bijuwa (sorcerer). He lived just below the school hill. He was a very popular performing sorcerer both between the Rai and Doyas. He had many ceremonial friendship (Mit-friends with Doyas) of Satakha. Besides him there were three other popular Rai Bijuwa in the locality. They all had their own Mit-friends among the Doyas.

12. Hirangkanchha

Hirangkanchha (60 yr.) was another Bijuwa. He was perhaps the most popular Bijuwa among the Doyas particularly in Lotukuchu. He was never to be seen at home unless on one was very lucky to see him very early morning at his home. I enjoyed a very good relation with him. He treated me like his own son. I often met him in the villages and at one occasion I accompanied him in his performances in one Doya family at Lotukuchu. His daughter, Maina was married to Tshering at Satakha. Maina was also a student up to class-IV before she ran away with Tshering. Their marriage was not solemnised in both the communities. Tshering and Maina lived separately in Satakha village. Hirangkancha wanted Tshering's parents to recognise the marital relation and pay some social abeyances but it was deliberately suppressed from Tshering's parents.

13. Sakab

Sakab was an active and hard working 40 yr. old man. I came to know him very closely through his daughter Gori (later changed as Lhassang) who was a student of class-IV when I left the school. Sakab married two Doya ladies in Lotukuchu and later joined forest services as guard in Chukha district. He got posted in a place near Phuntsholing among the Nepalese and there he married with another Tamang lady. He then, left his job came back home and settled at his natal place with his Tamang wife and two daughters. He built the best house in the whole of the village with his earnings. He was a very hardworking man. He divorced his previous two Doya wives one after the other after paying fines *(Nama)*. His Tin-sheet-roofed double storied house is maintained most neat and clean one among the Doyas. He was one who built such a permanent house in Lotukuchu. He shared one of the two rooms in the first floor of his house for my stay at Dillang. Sakab often criticises his own people of being 'Junglees', 'dirty and fools'. Sakab is a son of Setah who is Karbari of Lower Lotukuchu. He fought with his parents for a piece of land. Sakab has got many sisters and two brothers. But his own people excommunicated him for quite long time for bringing and getting married with other caste people. But he alone struggled, survived and prospered with his wife.

14. Setah and Yimjem

Setah and Yimjem are parents of Sakab. Setah has been a Karbari for Lower Lotukuchu for three consecutive terms of three years. He was over 70 and a respectable figure among the people. He brought his wife Yimjem from Sanglung through migration process. So all his children carry his own matrilineage title (Riih) called *Namba. Nambas* were the descendants of the past Doya king. He was knowledgeable person in the village in elders' council. He often called me 'Chan' (Son) and told me lots of stories about past and present of Doyas. He was an important resource person for me. He liked to keep in touch with national and international events and development for which he often ask me about many things. He was quite concerned about the Nepali upheaval during 1990 and 1993. He did not like disharmony in the inter-community relation with the Rai. He saw Paro Penlop when he was young. He knew certain political situations the country faced during the Penlops' time in the country. They were under the rule of Paro Penlop. He used to be one of the porters from among the Doyas for carrying the loads from India (Chamurchi) for the Penlops. They used to tend Penlop's and Maharani's Ponies and cattle, make baskets for carrying Areca nuts for the Penlop from across the border to Denchukha - a track of three to four days from Chamurchi (India). Setah is proud father of 11 children including eight daughters and three sons. Two of his three sons were my students.

15. Dangkachen

Dangkachen (60 yr.) was Setah's mother's brother's son. He was also at Dillang. He was a DYT (Dungkhag Yargey Tshogsung) or a Head of a block comprising of seven (several) Karbaris village. He came to this high position not because of his own merit but because the administration wanted a Doya man to take the position for a change. This position had been with the Nepalese for long time. He became a DYT after 2 years of Karbariship for upper Lotukuchu although he belonged to Lower Lotukuchu. He was married to two of Setah's step-sisters. Before becoming DYT when he was asked to hand over the charge of Karbariship to another person, called Dipraj Doya who belonged to Upper Lotukuchu. He put up a strong protest against it by not surrendering the records and files to Dipraj although the later was already nominated by the administration. The previous headmaster of the school, who was also made the 'charge de-affairs' of the village administration in those days directly under the instructions of District Authority, helped Dangkachen sympathetically to the post of DYT in place of a Rai old man, Misraj. Although, Dangkachen was not so authoritative in his post, he liked to be a responsible person in the administration. A sense of fraternity prevails in his decisions for which he often had to bear the unpleasantness of his superiors in the administration and own people at times. Once, Sakab outrightly challenged his competence and campaigned against him for an alternative. But on the whole Sakab had to give up for he won social stigma for marrying Nepali and divorcing his Doya wives and children.

Dungkachen's son, Ujey Tashi died recently. He was drowned in *Moti* River, which flows just below their residential area while fishing. He left behind his wife and two kids at Upper Lotukuchu.

Kaflam was Dungkachen's second daughter still unmarried at age over 30. She along with Konkilang. Kaflam often sent me presents of eatables like fish and cheese through his youngest brother who was a student in the school.

16. Aedu Tshering

Aedu Tshering (50+ yr.) was the eldest brother of Dankachen. He had large land property. In his drunken state of mind he often told me about many controversial cultural and political matters of the Govt. of Bhutan concerning his people which others always tried to gag him even before completing any story. He often sang me a song that was related with painful past history of his tribe. Others often used to admonish, him not to talk too much. Most of the time, he lived down near the bank of Moti tending his land and cattle and crops. He remained a peculiarly outspoken person with lots of things to tell but others discouraged and despised him.

17. Dip Tshering

Dip Tshering (50+ yr.) was called 'Dipraj' just a year ago but under certain socio-political pressures from the authority he had to change his name. Otherwise, he was a liberal man by nature. He did not mind to be called by his previous name. He was quite free and frank jolly to talk about things and about his people. He became Karbari of Upper Lotukuchu. He helped me a lot in recording their traditional songs. He believed in communal harmony as a soft-spoken person by nature.

18. Jimi

Jimi (40+ yr.) was a simple and hardworking local orange dealer in Upper Lotukuchu. His simplicity won confidence of the district administrator and once he was given a contract of opening out a rough motorable road along the 'Damti' (Chamurchi Khola) for extracting logs from the forest. Out of his earnings he built one pukka double storied house with tin roof but could not complete it for a long time as he suffered in his business. Soon after a rise in popularity among the people his simplicity attracted many scoundrels from outside and he went bankrupt with loan debt of few lakhs. He seemed to be losing confidence of the local orange orchard owners who are mostly his own people for keeping their payment due for long time. I stayed in his house at the Upper Lotukuchu for about three-four months together after shifting up from Dillang.

19. Yangku

Yangku (70+ yr.) was a rich man with plenty of land and orchards. He was also counted as one of the knowledgeable elders in the village council. He was happy with his wisdom and property. He rarely goes out of the village. He too, had built a tin roofed house near Jimi's with his own earnings from his orchards. Jimi was also one of his debtors. He was an inveterate drinker but at seventies also he was fit at works. Most of the time he worked and looked after his fields and orchards and rarely comes up to his main house in Burtlhang, Upper Lotukuchu. He talked about many things even without asking. He liked me because I was a good listener. Yangku had an elder sister called Budu. When she was young, she served Dasho Dung pa (SDO) for many years. Now, she was old over 70s and lived alone in a small hut without a spouse.

20. Singey

Singey (80 yr.) was Yangku's elder brother. He was always in debt unlike his brother. He lived in the uppermost part of Lotukuchu along with his wife and children.

21. Ajey

Ajey (40+yr.) belonged to *Binchat Riih.* Her forefather, 'Bindin' a Pama was the originator of her *Riih.* She lived in Lotok and had mothered 12 children. Two of her matured young daughters died recently between 1992 -93 suddenly after a short sickness. She called me *chan.* She talked very freely. Three of her small kids were in the school who she entrusts me. She was quite a good folksinger even in her mourning time she obliges me with songs. I often visited her house and look into her difficulties. Her house was perched on the top of a cliff from where one can have glimpses of Phuntsholing town at a far distance in a clear weather day. Nearby her house her sisters; Chewang, Lhadem and Kabo lived in their own houses along their spouses and children.

22. Lhadem

Lhadem (40 yr.) was married with Jochung. Jochung is Jimi's cousin brother. Her eldest son Ugyen (19 yr.) was studying in the school. She called me *Payu* of her children at the school. They are very nice and hospitable to me. They were good guides for me.

23. Purna

Purna (11 yr.) was a student in Class-II when I left. He was son of Kabo and his father Tshering. Purna was my best companion. He was ever ready to go with me anywhere. From him I learnt many interesting rhymes, riddles and beliefs. He calls me *Pu* (brother).

APPENDIX III
DOYA (LHOKPU) LANGUAGE

Doyas speak an East-Himalayish[1] language called Lhokpu different from Dzongkha/Zhungkha, the National language of Bhutan, which is the mother tongue of the Drukpa.

Lhokpu language belongs to East-Himalayish[1] sub-branch and Dzongkha belongs to Tibeto-Kanauri sub-branches while both the language take roots from Bodic sub-division of Tibeto-Burman family of languages.

Besides their own mother tongue Doya speak Nepali language fluently and some of them can read and write the language as most of the official communications were done in the Devnagari scripts (Nepali) in the south of Bhutan, and only about 3% of the population could speak Dzongkha language also.

Some Verbs

Bipu	To borrow	*Dall*	To beat	*Dem*	To fold (cloth)
Guih	To close/shut	*Hon*	To open	*Hal*	To *dry* things
Ho	To fry	*Hahk*	To stir	*Hoot*	To see
Hint	To ask	*Chem*	To stitch	*Kai*	To throw
Ken	To get tired	*Kuchen*	To steal	*Leh*	To wash clean
Jap	Pain	*Rig*	To tiggle	*Rhigel*	To send
Sai	To wash with water	*Wall*	To mix	*Ten weh*	To paste
Nhoh	To think	*Tan*	To bring	*Yuh*	Come/go down
Yuh the	Take out	*Jam*	To chop/cut	*Lang-teh*	To fetch
Wi	To sleep	*Toh*	To dig	*Ret*	To feel pain
Jom	Make/draw				

1. I had an informal personal interview with the Assistant Professor, Van Dreim George, of the Amsterdum University who came down to the Doyas to study their language during my stay at Lotukuchu in 1992. He calls Doya language as Lhokpu.

TIBETO-BURMAN LANGUAGE

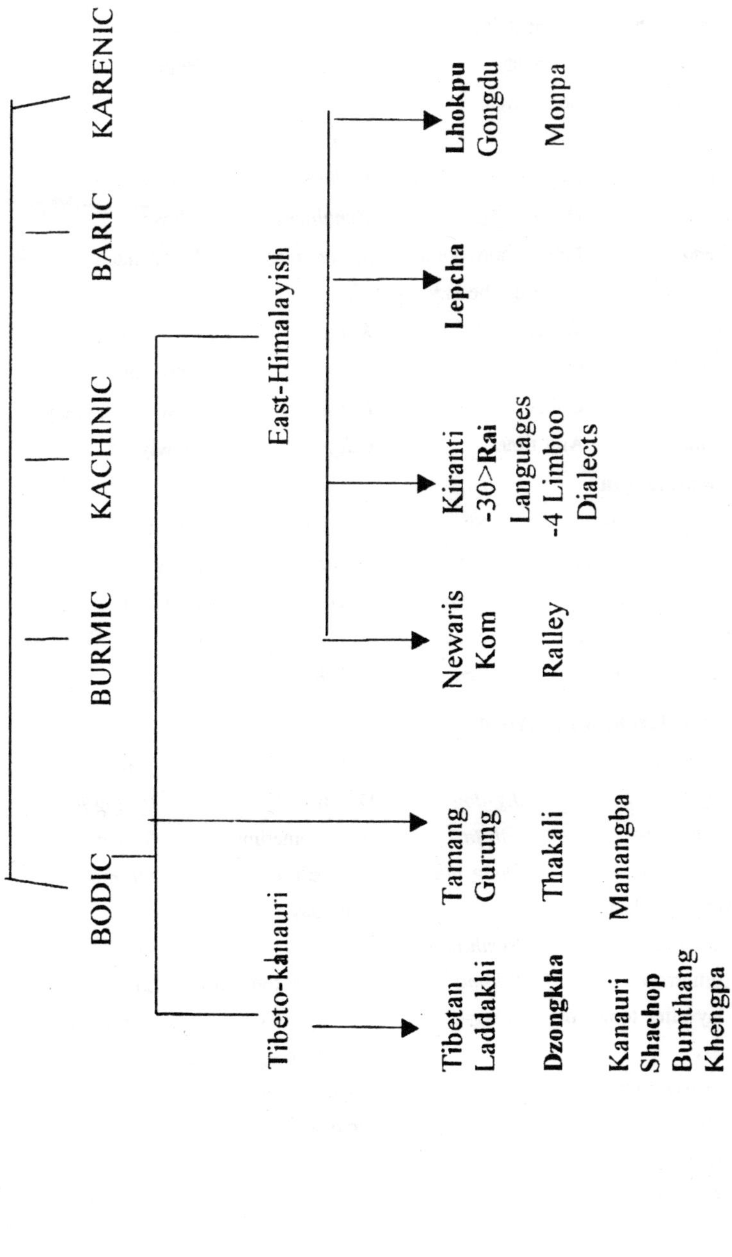

Some Grammar Words

Chitenjang	Always	*Ko*	She
Het la	When it is?	*Na*	You
Ne-ma	Everyday	*Na-ha*	Your
Reh-la-hela	Sometimes	*Ka*	I
Eyung	Little	*Ka-nga*	My/mine
Tah-ta	Right now	*Piklheng*	Below
Eley	Down	*Wenglheng*	Above
Kono	Lateral/horizontal	*Mang-yung*	More/much
Kowing	Towards the sky	*Eheng*	Up
Hetmi	Which one?	*Koley*	Downwards
Lamah	Quickly	*Koro*	Upwards
Nem	Cold	*Het-ten*	How much/many
Hetla-yang	Any time	*Odey*	Slowly

Numeration

One	*Itpo*	Six	*tukpu*	Twenty	*It kal*
Two	*Nihpo*	Seven	*Nit pu*	Forty	*Nihkal*
Three	*Sumpo*	Eight	*Getpu*	Hundred	*Itpul*
Four	*Lihpo*	Nine	*Kuhpu*	Half	*It chet*
Five	*Ha pu*	Ten	*Teh pu*		

Time Reckoning Words

Morning	*Rih-jig*	Evening	*Llpma*
Night	*Jig-dog*	Day time	*Hi-dog/hinting*
Right now	*Tah-ta*	After sometime	*Tah-yo*
Day before yesterday last	*Dong nih*	Day before yesterday	*Yar nih*
Yesterday	*Nemh-neh*	Today	*Tahi*
Tomorrow	*Rih-ma*	Day after tomorrow	*Eddi*
Day after tomorrow next	*Dong-di*	4th day from tomorrow	*Lah-di*
5th day from tomorrow	*Bed-di*	6th day from tomorrow	*Nuh-di*
Days	*Niih*	Year	*Nim*
Last year	*A-nim*	Next year	*Ben-nim*

Calendar Year

A cycle of years is made of 12 years. Each year is named after twelve animals which there own significance. A year is made of 12 months. The months have no name like that of English calendar but they are ordered in sequences of First, second, and third month, etc.

Doyas don't have their own calendar. They use this calendar, which commonly used by the Tibetan and Drukpa called the Dzongkha Calendar.

Words Relating to Environment

Sky	*Tirr bang*	Hill	*Teng*
Moon	*Tahli*	Soil	*Boh*
Sun	*Yarnhi*	Shifting fields	*Yonk*
North	*Chang*	Plain land	*Ding*
West	*Nup*	Uphill dwellers	*Ro-sant*
East	*Sar*	Downhill dwellers	*Ley-sant*
South	*Lho*		

Name of Some Diseases/Sicknesses

Cold and cough	*Choisma*	Cough	*Rohma*
Measles	*Seh ma*	Chicken pox	*Chutney*

Parts of Body

Head	*Puh-lum*	Back of head	*Jommui*	Hair	*Pu-sum*
Forehead	*Chewa*	Eye	*Miksey*	Eye brow	*Mik-mul*
Nose	*Nah*	Ear	*Natok*	Face	*Noi-tok*
Mouth	*Nio*	Cheek	*Ngom*	Teeth	*Sui*
Moustache	*Zau*	Nose drop	*Nah-ti*	Chin	*Khatok*
Fontanel	*Dorr*	Lower lip	*Weisa*	Neck	*Hat-teng*
Upper lip	*Nolsa*	Ear hole	*Nha burr*	Armpit	*Batok*
Wind pipe	*Oibung*	Back neck	*Takung*	Wrist	*Tibi*
Epiglottis	*Chupu*	Arm muscle	*Sat lum*	Palm	*Kur tak*
Shoulder	*Punga*	Upper arm	*Lan*	Elbow	*Koito*
Fore arm	*Koi lan*	Back palm	*Kur lap*	Nails	*Kur chin*
Fingers	*Kur hal*	Index finger	*Yug rhat*	Knuckle	*Chih tok*
Little finger	*Get cha*	Middle finger	*Lug rhat*	Ring finger	*Newa*
Muscles	*Dildon*	Chest	*Tang-tuk*	Breat	*Num bump*
Abdomen	*Leh-ma*	Belly	*Suk*	Left hand	*Dam Kurr*

Right hand	*Keh-kurr*	Lungs	*Eyosha*	Intestine	*Lhiring*
Heart	*Toi-mhu*	Liver	*Lhimiig*	Stomach	*Poh-tet*
Umbilical	*Ding di*	Anus	*Ae burr*	Testis	*Jig*
Penis	*Neit*	Scrotum	*Lau*	Vagina	*Tu*
Body	*Ju*	Buttock	*Etoi*	Waist	*Keypa*
Thigh	*Lateng*	Knee	*Chik puis*	Back of knee	*Koh tal*
Calf	*Dang lhan*	Shin	*Nga dong*	Ankle bone	*Tetlheng*
Ankle	*Gitong*	Heel	*Tingpa*	Sole	*Dong lhak*
Toe finger	*Dong ran*	Foot	*Dong jao*	Lehma-mike	*Pregnant women*

Clothings and Ornaments

Cloth(e)	*E-yem*	Ladies clothe	*Met-yem*
Gent's clothe	*Po-yem*	Red beads	*Ek-jig*
Black beads	*Nag-jig*	White beads	*Long-jig*
Finger rings	*Jukchi*	Ear rings	*Natok-ley se*

Some Food Items

Mushroom	*Bo-tang*	Puffball	*Jal-mhu*
Sweet potato	*Dung buhl*	Buckwheat	*Kersey*
Tapioca	*Loh-bul*	Banana	*Rissa*
Edible fern	*Sa-em*	Salt	*Dii*
Chilli	*Murr*	Butter	*Marr*
Fish	*Ha*	Meat	*sa*
Rice	*Amto*	Curry	*Aem*
Water	*Chio*	Sore cheese	*Tatchi*
Rhizomes	*Burr*	Cheese water	*Daudung*

Plants

Choksey	A soft and juicy bulb of a type of fern used for quenching thirst.
Gopey	A type of bamboo used for cutting umbilical chord.
Lehdeng	A wild scented leaf *(Tejpata* used as spices in India) used for roofing.
Lhi	Seeds.
Monh-bul	A rhizome of ginger family used for making liquor.
Ri-sing	Banana plants.

La	Leaves of plants.
Du-sing	A soft wood used as firewood (*Utish* in Nepali).
Punti	Flowers.
Changdon sing	A firewood tree
Lhui-sing	A medicinal plant used for stopping bleeding when bitten by leeches.
Salap	Oak leaves.
Tocha	Broomstick grass.
Nit-sing	Bamboo used for making tumblers and containers.
Li-sing	Medium size bamboo used for making fastener strings *kutong*.
Burr-bar	A leaf with rough hairy surface used for hastening delivery. It is also used for suppressing acute pain with swellings.

Animals

Malja	Peacock.	*Buk-sop*	Snell.
Pepchu	Bat	*Boont*	Locally prepared yeast for fermentation processes.
Jigjut	Shrew	*Ding-rip*	Ants.
Dechu	Porquipine	*Rongey*	Cicada.
Lhechu	Mouse	*Simpuk-rhal*	A nocturnal bird that feeds in mud.
Julep	Lizard.	*Echak*	Just born calf.
Pehchang	Iguana	*Be-chat*	Calf standing on four.
Tangjal	Crocodile	*Pasha Be-chat*	Juvenile calf.
Jalma	Viper/snakes.	*Lang-sha*	Ox.
Lhang	Eagle/Kite.	*Ba-lhang*	Grown up calf.
Lhuk	Jackal.	*Lang*	Ox for breeding.
Tong gong	Flamingo.	*Ba-ma*	Mother calf
Pehchu	Pelican.	*Mo-lang*	Ox for traction.
Hoonki	Pekinese.	*Chor-ba*	Milking cow.
Leyjey	Greyhound.	*Lang-an*	An aged ox.
Geyjig	Crab.	*Ba-gok*	An aged cow.
Ta-sjig	Lobster.	*Bo*	Castrated ox.
Kung	Tiger.	*Hrah*	Goat.
Jig	Leopard	*Hra-ping*	Grown up goat.
Eh-bale	Beetles.	*Nachu*	Flying squirrel.
Chuja	Swan.		

Household Articles

Middle pillar of house	*Bong dong*	Wooden milk churner	*Ausum*
Bamboo cylinder	*Belheng*	Bamboo ladle	*Changkulik*
Bamboo container	*Jup tek*	Fire place	*Jikpu*
Bitter guard shell	*Jopsey*	Bamboo blade for cutting umbilical chord	*Payung*
Sleeping cabin	*Boh chung*	Mortar and pistil	*Simteng*
Cane sieve	*Cha chang*	Bamboo Tray	*Seleh*
Twig stirrer	*Chatub*	Bamboo needle	*Rim*
Plant strings	*Jin*	Stone glinder	*Rak tag*
Bamboo cylinder	*Tibuk*	Baby carrier	*Tokrui*
Sleeping platform	*Tonk*	Letter	*Yi-gey*
Baby drapers	*Yonk yem*	Fermenting pot	*Yok*
Cooking pot	*Roug*	Basket carrier	*Wangnk*
A dish	*Porr*	Roofing grass	*Kerr*
Bed	*Yisa*	Door	*Goh*
Window	*Da-chong*	A fence	*Gah*
Wall	*Chapag*	Pillow	*Hang-u*
Cinder	*Buh*	Charcoal	*Masi*
Bamboo matt	*Lho*	Roof	*Jaru*
Winnow	*Tra*	Bamboo basket	*Sistong*
Copper pot	*Tumboo*	Measuring basket	*Rong tog*
Horn	Tang	Grain basket	*Kutong*
Bamboo tumbler	*Dung*	Bamboo straw	*Jiptong*
Sickle	*Goish*	Kitchen knife	*Chabu*

Miscelaneous List

Thief	*Aken*	Dream	*Mahnk*
Local Doctor	*Pama/Geypa*	Ceremonial friend	*Tochang*
A Miser	*Tekchum*	Children	*Ah-lum*
Village	*Ewuika*	Handsome/beauty	*simpsoan*
Woman	*Met-ma*	Man	*Ra-an*
Eldest son	*Thesod*	Eldest brother	*Pugan-sod*
Younger brother	*Huisod*	Yellow colour	*Lhing*

APPENDIX IV

GENEALOGICAL CHART OF LASKEY (L) RIIH

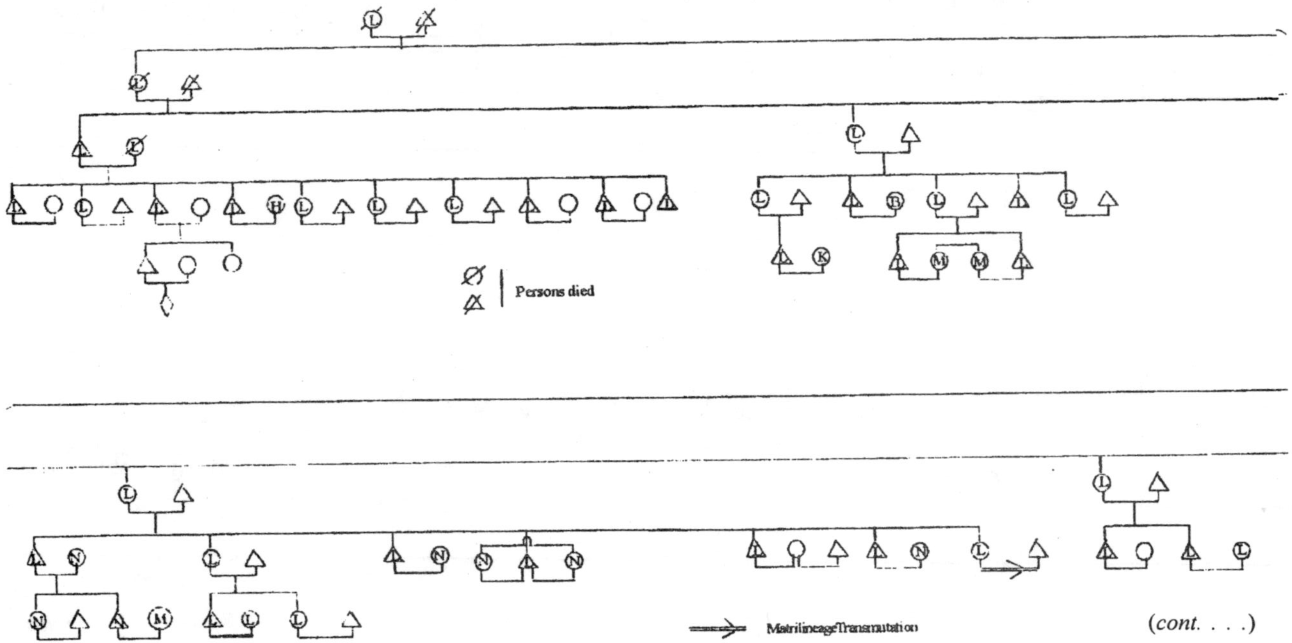

(*cont.* . . .)

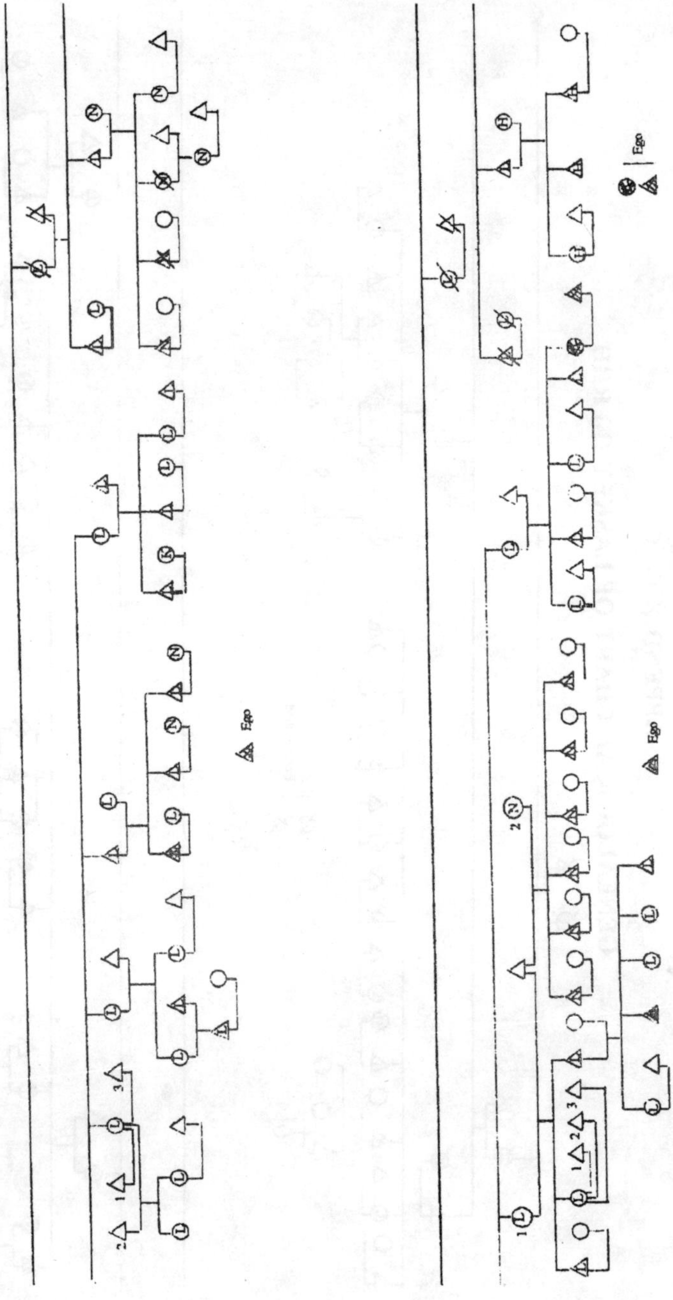

(cont. . .)

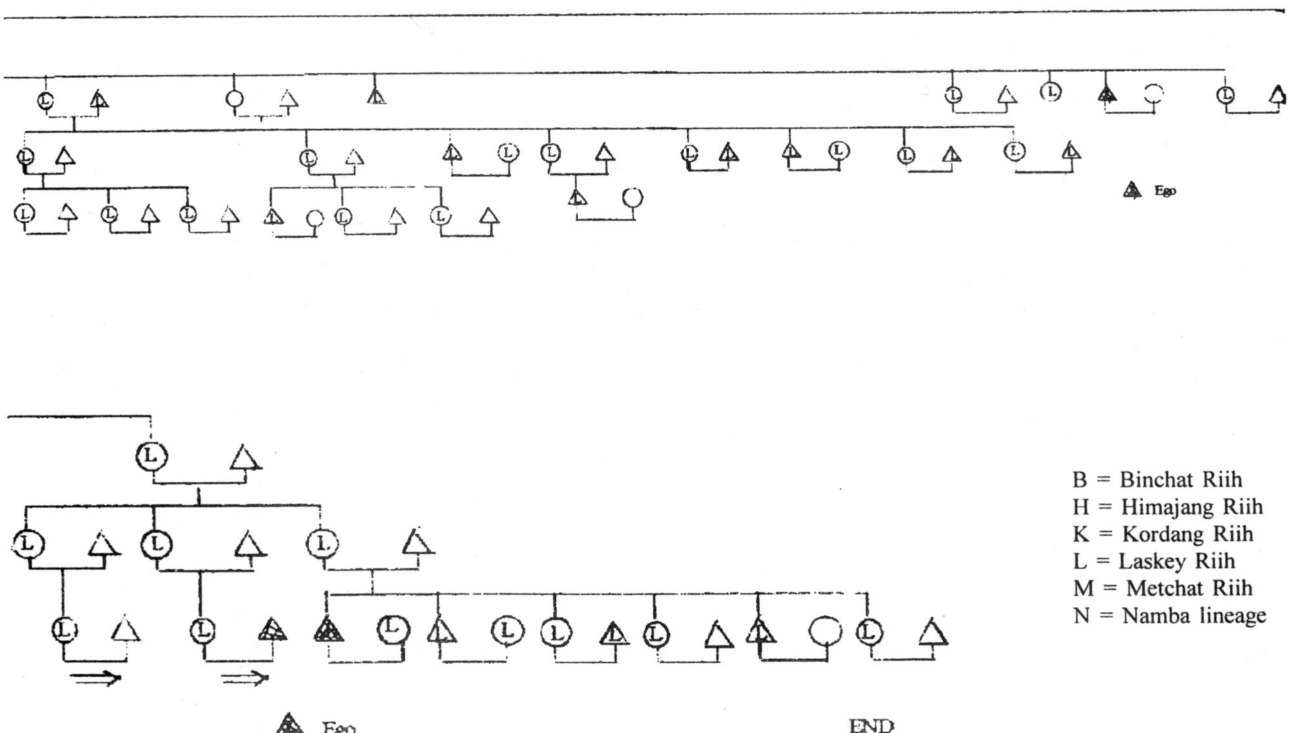

B = Binchat Riih
H = Himajang Riih
K = Kordang Riih
L = Laskey Riih
M = Metchat Riih
N = Namba lineage

1. School Children in the play ground.

2. Parents' Meeting at school campus.

3. School Annual Day Celebration.

4. A *La* at Sanglung with father and daughter.

5. Another *La* at Satakha with Mother and children.

6. *Makim* at Sataka with father and daughter.

7. Doya in their traditional dress at the: foreground.

8. An old Doya woman in her traditional dress—a rare sight! (Top shirt although is a part of the national costume).

9. A middle aged Doya woman fully adapted to Nepali costume.

10. Some Doya Women in Lotukuchu, at *Tokim* at the background.

11. Doya women in Lower Lotukuchu.

12. Doyas presenting folksongs.

13. A woman at Taba roasting flat bread.

14. A Doya man taking rest on the path after getting fully drunk.

15. An early morning prize catch of a wild cat at Lower Lotukuchu.

16. Sharing freshly slaughter cow meat at upper Lotukuchu.

17. A performing Doya *Pama* (witch doctor) with his second wife.

18. A Nepali *Bijuwa* performing rituals at a Doya home to cure a sick.

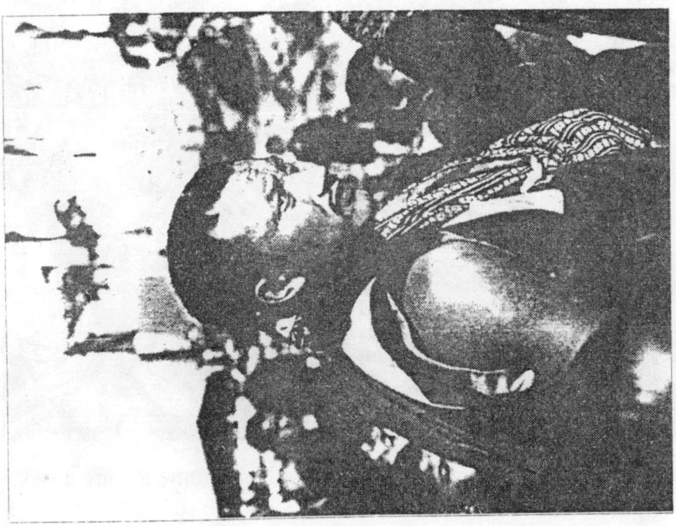

19. Sub-divisional head Lama visiting the School for special prayer.

20. A widower wearing long hair - at the background

21. Haoas *Nulak* (Tent) on the path to Samchi H.Q.

22. Hapas fleet ponies all set to go with loads of orange.

23. Doya Militia, newly recruited, taking oath to the King, the Country and the People (*Tsa-wasum*)

24. Doya elders proud to have a Royal Army from their community.

25. Doya getting used to plough and terrace fields.

26. Expecting good cash return from orange crop, Setah in his orange orchard, Lower Lotukuchu

27. My host family in Upper Lotukuchu.

28. An old Doyaman enjoying Yu.